YALE LAW LIBRARY SERIES IN
LEGAL HISTORY AND REFERENCE

Figure 1. Norman Lieber's bookplate, affixed to the inside cover of the notebook containing the manuscript. Source: National Archives.

To Save the Country

A Lost Treatise on Martial Law

FRANCIS LIEBER AND G. NORMAN LIEBER

Edited and with an Introduction
by Will Smiley and John Fabian Witt

Yale UNIVERSITY PRESS

New Haven and London

Published with support from the Lillian Goldman Law Library, Yale Law School.

Yale University Press books may be purchased in quantity for educational, business, or promotional use. For information, please e-mail sales.press@yale.edu (U.S. office) or sales@yaleup.co.uk (U.K. office).

Set in Minion type by Newgen North America, Austin, Texas.
Printed in the United States of America.

Library of Congress Control Number: 2018966490

ISBN 978-0-300-22254-8 (hardcover : alk. paper)

A catalogue record for this book is available from the British Library.

This paper meets the requirements of ANSI/NISO Z39.48-1992 (Permanence of Paper).

10 9 8 7 6 5 4 3 2 1

Dedicated to the judge advocates of the United States armed forces and to the civil liberties lawyers who engage them— bringing law to force for a century and a half.

Contents

Acknowledgments

This project began when one of us stumbled across a nearly unreadable and badly jumbled nineteenth-century manuscript hidden deep in the National Archives in Washington, D.C. Making the manuscript legible and decoding its many lost references has involved more than simply the work of the two editors. For more than a century, archivists and record-keepers in the United States Army and later at the National Archives and Records Administration cared for the manuscript. Little on the surface of it revealed its value, but the professionalism and commitment of these officials in the federal government preserved the manuscript nonetheless. The attention of these civil servants made our work possible. We are deeply grateful, too, for the excellent assistance of the archivists at the National Archives where we spent painstaking days and weeks photographing the manuscript.

The Yale Law Library performed with its accustomed brilliance, too, helping us locate difficult-to-find texts. Master librarians Julian Aiken, Lora Johns, John Nann, and Fred Shapiro were especially helpful, as were Teresa Miguel-Stearns and Blair Kauffman as heads of the library. The Hauser Library at Reed College was also helpful, particularly in researching the chapter annotations.

A small army of graduate and law students served as research assistants and made it possible for us to bring the project to completion. Arjun Ramamurti threw himself into the work of researching dozens of annotations. Samuel Breidbart, Michael Cotter, Berit Fitzsimmons, Chris Haugh, Tobias Kuehne, Jorge Bonilla Lopez, David G. Miller, Lauren Miller, Rob Nelson, Gabe Perlman, Todd Spencer, and Brandon Thompson provided indispensable assistance on the project: tracking down obscure references, scrutinizing the text, and translating the Latin and German passages that displayed the Liebers' scholarly erudition.

David Dyzenhaus, Gary Gerstle, Joel Isaac, Duncan Kelly, and Nomi Lazar offered invaluable comments at a States of Exception in American History conference at Clare College, Cambridge, in 2015. Heroically, members the same group offered still more reactions and ideas at a follow-up conference at the University of Chicago in 2018. The project began when both authors were at Yale, where Bruce Ackerman, Scott Shapiro, and student members of the reading group in the Yale branch of the American Constitution Society offered constructive feedback on the Lieber manuscript and our interpretation of it. Bernadette Meyler generously read the manuscript and suggested a brilliant addition. A workshop at the University of Southern California Law School led by Daria Roithmayr and Ariela Gross helped refine our thinking. The manuscript also benefited from an audience at the Lieber Institute of the United States Military Academy at West Point in October 2018, where Laurie Blank, Rich Gross, Jens Ohlin, Shane Reeves, Richard Salomon, Mike Schmidt, and others weighed in with a number of helpful suggestions. We are also grateful to Bill Frucht and Karen Olson of Yale University Press, and to the Press's two anonymous reviewers.

Editors' Note on the Text

This book consists of a lost manuscript by nineteenth-century political theorist and jurist Francis Lieber and his son G. Norman Lieber along with an introduction and editorial annotations. We found the Liebers' manuscripts on martial law and emergency constitutionalism in the U.S. National Archives and Record Administration's Judge Advocate General files, among the personal papers of Norman Lieber.[1] The manuscripts consist of two closely connected parts. The first (hereinafter GNL MS) is a manuscript that appears mostly to be in Norman Lieber's own hand. Longer excerpts from other sources appear to have been written by another person (perhaps an assistant or secretary). Based on references internal to the text, much or most of it was written or edited sometime after 1874.

The second manuscript is the beginnings of an annotated edition of General Orders No. 100 (hereinafter FL MS). Several paragraphs, cut from the printed order, are pasted separately on pages of stationery. Notes are attached, in what appears to be Francis Lieber's hand. Norman Lieber printed passages from these notes in two articles published during his own lifetime, referring to them as "a manuscript note" written by Francis Lieber and "found among his papers after his death."[2] These notes were almost certainly written between 1863, when Francis Lieber wrote General Orders No. 100, and 1872, when he died.

Preparing the texts of the GNL MS and the FL MS posed several challenges. For one, the manuscripts were in considerable disorder. They appear to have been relatively early drafts, with a number of different kinds of errors and much awkwardness. Errors include typographical errors, mistakes of citation, and omissions or inadvertent alterations in the Liebers' long quotations from other texts.

We have tried to act as fiduciaries for the reader, editing the text to make it readable while neither altering the Liebers' meaning nor sparing the Liebers from those mistakes or practices that bear on the significance of the text. Accordingly, we have fixed without comment minor typographical errors and obviously inadvertent errors. We have usually done the same with the Liebers' informal citations to earlier texts. Our practice with such citations has been to replace the informal manuscript citations with formal citations complete with editorial information to help the interested reader identify and pursue the text to which the Liebers meant to refer. We have done our best to locate the particular editions on which the Liebers most likely relied, though in some cases this involved some guesswork. We have also added citations where the Liebers' draft manuscript omitted them. Such citations appear in numbered footnotes interspersed among the Liebers' own citations and footnotes.

Most importantly, we have added to the manuscript a series of our own editorial annotations, usually offering short explanations for references in the text that might be obscure to the modern reader. The Liebers range widely over Anglo-American constitutional history in their account of the emergency power, and we aim to allow the reader who encounters an unfamiliar reference to understand the significance of the person or event under discussion.

To distinguish our own notes from the Liebers', the latter appear as numbered footnotes. When we added material to these existing notes, we note this by setting off our annotations in brackets and introducing them with the phrase "Eds. Note." When we have added entirely new explanatory notes, these are found in separate footnotes marked by symbols.

One final thing to note is that on a number of occasions, the Liebers (and especially Guido Norman Lieber) seem to have written about an old text while actually relying on some other, more recent text's account of the older text. We can identify such instances most readily when the Liebers' account of the older text includes one or more errors introduced by the more recent text. We identify such passages using editorial annotations and symbol footnotes. Similarly, when the Liebers' account tracks other, earlier works, we have likewise tried to note this for the reader.

Notes

1. National Archives and Records Administration, NM33 A, Entry 12A, Box 2, Folder 5, with other pages in other folders.

2. G. Norman Lieber, "What Is the Justification of Martial Law," *North American Review* 163, no. 480 (1896): 549–63; G. Norman Lieber, *Meaning of the Term Martial Law as Used in the Petition of Right and the Preamble to the Mutiny Act* (n.p., 1877).

Introduction

Over the past two decades, the problem of emergencies in constitutional democracies has come to seem ever more urgent. National security controversies, financial panics, natural disasters, and political turmoil have revived questions about what constitutions are for, about what they accomplish, and about what constitutionalism can accomplish in moments of emergency.

The experience of the United States in the American Civil War has been a recurring point of reference. As the great crisis of one of the earliest constitutional democracies in the modern world, the Civil War presents a leading case study in how constitutions work in extremis. And so for more than a century, the Civil War and its aftermath have been core cases for theorists of emergencies.[1]

There is good reason for the centrality of the Civil War experience in the literature on emergency, for it presents the single greatest example in American history of executive authority wielded in emergency times for the good. Lincoln's Emancipation Proclamation was, by its own terms, an "act of justice" founded "upon military necessity." It was a joinder of righteousness and emergency authority. Since September 1862 it has stood as an electric, and sometimes dangerous, example of the uses of executive power.

Yet for virtually the entire period, a key contribution has been missing from the study of the Civil War. Francis Lieber was one of the key architects of the Lincoln administration's approach to the law of emergencies. A professor at Columbia College and in Columbia's new law school, Lieber rose to prominence early in the war as an insider in the administration's defense of Lincoln's suspension of the writ of habeas corpus. Later in the conflict, he parlayed his military experience in the Napoleonic wars into a commission from the Lincoln administration to draft a code of instructions in the international laws of war for the Union Army. His code was notoriously severe. Organized around a fierce commitment to the righteousness of just wars and a tough conception of military necessity, Lieber's code aimed to legitimate Emancipation and to authorize the newly aggressive Union campaigns of the second half of the war. Lieber became one of the administration's chief strategists for the exercise of military authority, including Emancipation, under the Constitution.[2]

But Lieber did more. While the war raged on, he proposed to General in Chief Henry Halleck that he develop a more extensive account of the problem of law in wartime. Indeed, the ink was barely dry on the first print run of General Orders No. 100 when he proposed an annotated and expanded edition. A year later, he offered to develop his wartime instructions for the Union armies into a series of lectures at the United States Military Academy at West Point.[3] When the war ended, Lieber continued to work on the text. Reconstruction offered new questions and issues to address. The Supreme Court's 1866 decision in *Ex parte Milligan* posed new challenges to the aggressive forms of military authority that Lincoln had advanced and that Lieber's writings had supported. And so Lieber expanded the scope of his work, aiming to turn it into a broad argument about the role of law and constitutions in periods of emergency.[4]

Lieber was never an organized writer, however. The work was never finished. It was more a collection of arguments and insights than a coherent text. In 1872, with his work still badly disorganized, he died suddenly, leaving among his papers what seems to have been a mass of hastily assembled and disconnected chapters on the problem of martial law. Had the manuscript been finished, it might have served as the culmination of the Civil War debates on emergency constitutionalism. Lieber had hoped it would be a definitive statement on the controversies between Lincoln's assertion of war powers, on the one hand, and the critics, on the other, ranging from Chief Justice Roger Taney in *Ex parte Merryman* at the conflict's outset to the Supreme Court's nine justices in *Ex parte Milligan* at its close.[5]

After Lieber's death, his oldest living son, Guido Norman Lieber, took the manuscript in hand.[6] Norman Lieber worked to finish the text, elaborating its arguments and developing its implications. Twice in 1877 and again in 1896, he published small pieces of it in pamphlets and articles of his own.[7] Norman became the chair of the law department at the United States Military Academy at West Point. He served as the longest-sitting judge advocate general of the United States. He was a leading commentator in his own right on the role of the military in a peacetime democracy.

At some point in Norman's career, a book-length manuscript emerged. The text was still not complete. It remained undisciplined, and it retained the elder Lieber's tendencies to decadence in parts, but its basic structure and argument had taken form. The manuscript represented a meditation on the problem of emergency constitutionalism in democratic systems, inspired by the great constitutional conflicts of the American Civil War. Yet Norman Lieber again put the manuscript in a file. And there it rested for decades, until eventually it was transferred at some point in the middle of the twentieth century to the National Archives and Records Administration in Washington.

The Liebers' manuscript offers a fierce yet law-bound argument about emergency constitutions. For one thing, it substantially revises the conventional wisdom about the Civil War conception of emergencies and the law. The Liebers' manuscript suggests that American observers and jurists have misunderstood the basic legal logic of the Lincoln administration's approach to the war. But the manuscript does more than this. It offers deeper roots for a tough but liberal view of constitutional democracies in crisis, one that finds continued significance for the law even as—if not especially as—the republic is at risk.

Abraham Lincoln's message to Congress on July 4, 1861, has come for many to stand as the ultimate American example of what we may call the realist view of emergency constitutionalism. What, Lincoln asked, is a president to do when facing an emergency that presses the executive to break the law? Are "all the laws, *but one*" to fall so that one or more rules may be followed?[8] The conventional answer, ascribed to Lincoln, is emphatically no. The Constitution gives way to something organic and external to law.

Imagining themselves in the tradition of Lincoln, leading American statesmen and jurists in the century and a half since have promised to defend the republic even if it means abandoning the Constitution. In the Second World War, John J. McCloy in the Department of Defense observed that the Constitution was a mere "scrap of paper," one he would readily discard if rescuing the nation so required. In the Cold War, Justice Robert Jackson of the U.S. Supreme Court reminded the country that the Constitution was not "a suicide pact."[9] More recently still, officials in the White House of George W. Bush made clear their disdain for legal limits that interfered with the self-defense of the state. Any number of observers, on the left and on the right, claimed that the presidency of Barack Obama exhibited similar tendencies.[10] A disrespect for the law seems built into the "America First" policies, and indeed the very temperament, of President Donald Trump.[11]

The tradition of American realism in the moment of emergency has served as an American version of Carl Schmitt's theory of the state of exception. In this view, emergencies set aside the law, leaving nothing but the power of the sovereign to do what is necessary to rescue the state. This was the source of Schmitt's uncompromising dictum: "Sovereign is he who decides on the exception."[12] Schmitt contended that in the moment of crisis, the sovereign who invokes the emergency and seizes the authority of necessity has the power to remake the very identity of the state. The conclusion seemed to follow as a matter of logic. To determine the means necessary to defend the state, a decisionmaker needs first to decide on the ends for which the state exists. Some sovereigns might act to preserve the preexisting identity of the state. These Schmitt called "commissary dictators." But others would be "sovereign dictators"; they would seize the moment of the emergency to recast the state as they chose, and no legal or constitutional mechanism would constrain them.[13]

In the wake of the United States' great existential emergency, however, the Liebers articulated a different view, one that challenges a certain strand of Schmittian thinking about emergencies and promises to revise the conventional view of Lincolnian realism.

Emergency, the Liebers contended, does not throw a constitutional regime back into the state of nature, and certainly not when the regime is a complex constitutional democracy. The Liebers' crucial insight was that the moment of emergency poses a distinctive problem in collectivities that constitute themselves through the law. Schmitt imagined that the emergency allowed the sovereign to reorganize a collectivity that already had some "telluric" identity independent of the law. The paradigmatic case for Schmitt was the ethnically homogenous nation. But in legally constituted communities there is no collective entity existing *prior* to the laws to be saved by transforming the law. Law makes the community, so there is nothing for the sovereign to rescue other than that which the law has made.

Schmitt's argument comprehends part of this. The openness of the state to radical revision in the moment of emergency motivated his claim that the sovereign is he who decides upon the exception. The Schmittian exception is a moment of extraordinary power precisely because the determination of the means also requires decisions about ends.

But the Liebers grasped two closely connected things that seem to have evaded Schmitt and also theorists like Giorgio Agamben who have glossed and elaborated on his arguments in more recent years. The first is that as a descriptive matter, the moment of exception cannot escape the assumptions, cultural codes, and folkways of the regime. It is, after all, only the preexisting law that singles out some as leaders in the moment of emergency, that tells those leaders who is in and who is out of the regime, and that sets territorial boundaries on plausible claims of power. Foundational features of the regime inevitably shape the projects, interests, and identity of those who seize authority in the emergency. The basic values of a community's law thus travel into the very depths of a crisis. Indeed, they do so inevitably. Agamben's notion of a moment of bare and unmediated power simply does not come into being.

This descriptive insight led the Liebers to a prescriptive argument about how emergencies ought to be handled. The Liebers were no mawkish liberals; they rejected what the elder Lieber called, with a little too much disdain, the "namby-pambyism" of the traditional liberalism. With Lincoln, they were committed to identifying the kinds of power that would save a country worth saving. But they disagreed with Schmitt, too. When the leader of a community constituted by law asks what is necessary to rescue that community in a moment of existential crisis, the Liebers contended that the legal resources of the community offered a standard that held off Schmitt's naked moment of exception. The distinctive cultures of reason in self-constituted republics, they argued, set limits on the means and the ends their leaders could legitimately adopt.

The Liebers' account of the distinctive functions of *reason* in emergency constitutionalism illuminates a way of rethinking the basic structure of Lincoln's ideas on the law in crisis times. It also sheds light on the theory of constitutional emergencies in our own day. The manuscript only begins to plumb the depths of such theories, and it only offers the prologue for a revision of Lincoln's thinking. Lieber the son was not quite up to the task of finishing what Lieber the father began. But in what follows, this introduction develops the significance of the lost manuscript. We put the manuscript into the twin contexts of the intellectual history of emergency powers and the controversies of Civil War–era America. But to understand where the manuscript comes from, to understand its significance, we start with the lives of the authors themselves.

Authors and Manuscripts

Francis Lieber was born in Prussia in 1798. As a youth, he watched Napoleon march through Berlin. Like an entire generation of Prussians, Lieber organized much of his political thinking around the lessons of Napoleon's humiliating victories. In 1815 he fought against Napoleon's resuscitated forces near Waterloo. Chasing Napoleon back toward Paris in the days thereafter, Lieber was shot through the neck and again in the chest. He was left for dead in a Belgian field. Peasants rooted through his pockets for valuables. And yet somehow he lived. After the war, Lieber became a garrulous intellectual in liberal nationalist circles in Berlin. But liberal nationalism, forged in the furnace of Napoleonic domination, soon fell out of favor in the reactionary mood of Metternich's Europe. Arrested and threatened with prison for his dangerous liberalism, Lieber traveled to Greece to fight against the Ottoman Empire in the Greek War of Independence. Disgusted with what he perceived as the decadence and irresponsibility of the modern Greeks (nothing like their ancient predecessors, he moaned), he returned to Prussia only to be forced once again to flee, this time for England in 1826, and a year later for the United States.

   In the United States, Lieber spent eight years looking for serious employment. He ran a German-style gymnasium in Boston for a year. (John Quincy Adams was one of his visitors.) In Philadelphia, he edited and published the fabulously successful thirteen-volume *Encyclopaedia Americana*. He angled for a position teaching history at Harvard, but much to his chagrin, none materialized. In 1835, he took a faculty post at South Carolina College (now the University of South Carolina) in the state's capital city of Columbia. He taught there for more than two decades, writing books and treatises on politics, interpretation, and culture. He never acclimated to life in a provincial southern town. He spent summers in New York and Cambridge, currying as much favor as he could with the northern cultural and literary elite and scouting out the prospect of new positions in the North. His efforts never came to fruition, and so he and his wife, Madeleine, settled down to raise three sons in South Carolina: Oscar, Norman, and Hamilton. Finally, with his boys grown and after being passed over for the institution's presidency, Lieber resigned in 1856 and moved to New York City.

In New York, good fortune struck. Columbia College (now University) was expanding its faculty and was also in the early stages of founding a new law school. In 1857 Lieber took a position there as professor of history and political science. By the time the Civil War began, Lieber had settled into Columbia as a garrulous and influential theorist of the history and theory of republics.

The Civil War dealt a shock to the Lieber family and split its allegiances. Oscar, Francis's oldest son, signed up to fight on the side of the Confederacy in which he had grown up. Hamilton and Norman, the younger and middle sons, respectively, joined the Union Army. Francis's sympathies lay strongly with the latter. He quickly found his hard-won expertise on republican political theory in high demand. Lieber hurriedly put together a lecture course on the laws of war at Columbia's new law school. *The New York Times* picked up the lectures and reprinted them weekly.[14] Meanwhile, Lieber deepened his connections to key figures in the Union command—connections he had forged in his many summers in the North.

The first year of the war was a trying time. Lieber's son Hamilton lost his right arm at Fort Donelson in February 1862. Oscar died resisting the Union effort to take Richmond later that spring. But in the Union war effort, the elder Lieber gained influence. He served as a key figure in the Lincoln administration's defense of its suspensions of habeas corpus, connecting Lincoln with the Philadelphia lawyer Horace Binney, whose argument in favor of the president's suspension authority became more important than the defense offered by Attorney General Edward Bates. In 1862, Union General in Chief Henry Halleck asked Lieber to draft a short text on the law and history of guerrilla warfare. Lieber responded with a short and often underappreciated essay that anticipated the main features of modern humanitarian law on the irregular fighter.[15]

In the winter of 1862–1863, as the Union moved toward Emancipation and as Lincoln aimed to step up the aggressiveness of its war effort, Halleck called upon Lieber to restate the entirety of the laws of war rules into a single, concise package. Lieber did so in a pamphlet of 157 articles, whose basic terms treated questions such as the law of occupation, the treatment of prisoners of war, the use of poisons and torture (both were prohibited), the targeting of cultural monuments, and more. Most significantly, the Lieber Code, as the pamphlet later came to be known, defended Emancipation and the arming of black soldiers. In the spring President Lincoln published Lieber's text under Lincoln's own signature as U.S. Army's General Orders, No. 100.[16] The code became the basis for later international restatements of the laws of war and helped smooth the political path for multilateral treaties on the laws of war, beginning with the 1899 Hague Convention.[17]

Guido Norman Lieber (1837–1923) was the only one of Francis Lieber's three sons to escape the war unwounded. An 1858 graduate of Harvard Law School, Norman fought on the front lines in the war's early campaigns; his father thought for some time that Norman had been captured in the Seven Days' Battles outside of Richmond in 1862. Beginning the next year, Norman served as a judge advocate. After the war, he joined his father in the Confederate archives in Richmond to investigate war crimes. In the 1870s, he served in the Indian conflicts in the Department of Dakota and then taught law at West Point. In 1884 he became acting judge advocate general of the U.S. Army; the War Department promoted him to judge advocate general in 1895, and he became the longest-serving person to hold the post.[18]

Norman Lieber carried on the family tradition of writing, in a fashion. He published important articles on martial law during the second half of the century. But most of all, Norman was an institutional man, not a theorist. He was a better navigator of bureaucratic institutions than his irascible father, but he lacked his father's erratic brilliance and theoretical electricity. And one result is that he carried with him for much of his life a set of manuscripts that he never published, but that he seems to have worked on and worried over from time to time.

The manuscript published here consists principally of two connected parts. The first (the GNL MS) is mostly in Norman Lieber's own hand; from internal references in the text, it appears to have been written or edited after 1874. The second part consists of a fragmentary annotated version of Francis Lieber's

General Orders No. 100 (the FL MS), which was written sometime between the drafting of General Orders No. 100 in 1863
and the older Lieber's death in 1872.

The GNL MS is divided into seven numbered chap-
ters. The first distinguishes "military law" from "martial law,"
while the second traces the development of military law in
English history and shows its distinctive characteristics. The
third chapter discusses *martial* law in English history, and
the fourth traces the views of early English legal authorities
on this issue. The fifth and sixth chapters, respectively, take
up the relevant Acts of Parliament on martial law, and several
late-eighteenth- and early-nineteenth-century British cases.
Further miscellaneous materials are mixed in. One extended
section, found among the numbered chapters, may have been
intended as a chapter of its own on American precedents for
the use of martial law from the Revolution through the 1840s.
We have included it here as the seventh chapter of the book,
fitting it in chronologically and conceptually with the rest of
the manuscript. An eighth chapter—denominated as the seventh in the GNL MS, but converted to the eighth here—turns
to the content of martial law in the United States during and
after the Civil War.

The chapters work out the implications of the principles
laid out in the FL MS, while engaging later developments and
publications, so much so that the two manuscripts set forth a
single theory of martial law in the Anglo-American constitutional tradition. Because the two manuscripts are so closely
linked, we include the fragmentary FL MS as an appendix to
the GNL MS. Both manuscripts share the characteristic features of Lieber *père*—his distinctive combination of erudition,
historical learning, and theoretical flights of fancy, with frequent bouts of literary decadence and disorganization. More-

over, the writing that appears in Norman's hand is uncharacteristically ambitious of the younger man. Norman's work in the years after his father's death was almost entirely based on the basic principles laid down by his father. It is not clear whether Francis would have agreed with all of the particulars of his son's elaborations. But the general theory seems to be unchanged. Norman appears to have completed the manuscript as a labor of love in fidelity to his father's thinking.

The Liebers' Theory of Martial Law

A long Anglo-American tradition associates martial law with no law at all. Matthew Hale asserted in the seventeenth century that martial law was "not a law, but something to be indulged, rather than allowed, as a Law." Writing a century later, William Blackstone glossed Hale, adding that martial law had "no settled principles" and was "entirely arbitrary." A robust tradition ever since insists that martial law is a lawless form of authority, not worthy of the label "law" at all.[19]

The Liebers disagreed. Their view of martial law flowed logically from Francis Lieber's heterodox orientation to the Enlightenment laws of war. Lieber's position was in one sense a throwback to the just war tradition of the Middle Ages and Early Modern period. For a century and more, European thinkers on the laws of war had jettisoned analysis of the righteousness of one side or the other in battle. Jurists accounted both sides as just in the hopes that they would thereby be able to develop rules that both sides could respect. (In the words of the Swiss jurist Emmerich de Vattel, "in every case susceptible of doubt, the arms of the two parties at war are to be accounted equally lawful, at least as to external effects, and until the decision of the cause."[20]) By recognizing the sovereign equality of warring states, the European authorities had been able to accept "a dizzying array of rules" about which forms of violence were allowable, without regard either to who was inflicting the violence or to what end the violence was directed.[21]

In writing General Orders No. 100 for the Union, however, Francis had turned away from the eighteenth-century European tradition. Echoing his fellow Prussian Carl von Clausewitz, who famously described war as "politics by other means," Lieber spoke of conflict as "the means to obtain great ends of state."[22] Actions within war had to be understood, and judged, by reference to their ends. The central test for the legality of wartime conduct was thus "military necessity," a quality that "consists in the necessity of those measures which are indispensable for securing the ends of the war, and which are lawful according to the modern law and usages of war," including a wide range of violence against life, limb, and property.[23]

What did necessity permit a state to do in wartime? In discussing the occupation of foreign territory, General Orders No. 100 laid down a stern injunction: "To save the country is paramount to all other considerations."[24] It was the starkest line of General Orders No. 100. Lieber did not relish the suffering righteous combat often entailed. He had experienced far too much of it in his life to be blithe about it. But he accepted suffering in a just cause as unavoidable. Even more, he viewed suffering for righteousness as a wellspring of republican virtue. To suffer for a good cause was to be reminded of what was at stake in the realm of the political.

The Liebers adopted the severe approach of General Orders No. 100 in their writing on martial law and emergencies. In the *New York Times* in the second year of the Civil War, the elder Lieber had announced that "nations in utmost need are never saved by legal formulas." Lieber warned the *Times*'s readers that if the "fundamental law of a nation omits to provide for these exceptional cases," the people would inevitably seize the power to answer the crisis. "Power will be arrogated," Lieber concluded, "as people arrogate power in cases of shipwreck."[25]

In their postwar treatise, the two Liebers carried forward their fierce view of an elastic necessity power. Quoting General Orders No. 100, they repeated its starkest line: "'To save the country,' say the Instructions already cited, 'is paramount to all other considerations.'"[26] The basic proposition, they continued, followed from what it was to be a state. Quoting the legal scholar Joel Bishop, they argued that for governments as for individuals, "self-preservation" was the "first duty," one that took precedence over all others. This was "a principle inherent in all politics." Martial law was therefore "the necessity of employing the means which will render the resort to force effective" in those instances where, as Alexander Hamilton had written in *The Federalist*, "seditions and insurrections" had become "maladies as inseparable from the body politic, as tumours and eruptions from the natural body." Simply put, martial law was "the law of necessity applied at home," and it provided for "the legality of everything absolutely demanded by military necessity" when the requisite emergency arose.[27]

Martial law, they observed, had been widely misinterpreted and confused with other types of law. In particular, commentators were prone to confuse three different types of "military jurisdiction": first, there was "military law," the body of rules that governed members of the U.S. armed forces in peace or war—such as the Articles of War, enforced by courts-martial and the standing orders of commanding officers.[28] Second, there was "the Martial Law of hostile occupation," exercised by military forces in enemy territory.[29] G.O. 100 provided some guidelines on the law of occupation, and it was these sections that Francis Lieber annotated in his manuscript.[30] Finally, there was "Martial Law applied at home," or "Martial Law Proper," which formed the main topic of the Lieber Theory.[31]

Martial Law Proper was not the application of Military Law to civilians. As Daniel Hulsebosch's scholarship on the constitutional history of the War of Independence has recently observed, the distinction between martial law and military law was one that British officials had observed from time to time.[32] But the Liebers made the distinction between the two forms of military authority the core of their argument. As they saw it, Martial Law Proper represented the legal authority of the government to set aside otherwise binding principles of law when necessity so demanded. This authority arose not from enumerated constitutional powers but from what the Liebers called "natural law," which meant the demands of necessity. Just as "the law of trespass is inoperative against those who forcibly enter a house in a case of conflagration," they contended, so the "salvation of a country is like the saving of an individual life."[33]

In the face of threat, they argued, a right to collective "common defense" was "an attribute of sovereignty inherent in all polities."[34] Thus, "[t]he right of self-defense being a necessary attribute of sovereignty, recognized by our Constitution, and Martial Law Proper a necessary means of self-defense, its rightful exercise must rest somewhere, whether or not mentioned amongst the enumerated powers."[35] The Liebers recognized that such an unenumerated power was "apparently forbidden by the Constitution." After all, the Tenth Amendment provided, "the powers not delegated to the United States by the Constitution, nor prohibited by it to the States, are reserved to the States respectively, or to the people."[36] But the

Constitution's text did not and could not end the analysis, for certain rights of states in the international order were non-delegable. The "law of necessity," they wrote, "cannot be controlled. Statutes cannot be framed, nor can human ingenuity devise the means, to evade it." Indeed, the Liebers believed that in its own halting and uncertain way, the Constitution did recognize such power. It authorized suspension of the writ of habeas corpus during rebellion or invasion. It permitted the forcible quartering of soldiers in civilian homes in wartime. It contemplated the prospect of insurrection, invasion, and domestic violence. "The law thus recognized," the Liebers held, "is, in fact, the law of necessity as applied to a time of war[.]"[37]

The Liebers were influenced, as were many who wrote on martial law, by John Locke. We know this because the Liebers say so in the first chapter of the manuscript itself. We can also see it in the structure of their argument. As political theorist Nomi Lazar has argued, Locke developed an internal conception of the prerogative power of government.[38] The power of self-preservation, in his view, was not in derogation of the system of government but rather part of it. To be sure, sometimes self-preservation required a government to do something "against the direct letter of the law, for the public good." But because "a rational creature cannot be supposed, when free, to put himself into subjection to another, for his own harm," it necessarily followed that the power of self-preservation was a core term of the social compact, not something external to it.[39]

The Liebers also followed Locke in seeing the necessity power as inevitably and properly an executive branch power. The president was distinctively positioned to act effectively when emergency so required. This was partly a product of the president's commander-in-chief authority over the armed forces. It was in part a result of the institutional character of an executive branch that never went out of session and that did not have to make decisions collectively like the Congress. But it also followed logically from the basic theory the Liebers articulated. Martial law, in their view, was a kind of background principle, one that always authorized actions necessary to defend the republic. As the chief executor of the laws of the republic, the president was always already charged with enforcing necessity's mandate. No Congress could withhold from the executive the power to do what was necessary for the country's self-preservation.

The association of necessity with the executive was vital to the Liebers for two further reasons. The first was judicial review. Norman, for one, would later argue explicitly that the Congress did not have the authority simply to declare Martial Law Proper—to suspend the ordinary law—when it saw fit, because he believed this would cut off after-the-fact review in the courts.[40] It was vital, the Liebers contended, that people whose rights had been violated by actions taken under Martial Law Proper be able to file suit. Courts would then evaluate a president's actions (or those of his subordinates) for their necessity justification after the fact. A president could do nothing to immunize executive officers' actions from such scrutiny, at least not in civil suits. But Congress, by legally declaring Martial Law Proper, *could* issue such immunity—and this must not be allowed, the Liebers believed. "Congress in enacting such a law would be acting under a constitutional political power; the act would be a political act; Congress would be the judge of its necessity; and the necessity could not be inquired into by the courts."[41] Congress could thus abuse its power, "and the person injured would be without remedy."[42] Therefore only the executive, and especially the military, could act according to Martial Law Proper, because only their particular actions could be challenged by litigation.

In setting the standard of review in such cases, the Liebers quoted approvingly Chief Justice Roger Taney's majority opinion in *Mitchell v. Harmony*, an 1851 case dealing with the powers conferred by necessity during operations in Mexico during the Mexican-American War.[43]

> [I]f, with such information as he had a right to rely upon, there is reasonable ground for believing that the peril is immediate and menacing or the necessity urgent, he is justified in acting upon it, and the discovery afterwards that it was false or erroneous will not make him a trespasser. But it is not sufficient to show that he exercised an honest judgment, and took the property to promote the public service; he must show by proof the nature and character of the emergency, such as he had reasonable grounds to believe it to be, and it is then for a jury to say whether it was so pressing as not to admit of delay; and the occasion such, according to the information upon which he acted, that private rights must for the time give way to the common and public good.

The Liebers would not often agree with Lincoln's nemesis, Taney, who, ten years after *Mitchell*, famously ruled against the administration on the question of habeas corpus suspension in *Merryman*. But they concurred completely in his *Mitchell* view that the law of necessity established the content of Martial Law Proper.

The Liebers perceived a second, and related, danger if Congress were invested with the power to declare Martial Law Proper. Following the reasoning of Philadelphia lawyer Horace Binney, whose argument for Lincoln's authority to suspend habeas corpus had been highly influential in 1861 and 1862, the Liebers observed that resting the necessity power in the executive rather than in the legislative branch served a further vitally important goal in moments of emergency. Disempowering the Congress separated the necessity power from the legitimate lawmaking body of the republic. A legislative branch with the authority to act on the emergency and determine the scope of necessity, the Liebers contended, posed a distinctive danger. The executive acted within a legal regime whose content was largely fixed by others. The legislature, by contrast, substantially shaped the legal regime itself. A legislature was thus more likely to disrupt and transform the identity of the state in the moment of an emergency.

The risks were all the greater because the necessity power the Liebers contemplated was an awesome one. Necessity could arise from "immediate and direct physical necessity" during combat—but it need not. Indeed, necessity could arise any time there was a threat to the republic. It could not, therefore, be completely specified in advance. "The salvation of a country," Francis Lieber recorded in his own hand, "is like the saving of an individual life. It is paramount to all else."[44] This statement mirrored his broad, ends-based definition of "military necessity" in General Orders No. 100. Necessity was always to be determined by the circumstances of each case. No general rules could be stated, because a reason that "would justify one act might be totally inapplicable to another."[45]

In the "immediate neighbourhood" of active hostilities, Martial Law Proper had "full sway." Tactical necessity could allow the military to "demolish or seize property, and . . . arrest persons, if indispensable for the support of the army or the obtaining of the military objects."[46] This also meant that Martial Law Proper, through trials before military commissions, could punish violations of the "common law of war"—in other words, offenses that did not exist in peacetime, and over which civilian courts could not exercise jurisdiction. When warfare forced civilian courts to close, the necessity of continuing to enforce ordinary laws justified "extend[ing] the protection of military authority to the inhabitants of districts within the theatre of active military operations in which the civil administration has been displaced."[47]

Martial Law Proper thus conferred broad authority to take or destroy property and lives, either summarily or through trials for crimes, and either on the battlefield or distant from it. Only necessity itself could constrain the exercise of Martial Law Proper. Because "Martial Law Proper is a law of necessity," the Liebers wrote, "its jurisdiction must extend wherever the necessity exists. It cannot be restrained within territorial limits."[48] Here lay the Liebers' critique of the famous *Milligan* decision in the Supreme Court in 1866, about which we say more shortly. The important thing here is that the Liebers believed emergency law was constituted by elastic standards, not hard-and-fast rules. The kinds of extraordinary actions warranted by Martial Law Proper would differ depending on the circumstances, location included. In places where the civilian courts were closed, the power would be broader; military necessity there would typically allow military tribunals to take cognizance of crimes that civilian courts would ordinarily have punished.[49] This was necessary because if Martial Law Proper did not enforce the law, no one else would.

This did not mean that Martial Law Proper's military tribunals could try individuals for *any* crime. American military tribunals, the Liebers noted, had no jurisdiction over the ordinary crime of treason, which the Constitution reserved for the federal courts. Such a hard-and-fast limit on military commission jurisdiction, however, was itself nothing more than an artifact of the necessity power. Where the ordinary legal processes provided adequately for some contingency, no new necessity power came into being. Where the law of the land was sufficient and not unduly obstructed or impaired, "it cannot be set aside by the war power. The object being attainable without a resort to it [martial law], the reason of necessity in which it is grounded fails."[50] And in the event the ordinary law was insufficient in fact, the common law of war offered military commissions the power to punish the same behavior and conduct, even if treason as such could not be charged.

Of course, the vast necessity power the Liebers contemplated needed to be confined in some manner; it could only be properly invoked in situations of true crisis. Martial Law Proper, they cautioned, was "an exercise of military power *in time of war, insurrection or rebellion.*"[51] Martial Law could not exist in peacetime.[52] But the Liebers made clear once again that necessity was the ultimate measure of its own power. It did not wait on the declaration of formal war. And so the Liebers went to great lengths to make clear that a domestic insurrection, when it reached a certain intensity, could be considered war under both domestic and international law. Francis Lieber had made such a point as early as 1861, writing about the status of Confederate prisoners in the *New York Times.*[53] In their manuscript, they drew further upon the U.S. Supreme Court's clear statement in the 1863 *Prize Cases,*[54] and upon an opinion written by Chief Justice Salmon P. Chase while sitting with the District Court for North Carolina in 1867.[55] Both opinions held that the Civil War *had* been a war, entitling the Union to exercise necessity's powers even without recognizing the Confederacy as a sovereign state with its own right to wage war.

The American Context

The story of martial law in America went back to the Revolution and before. British invocations of the concept in the War of Independence prompted protests from rebels and loyalists alike.[56] In the War of 1812, Andrew Jackson's use of martial law in New Orleans produced controversy that persisted for decades.[57] In the antebellum years, martial law produced a series of debates and anxieties about the relationship between military authority and slavery.[58] The Liebers were influenced by all of these episodes. But most of all they wrote against the backdrop of the Civil War experience and its culminating martial law experience in the Supreme Court in 1866. The Court's opinion that year on executive powers during the Civil War, *Ex parte Milligan*, stood at the center of the postwar debates out of which the Lieber manuscript emerged.

The *Milligan* case arose when Union troops arrested Lambdin P. Milligan in Indiana in October 1864. Milligan had been a member of a shadowy pro-Confederate organization known as the Sons of Liberty.[59] Together with his fellow members, he plotted to free Confederate prisoners of war and lead a secession movement in the Upper Midwest. But Union intelligence foiled the conspiracy. Milligan and five others were arrested and tried before a military tribunal of Union Army officers.[60] On the testimony of a coconspirator who turned against him, Milligan was sentenced to death. In May 1865, his lawyers petitioned for a writ of habeas corpus in the Indianapolis federal court, where two judges (one of whom was Supreme Court Justice David Davis) disagreed on the question, and certified it to the Supreme Court. Oral arguments were heard in early 1866, and on April 3, the Court ordered Milligan discharged. Nine months later, on December 17, the Court released its majority opinion, written by Justice Davis. Davis's opinion rejected the government's power to apply martial law in areas like Indiana, where there were no active military operations and where the civilian courts were open. Chief Justice Salmon Chase, writing a separate concurring opinion, agreed with the result, but differed with the majority in arguing that *Congress*, if it wished, could have authorized such an exercise of martial law.

All the lawyers arguing *Milligan* before the Supreme Court grounded their arguments on enumerated constitutional powers, either implicitly or explicitly. As the Court held in *McCulloch v. Maryland*, "[t]his government is acknowledged by all, to be one of enumerated powers. The principle, that it can exercise only the powers granted to it . . . is now universally admitted."[61] Accordingly, the government contended that the legality of Milligan's detention and trial flowed from the president's constitutional authority as commander in chief and asserted that this power authorized a president to do whatever the international law of war allowed. Benjamin Butler, arguing for the government, asserted that Lincoln had authorized the trial of offenders like Milligan by military commission under a power "which is vested by the Constitution in the President."[62] What was that power? Butler quoted the Duke of Wellington, who had written of martial law as "the will of the commanding officer of an armed force."[63] That power was not mere will, Butler cautioned. It was a constrained power. It ran only so far "as necessity demands and prudence dictates."[64]

Properly understood, Butler continued, this necessity power had authorized the trial of Milligan by military commission. Any other view would lead to a logical absurdity. Lincoln had suggested as much when he asked, "Must I shoot a simple-minded soldier boy who deserts, while I must not touch a hair of a wiley agitator who induces him to desert?"[65] Butler echoed the same view, asking the Court to consider that,

> In time of war, to save the country's life, you send
> forth your brothers, your sons, and put them under
> the command, under the arbitrary will of a general
> to dispose of their persons and lives as he pleases;
> but if, for the same purpose, he touches a Milligan,
> a Son of Liberty, the Constitution is invoked in his
> behalf—and we are told that the fabric of civil gov-
> ernment is about to fall![66]

Properly understood, Butler insisted, the fabric of government included, and indeed was held together by, a necessity power that had provided Lincoln, as it provided all presidents, the authority to do what necessity required under the circumstances.

Arguing for Milligan, leading lawyer David Dudley Field rejected Butler's necessity theory. Field conceded that otherwise illegal actions might be permissible in cases of necessity; as examples, he cited private citizens tearing down a house to prevent fire from spreading, and a military garrison commander suppressing a mutiny. In such circumstances, "necessity alone" could justify executive actions.[67] But in Milligan's case, Field insisted, "there was in fact no necessity."[68] The government had charged Milligan with crimes for which he might have been tried in the federal courts. If those courts were open, how could necessity warrant a military commission? How, moreover, could necessity ever justify the trial and punishment of detainees if temporary detention alone would suffice to remove them from the contest? Congress had authorized the president to suspend the writ of habeas corpus in March 1863. The Union could therefore have held Milligan without trial under the "capacious powers" already afforded to the president by the Congress. No reliance on a further necessity power was required to accomplish the goals asserted by the government.

Field's cocounsel, Jeremiah Black, former attorney general of the United States under James Buchanan, went a step further in his arguments before the Court. If war granted the power to skirt the Bill of Rights, the federal courts, and trial by jury, then emergencies would serve as invitations to tyranny. A designing president could "provoke" a crisis and "keep it going even after the actual conflict of arms is over." Emergency powers "could make war a chronic condition of the country, and the slavery of the people perpetual."[69] Indeed, Butler's arguments in favor of the military commission, Black contended, inadvertently revealed a grave flaw in the government's reasoning. If Butler's account were correct, Black emphasized, then

> we are at the mercy of any foreign potentate who may envy us the possession of those liberties which we boast of so much; he can shatter our Constitution without striking a single blow or bringing a gun to bear upon us. A simple declaration of hostilities is more terrible to us than an army with banners.[70]

The government's emergency power theory, Milligan's lawyers contended, seemed to have opened the door to the end of constitutional self-government.

In an opinion issued nearly a year later, Justice David Davis sided with Milligan but tried to find a middle space between the divergent arguments of the government and defense counsel. Davis recognized the force of the necessity power. The government, he wrote, "has all the powers granted to it, which are necessary to preserve its existence." That necessity power, in Davis's view, arose "within the Constitution," not outside of it. Its efficacy had been "happily proved by the result of the great effort to throw off its just authority."[71]

But the power of necessity required limits, Davis contended. It was one thing to allow for executive actions against property when they were subject to review by the courts in damages actions after the fact. But Lambdin Milligan had been sentenced to death. No damages action could restore his life. And so Davis was compelled to reach the constitutional question of the executive's power to try Milligan by military commission. Reviewing the trial protections of the Bill of Rights, as well as the Article III guarantee of a jury trial, Davis observed that the military commission had failed to afford Milligan the basic protections provided by the Constitution. That failure might be justified if the "laws and usages of war" or the necessity of martial law authorized the president to act. But no such necessity could be found. The courts were open and in "proper and unobstructed exercise of their jurisdiction." Indiana was not "the locality of actual war." And so, Davis concluded, no necessity could be cited to sustain a trial by military commission outside the ordinary channels of the federal courts, trial by jury, and the Bill of Rights.

Chief Justice Salmon P. Chase and three of his colleagues concurred in the judgment, but still disagreed on an important point. Chase insisted that although the commission that had sentenced Milligan to death lacked the lawful jurisdiction to try and punish him, it was nonetheless the case that Congress *could have* authorized such a commission. "Congress," he wrote, "had power, though not exercised, to authorize the military commission which was held in Indiana." No one doubted, Chase continued, that the Bill of Rights did not embarrass the government's power to try members of the armed services; the Fifth Amendment to the Constitution had an express carve-out for "cases arising in the land and naval forces, or in the militia in actual service in time of war or public danger." Chase and his colleagues in the minority went further. Surely, they reasoned, the same exception that explicitly applied to members of the armed services also applied implicitly to "citizens conspiring or attempting the destruction or great injury of the national forces." Chase's reasoning on this point was crucial. Congress, Chase wrote, "is but the agent of the nation." The "security of individuals" against tyranny thus depended "on the intelligence and virtue of the people," who by "frequency of elections" would guarantee their own freedom through the ballot box.

The victorious petitioners in *Milligan* hoped that the decision would bury the war power once and for all; future president James Garfield, who served as Field's cocounsel in the *Milligan* arguments at the Court, wrote that he hoped the Court's decision would be "the just and final settlement of this great question."[72]

But the Liebers rejected much of the *Milligan* decision's effort to bring closure to the war. Norman and Francis believed that both of the opinions in the Court's *Milligan* decision threatened the powers the Lincoln administration had asserted, and the elder Lieber had defended, during the war.

Accordingly, the Liebers developed a creative reading of *Milligan* that aimed to rescue the basic theory of necessity, on the one hand, while accommodating the Court's authoritative opinion, on the other. The Liebers argued that all sovereign states have an inherent natural right of collective self-defense.[73] Butler had said as much while arguing for the government, quoting John Quincy Adams's 1836 claim that "the powers incidental to war are derived, not from any internal, municipal source, but from the laws and usages of nations."[74] Even Field, in arguing Milligan's side of the case, had conceded that necessity might allow departure from the ordinary law. But if that were right, the Liebers reasoned, the Court's effort to draw crisp confines around necessity's exercise was doomed from the start. The limits of self-defense were inevitably situation-specific; emergency powers, as political theorist Clement Fatovic has recently observed, are highly contingent on circumstances.[75] Whether Lambdin Milligan's trial by military commission was necessary in the relevant sense was something that could only be determined on the basis of the specific facts at issue. No court could say—no commentator or observer or jurist could say—that necessity *never* authorized a military tribunal outside the theater of active combat or where the courts were open. Active fighting and the courthouse door might be evidentiary proxies or guides for the inquiry into necessity for a given set of circumstances. But when the stakes were high, no proxy for actual necessity could suffice.

The Liebers contended that the government's arguments and the opinion of the Court had conflated military law, the law of military occupation, and Martial Law Proper. The government's lawyers as well as Justice Davis had relied on Sir Matthew Hale's seventeenth-century common-law idea there could be no "martial law" where the "King's courts are open for all persons." But in modern parlance, Hale had meant "military law," not martial law. Continuing the mistake, Butler had contended that necessity gave the government the same authority over civilians that it already had over soldiers. But once again the Liebers denied that this was so. For unlike military law, Martial Law Proper conferred only the power that was necessary under the circumstances and nothing more. "Whatever is done by virtue of this power," they wrote, "must be connected with the necessity which is looked to for its justification."

The Lieber Theory therefore rejected any geographic test. Necessity alone provided boundaries for martial law; it might authorize different kinds of conduct in areas of active combat than in more peaceful areas like Indiana, but only because necessity's imperative varied from setting to setting. *Milligan*'s geographic limits were thus a doomed effort at "attempting to confine [martial law] within impossible bounds." A standard of necessity, not a bright-line rule, would determine where Martial Law Proper could have sway.

The Liebers also challenged Chief Justice Chase's contention that Congress could have authorized Milligan's detention and trial. Chase had claimed that as the lawmaking agent of the people, the Congress could be trusted to protect the people's liberties; his view that Congress is less dangerous in moments of emergency has been widely accepted in American constitutional culture before and since.[76] But the Liebers insisted that this institutional feature of the Congress cut in exactly the opposite way. It was precisely because congressional action carried something akin to the authorization of "We the People" to change the law that the Constitution allocated emergency powers to the executive branch rather than to the legislative. Congressionally created emergency powers would come with immunity provisions insulating government officials from challenge. The very fact of legislative action would thus make necessity "a justification which could not be impeached."[77] By contrast, executive action pursuant to a purported necessity justification would be subject to after-the-fact review.

But if the Court got the analysis of *Milligan* wrong, it had the outcome right. In Milligan's case, the Liebers believed that the government's actions were not within necessity's warrant.[78] At oral argument in the Supreme Court, Butler had enumerated a set of warlike factors that, he argued, were sufficient for the war power to "attach itself."[79] Lambdin Milligan, he noted, had been arrested, detained, and tried

> within a military district of a geographical military department, duly established by the commander-in-chief; within the military lines of the army, and upon the theatre of military operations; in a State which had been and was then threatened with invasion, having arsenals which the petitioner plotted to seize, and prisoners of war whom he plotted to liberate; where citizens were liable to be made soldiers, and were actually ordered into the ranks; and to prevent whose becoming soldiers the petitioner conspired with and armed others.[80]

For the Liebers, however, these facts did not get to the point: the question was whether there had been a *necessity* for Milligan's trial for those particular offenses. There was no actual war in Indiana, because the civil authorities remained intact. And under the circumstances, properly evaluated, there had been no military necessity to punish acts for which the civil law offered a remedy. Thus, as the Liebers wrote specifically in reference to *Milligan*, when "the courts are in the uninterrupted discharge of their functions, and furnish adequate protection against the wrongs alone referred to, and there is no necessity for a more speedy and certain remedy, trial by martial law is unauthorized."[81] If Milligan were to be tried for crimes outside the common law of war, that trial would have to occur in a civilian court.

Indeed, the Liebers went further, for it was not clear that necessity would ever warrant executions by military tribunal; at the very least, it would warrant executions only rarely, as perhaps in the case of Henry V's orders to kill prisoners of war whom he thought he had no way of detaining.[82] The Liebers ran through a litany of men executed under the alleged authority of martial law in the British Empire. But none of these executions, as the Liebers saw it, had been lawful. Necessity, they wrote, did not reach "the trial of offenders, under the common law of war." In wartime, no "war power springs up" automatically assuming "supreme and exclusive jurisdiction over all acts, wherever committed." To the contrary, so long as the ordinary legal processes were available for the administration of such punishment, and so long as detention without trial was a continuing option, the government would be hard pressed to show that necessity required punishment by military commission.

The Lieber view of *Milligan* reveals an important moment in the history of Reconstruction. The great subtext for *Milligan* was the fate of freedom for the former slaves. Butler could have defended the military commission trial of Lambdin Milligan by focusing on Milligan's violations of the laws of war. Nearly one thousand military commission trials had charged violations of the laws of war during the conflict, and virtually everyone agreed that violations of the rules of war could be tried by military commission. But Republicans in

Congress aimed to use military commissions in the effort to bring freedom to the occupied South. As a result, the government defended Milligan's military commission on a basis that would lay a precedent for the commissions still under way in the occupied South. These commissions were an extension of Lincoln's Emancipation project, the same effort that Lieber's General Orders No. 100 aimed to advance.[83]

In the years after *Milligan*, Congress and the Court would play a cat-and-mouse game, with the Court aiming to limit military commissions and the Congress trying to find creative ways to authorize their use and insulate them from review in the courts. The Liebers had been central to the strategy of invoking the power of military necessity on behalf of Emancipation. Forceful advocates for the freedpeople saw Reconstruction-era military commissions as crucial to the progress of freedom. (The elder Lieber's friend Charles Sumner adopted this view.[84]) But like many in the North, the Liebers pulled back from applying the full weight of the necessity power to Reconstruction. By 1868, when the Supreme Court ruled that it had the authority to decide on the legality of military commissions, such tribunals were essentially foreclosed as a vehicle for bringing justice to the relations of the freedpeople and their former masters.[85]

The power of military necessity, however, soon found a new home. As legal scholar Sarah Cleveland has shown, the Supreme Court would soon begin to emphasize the Lieberian idea that the federal government, and in particular the executive, possessed a set of unchecked "essential sovereign powers." The Court would begin to do so in cases relating to the federal government's inherent authority to regulate Indian tribes. That same inherent and plenary power soon thereafter would be extended to the regulation of immigration and the governance of the territories. In 1936, the Supreme Court would state baldly in *United States v. Curtiss-Wright Exp. Corp.* that these powers, even "if they had never been mentioned in the Constitution, would have vested in the federal government as necessary concomitants of nationality."[86] Here was a variation on the Lieber Theory of martial law, which had contended that military necessity was one such power.

The Global Context

While Americans were debating the scope of the federal government's martial law power in domestic civil war, events in the British Empire were producing parallel arguments.[87] In particular, developments in Jamaica touched off a fierce debate about the place and limits of martial law in the British Empire. The Liebers' manuscript linked these two debates together into an extended account of emergency in Anglo-American constitutionalism. Father and son discussed the historical precedents the British partisans relied on, ranging from the Middle Ages to more recent incidents in the Caribbean. In particular, the Liebers took up the work of one of the most important writers in the British debates, a man named William F. Finlason. If the Court's *Milligan* decision aspired to put new constraints on martial law in Anglo-American constitutional law, Finlason purported to find in martial law a source for a terrifying new power of imperial governance.

In 1865, revolt broke out in the town of Morant Bay, Jamaica. Slavery had been abolished in Jamaica, as in the rest of the empire, in 1838. But freedom had brought new challenges. White planters bemoaned falling agricultural productivity. Freedpeople and their descendants—350,000 out of a total population of 440,000—chafed at the constraints imposed by their white landlords and resented the persistence of planter power. Most of all, the freedpeople continued to live in desperate poverty. For many of them, their resentment came to focus on the local courts. Typically run by the island's few white citizens, who numbered only 14,000, the courts served as key sites for the reproduction of the power of the colonial elite. The courts were where white landlords evicted their black tenants, and in Morant Bay there had been a steady drumbeat of evictions running back years.[88]

Matters came to a head after Governor John Eyre and the white-run assembly rejected a series of reform proposals. On October 11, 1865, several hundred black residents of the town of Morant Bay stormed the local courthouse, killing eighteen people, including the chief magistrate, and burning down the building. Governor Eyre responded by proclaiming martial law in the area of Morant Bay. His forces loosed a reign of terror on the local population. In the days after the uprising, Eyre's militia detained, tortured, and executed hundreds of Jamaicans, mostly black.

In England, the events of 1865 Jamaica touched off fierce debate. Leading lights turned out to take sides. John Stuart Mill and Charles Darwin joined a hastily formed Jamaica Committee protesting that Eyre had been unjustified in the violence he exercised.[89] The committee sponsored private criminal prosecutions against Eyre and two subordinate military officers, Abercrombie Nelson and Herbert Brand.[90] Though ultimately unsuccessful, the prosecutions brought leading jurists into the debate. Pamphlets poured off the presses with argument and counterargument.

The debate was about more than Jamaica. By the mid-nineteenth century, constitutional government was an important part of British ideology; martial law in England itself was

unthinkable. But at the same time, Britain had acquired a vast
overseas empire, maintained by often-brutal coercion of indigenous populations, restive settlers, military deserters and
mutineers, and forced laborers. The debate over martial law, as
scholars like Rande Kostal and Thomas Poole have shown, was
in many ways an attempt to reconcile the demand for law at
home, but tyranny abroad.[91] This had profound consequences
for the legal and political history of much of the rest of the
British Empire. Arguments in favor of a special colonial theory of martial law created two very different legal regimes in
the empire, one for England and the other for its colonies—a
factor that political theorist Nasser Hussain argues powerfully
shaped British India and its modern successor states.[92]

Indeed, in British India in the late nineteenth century,
British rule was enforced through a sort of permanent state of
exception, in which British officers claimed the right to exercise authority summarily and often brutally.[93] But paradoxi-
cally, despite or perhaps because of India's particular importance, and its different legal situation, much smaller colonies
loomed much larger in the martial law debate. Throughout the
empire, questions about martial law often arose where small
groups of settlers exercised control over much larger groups
of enslaved or subjugated laborers. Many of these island colonies were sites of agricultural production. Others, like Aus-
tralia, the Andaman Islands, or Norfolk Island, housed penal
colonies and military bases, in which regular civil administration had little role. As Lauren Benton has argued, such islands
were in one sense models of the type of absolute control over
bounded spaces that imperial states sought to impose generally. In another sense, they were also anomalies, set off from
the rest of the empire.[94] This latter feature made them susceptible to particular legal arrangements. Men like Governor

Eyre saw the remoteness of island possessions as grounds for thinking that extra-constitutional military authority could be confined. But for critics associated with the Jamaica Committee, the great danger was that distant islands might serve as "'nurseries' of martial law."[95] Victorian Englishmen feared that such exceptions to ordinary legal norms "might allow tyranny to migrate to other parts of empire."[96]

Thus, in a sense, the British debate over martial law, like the American debate, was about geography. Just as the Supreme Court worried that the law applying to persons in the rebellious southern states might move north into Indiana, so British observers worried that the law applying to ex-slaves and their children in Jamaica might move back to the imperial metropole. There were important differences, however. For one, post–Civil War military commissions sought to help ex-slaves, while martial law in Jamaica sought to suppress their demands. Moreover, the U.S. South was still—thanks to Union victory in the Civil War—part of the same nation as the North. As the end of Reconstruction proved, the white residents of these states could be readmitted to the Union on equal terms. The same was not true in India or Jamaica.

The influential British writer and jurist William F. Finlason played an especially important role in the debates that followed the Morant Bay insurrection. Now largely forgotten outside his role in the Jamaica affair, Finlason was among the best-known commentators on the British legal scene in the second half of the nineteenth century. The beginnings of his career were modestly promising, though hardly auspicious. Rising from an obscure family, Finlason was admitted to the bar in the prestigious Middle Temple, one of the exclusive English Inns of Court. Yet he never became more than a junior barrister, or "stuff-shirt barrister," as low-ranking members of the bar were known. Indeed, Finlason rarely went beyond the low-level work of drafting pleadings. But he did not let his middling status at the bar interfere with his career ambitions. Instead, Finlason found his real talent as a writer about the law. He became *The Times* of London's chief writer on legal affairs. Virtually inventing the role played a century and more later by American journalists like Anthony Lewis, Linda Greenhouse, and Adam Liptak, Finlason wrote *The Times's* legal coverage for nearly fifty years.

In particular, Finlason developed a fascination with one of the great legal questions of Victorian empire: the law of emergency in the colonies. After Morant Bay, Finlason wrote no fewer than five books on the subject of martial law.[97] As Rande Kostal has observed, Finlason's work in this area was especially concerned with "the military, demographic, and racial exigencies of the expanding empire."[98] For Finlason, the prototypical colonial rebellion pitted "a small loyal community" (usually white) against a much larger number of rebels (usually black or Indian). Martial law, in his account, was the legal regime in which colonial elites could maintain their power when insurrectionary violence broke out.

Accordingly, Finlason offered a stunningly ferocious account of martial law. In his view, martial law was the equivalent of "a declaration of a state of war." It was a kind of "arbitrary military power" that "suspends the common law." Not even necessity could constrain it, strictly speaking. "For what is necessity," Finlason asked, "and who is to judge of it?" Finlason stated the key question for a regime of necessity as crisply as it could be put: necessity with respect to what? It mattered immensely whether necessity was measured by "reference to the instant exigencies of the particular time or place," or instead with respect to "larger considerations" and the strategic goals of the state. Finlason came to a forceful answer. The common law, he argued, had the requisite authority for dealing with "actual outrage or insurrection." The common law had been built, after all, to remedy unlawful resort to force and arms. The distinctive feature of martial law was that it dealt in "measures preventive or deterrent."[99] Martial law, Finlason said, made available "the deterrent effect of the terror inspired by the terrible severities of military law[.]"[100]

In Kostal's words, Finlason was "the mid-Victorian era's foremost authority on the legal technology of terror."[101] Indeed, terror was Finlason's central strategy of authority for the empire. As in Jamaica, only force could ultimately permit an "inadequate force" of colonial militia to manage "a much larger" group of rebellious subjects. Martial law would thus use "summary executions, according to the stern severity of military law" in order to "inspire a terror" into rebels. Terror, Finlason reported, was "of the very nature of martial law," and "measures deterrent by means of terror," including what *The Times* of London's chief legal writer called "great severities," were martial law's "very essence."[102]

Finlason was not only the most prolific of the martial law writers during the 1866–1867 debates about Jamaica. He was also one of the most influential. His work was, to be sure, a polemic in support of Governor Eyre's position. It was often poorly written and repetitive—not surprising, as Finlason wrote with astounding speed.[103] But it was, at the same time, "the most comprehensive discussion of martial law that had ever been written in English."[104] At a time when the precise bounds of martial law were largely a mystery to British legal and political elites, Finlason laid down a powerful account of what martial law was and what it did in Anglo-American constitutionalism.

It is not clear from Finlason's writings on martial law whether he ever read Francis Lieber's work on the laws of war. Finlason's work, however, echoed the elder Lieber's emphasis on military necessity. Finlason, too, insisted that short and sharp wars were ultimately more humane than wars fought with one hand tied behind the back. A harsh application of martial law, Finlason argued, "even when inflicting military executions, is really merciful, for it is certain to save life in the long run."[105] If Francis Lieber drew on Clausewitz's work, so too did Finlason. (One historian has called Finlason's treatise "a Clausewitzian rumination on the harsh racial and political realities of the burgeoning empire."[106]) Parallel to Lieber's view that "[t]o save the country is paramount to all other considerations,"[107] Finlason's vision of martial law sought "to prevail at all costs," saving white settlers from annihilation by nonwhite majorities.[108]

It is clear that the Liebers read Finlason.[109] Given the British writer's influence, it would have been surprising if they had not. And yet the Liebers' approach was radically different in important respects. The Lieber Theory rested on the natural law right of self-defense. Their argument explicitly began with the inalienability of that right, inherent in all sovereign states. From there, they reasoned that the right of necessity in cases of self-defense must exist in the United States, even though some plausible readings of the Constitution seemed to deny this. This was the logic of the Lieber Code's fierce refrain: "to save the country is paramount to all other considerations."

Finlason, however, reversed the basic structure of the Lieber account.[110] The British jurist began with the historical authorities, drawing on a wide variety of cases, official legal opinions, and treatises. From these precedents, Finlason argued that martial law was "the *law of war*."[111] This meant that the government could exercise arbitrary power, through the military, in wartime and sometimes in peacetime. Unlike the Liebers (and Justice Chase in *Milligan*), Finlason did not sharply distinguish "military law" from "martial law"—at least not in wartime. Everyone agreed that the Crown's discretion (the "prerogative") allowed the monarch to go beyond the common law, establishing the Articles of War and enforcing these through courts-martial. Finlason also believed that the 1628 Petition of Right, and elements of British practice, authorized more than this. In his account, martial law extended the authority of military law to civilians. The Crown could therefore exercise "not merely the regular authority of military law as exercised in peace, but also all that military power which is exercised towards an enemy or armed rebel in time of war."[112]

To the Liebers, this was a category error, for it mistook martial law for military law. Finlason made the same mistake as the Duke of Wellington, who famously remarked (as the Liebers note in their manuscript) that martial law was nothing other than "the will of the general who commands the army."[113] In Wellington's conception, the Liebers observed, "martial law was no law at all." But as a description of martial law as opposed to military law, Wellington's dictum was crucially wrong. The difference between the two was vital, for the former was governed by the constraint of necessity, whereas the latter was the unconfined will of the military commander. Martial law and military law were thus entirely distinct.[114]

This seemingly obscure point mattered greatly, for it was the difference between a regime of law and a regime of lawlessness. Indeed, it was important enough that the Liebers spent five chapters discussing British history. They sought systematically to demolish Finlason's arguments, first tracing the history of military law and arguing that neither the Petition of Right

nor the preamble to the 1703 Mutiny Act allowed military law
to be applied to civilians, in war or peace.[115] (Norman Lieber
also made this argument in a later standalone pamphlet.[116])
The Liebers went on to trace, in some detail, instances of British state practice that might have been seen as exercises of a
prerogative right of martial law. They mentioned a number
of others more briefly, including many that had been cited by
Finlason as examples of martial law in British history.[117] But
the Liebers distinguished all of these. In much of the late Middle Ages and early modern era, they argued, "the prerogative
was at its highest power, or rather, was exercised without regard to law. Its illegal exercise can never be cited as precedent
to qualify a repetition of the abuse."[118]

Properly understood, the Liebers continued, martial law
in the modern sense had only come into existence since the
rise of modern constitutional states in the seventeenth and
eighteenth centuries. Indeed, the category of modern military
law presupposed a distinction between the soldier and the
subject that had only been invented in the Mutiny Acts, which
beginning in 1689 had authorized discipline within the military. Viewing the matter this way, the Liebers concluded that
the only proper precedents for *true* martial law, or Martial Law
Proper, came from the Irish uprisings of the late eighteenth
and early nineteenth centuries. There and only there had
Parliament recognized the inherent prerogative conferred by
necessity itself. Significantly, the Parliament had indemnified
officers who had violated the law, something that would have
been necessary only if the officers had been acting under a
legal limit on their authority—namely, the necessity constraint
imposed by Martial Law Proper.[119]

The Liebers also traced four modern cases that had
loomed large in the British debate—the trial of Joseph Wall

for harsh disciplinary measures he took while commanding a garrison in Senegal in 1782; the suppression of revolts on Demerara (an island in the Caribbean) in 1823 and on Sri Lanka (then called Ceylon) in 1817–1818 and 1848; and the 1865 Morant Bay incident itself.[120] They did not systematically take positions on these cases, but they did distinguish Wall's case from any present issues, and they explicitly challenged one of the judicial opinions arising out of the Morant Bay case. In the midst of an epic five-hour charge to the grand jury in the case of Nelson and Brand, Lord Chief Justice Sir Alexander Cockburn—even while repudiating many of Finlason's views—had suggested that in the limited circumstances martial law was permissible, it would resemble military law applied to civilians. The Liebers, of course, rejected this, for the same reason they rejected Finlason's dangerous conflation of military law and martial law. The former was a regime undisciplined by necessity, a regime of vast and arbitrary disciplinary authority for commanders in a hierarchical organizational structure for the governance of armies.[121]

The Liebers devoted great energy to refuting Finlason's views because, as they saw it, the British jurist imagined a state of exception in which there would be no meaningful constraint. For Finlason, martial law meant the nonreviewable discretion to do "anything which possibly could be deemed necessary or expedient, by the military authorities, for the carrying out its object."[122] As long as Parliament, or an appropriate Crown official, had a good-faith belief that martial law was necessary, Finlason insisted that they had unreviewable authority to act, just as a military commander had unreviewable authority to discipline the men under his command. This set a much higher bar for *ex post* review than the Liebers thought appropriate. As the Liebers saw it, officials who defended their actions on the ground of military necessity needed to show *more* than simply a good-faith belief in necessity. In *Mitchell v. Harmony*, the U.S. Supreme Court had held that "an honest judgment" and the desire to "promote the public service" was insufficient; officers "must show by proof the nature and character of the emergency, such as he had reasonable grounds to believe it to be ... [that] it was so pressing as not to admit of delay[.]"[123] Mere good faith was insufficient; instead, an official invoking military necessity had to act in good faith and reasonably. Good faith pursued unreasonably would be no defense.

The after-the-fact scrutiny defended by the Liebers could not be reconciled with the dichotomous regime Finlason advocated. For Finlason, the common law gave way, under the force of necessity, to a blanket privilege. But for the Liebers, it persisted in the form of an obligation to make necessity determinations according to an objective standard of reasonableness. This key distinction prepares us to see the most distinctive contribution of the Lieber manuscript to the debates over emergency constitutionalism.

The Lieber Theory of Emergency Constitutionalism

Finlason's writing on martial law anticipated a number of features in Carl Schmitt's theory of the state of exception. For Schmitt, the moment of necessity takes its shape precisely because it is radically unconstrained. Like the judge who confronts a question with no doctrinally required answer, the sovereign in the moment of necessity faces a moment of unbound power. In the emergency he does what is necessary to defend the state. And to know what means are necessary to defend the state, logic requires that he decide upon the character and identity of the state as well. Here, then, is the radical power of the Schmittian moment of necessity. In the moment of crisis the sovereign does more than decide on the collective tactics of self-defense; the sovereign's choice of tactics revises the very identity of the state.

Finlason was no Schmitt. He lacked the clarity of the German jurist. He was no theorist. He was, in world-historical comparison, a kind of hack. But his approach to martial law in empire carried some of the same implications. For in the moment of colonial crisis, Finlason thought necessity offered no constraint. In his hands, as we have seen, the necessity power became a tool of terror.

The Liebers, by contrast, developed an alternative way of understanding the emergency that was at once subtle and powerful, one that responded to Finlason's provocations and anticipated the limits of Schmitt's approach. Ironically, they drew it in part from the *Mitchell v. Harmony* opinion of Chief Justice Roger Taney, whose *Merryman* opinion on habeas corpus in 1861 had helped touch off the elder Lieber's engagement with Civil War constitutionalism.

In the case of Governor Eyre at Morant Bay, Mr. Justice Ker had instructed the grand jury that "public safety" "confides to the supreme authority in every country the power to declare when the emergency has arisen."[124] But the Liebers rejected this conclusion. Their alternative approach began with the proposition that the problem of emergency constitutionalism has a special structure in republics constituted by the law. Some regimes are built out of a collectivity with an identity prior to the state—an identity stemming from religious affiliation, perhaps, or an imagined ethnic or racial heritage. But others are self-constituted by the law. The United States, they contended, is of the latter type. It is the recursive construct of "We the People." This meant that in the moment of crisis the

United States had a distinctive question to ask. It could not in any simple way set aside the laws to preserve a conceptually independent collective. The collective was itself constructed by those laws; they could not be set aside without completely undoing the thing their relaxation was meant to defend.

The idea that martial law posed an existential danger to a regime constituted by law had been the central feature of the raging debates over emergency constitutionalism and slavery during the decades leading up to the Civil War. Beginning with John Quincy Adams in the 1830s, some from the North had contended that emergencies and the necessity power they carried with them held the potential to undo slavery. Southern critics responded by insisting that the end of slavery would so radically transform the identity of the republic as to leave it unrecognizable. This would not be a form of constitutional self-defense, they insisted; it would be a form of constitutional aggression. For their part, slavery's opponents answered that the federal government surely had to have the power to emancipate slaves if doing so was necessary to defend the republic. Indeed, the arguments made by Adams (whom the elder Lieber had known as president in the 1820s) anticipated by nearly thirty years Lincoln's Emancipation Proclamation, an order that relied for its authority on the military necessity power that Adams had raised and that the Lieber manuscript would later elaborate.[125]

The Liebers took the point a step further. If the republic had no collective identity independent of the laws, then neither did the republic's leaders have a position outside the law. Those with power in the regime held that power in virtue of the regime. Their projects and interests and strategies were inevitably conditioned by the regime. How, after all, could it be otherwise? There was, then, no clean moment of terror (Finlason) or bare power (Schmitt). There were only problems and actors situated in and constructed by regimes.

As a descriptive matter, the observation that the law accompanied emergencies was vitally important. It rebutted the bitter nihilism of Finlason's state of terror and anticipated the critique offered by scholars like David Dyzenhaus, Benjamin Straumann, and others of Schmitt's state of exception.[126] It foreshadowed the contention of British legal theorist Thomas Poole, echoing the American lawyer Philip Bobbitt, that the logic of raison d'état is inescapably contingent on the particular kind of regime in which the claim of necessity arises. And it resonated powerfully with the argument offered by Canadian political theorist Nomi Lazar a century and a half later that a regime's norms inevitably condition its responses to emergency. "There is no exception," declares Lazar. The Liebers would have agreed.[127]

Yet the Liebers' theory did not deny that emergencies left vast room for powerful men to transform the character and identity of self-constructed republics. So the Liebers added a prescriptive argument that followed closely from their descriptive insight. What could a state do in the moment of emergency? The appropriate question, argued the Liebers, was whether the conduct in question was necessary as measured by the commonsense judgment of a reasonable citizen. The acts of officials in moments of emergency, they wrote, "should be adjudged to be necessary in the judgment of a moderate and reasonable man." As they saw it, "reason and common sense must approve the particular act." If "these conditions are not fulfilled, the act becomes unlawful, with all the consequences attending to illegality."

Invoking the reasonable man—what we would today call the reasonable *person*—at this stage of the argument was a subtle but powerful move. Doing so not only created a standard for deciding whether the means chosen were permissible or not, it also implicitly shaped and constrained the ends toward which necessary means might be deployed.

John Locke's prerogative power, which was so important to the Liebers' theory, had been subtly different. Locke had constrained the prerogative by reference to the "publick good and advantage." In Locke's conception, the executive power was authorized to act without or against the law so long as those actions promoted "the preservation of all." The Lockean citizen, after all, had entered into a social contract to protect his survival.[128]

In the Liebers' theory, the ends invoked by the reasonable citizen analysis were not the same as biological survival. The reasonableness standard brought values along, too: an entire cluster of values and principles drawn from the constitutive commitments of the republic. For the Liebers, the ends from which one might derive permissible or necessary means thus included the public values of the regime, embodied in the perspective of the reasonable citizen.

How else, after all, can we explain the Liebers' firm stand against torture? The elder Lieber's G.O. 100 made it a point to prohibit torture without exception during war. Very few acts, even terrible acts, were categorically prohibited in his view. But torture was. "If, for instance, it be true," he wrote to Halleck in 1864, that "one of our officers was nailed to a board and roasted, we could never retaliate by roasting." Warning against strong retaliatory measures near the end of the war, the elder Lieber put it this way to his friend Charles Sumner: "If we fight with Indians who slowly roast their prisoners, we cannot roast in turn the Indians whom we may capture." Sumner read the letter on the floor of the Senate.[129]

The moment of necessity, as Schmitt would later understand, was one in which the ends and means of the republic—its very definition of the Lockean "publick good"—were plastic and up for revision. But the Liebers' earlier and deeper observation was that the public reason of the republic conditioned the process by which ends and means evolved. The two were mutually constitutive. Necessity, in the Liebers' hands, was thus not merely a warrant for harsh measures, though it could sometimes be that. It was instead a discursive frame for organizing and structuring the process by which "We the People" decide what matters in the midst of an emergency.[130]

Conclusion: Rethinking Lincoln and Emergencies

The Liebers' insights substantially revise the tradition of American thinking about moments of emergency. In particular, the Liebers crafted an alternative to the indigenous American tradition of Schmittian realism. In their hands, the Constitution was no scrap of paper, as John J. McCloy would later have it, to be discarded when the defense of the entity known as the nation so required; nor was it a mutual security pact among actors who existed before and outside the document, as Justice Jackson's "suicide pact" conception suggested. As the Liebers understood it, the self-constituted character of the American republic meant that there was no such entity to defend and no such actors to secure. A legally constructed collective organized around a particular culture of normative reason was all there was.

Understood this way, the Lieber manuscript offers an alternative way of making sense of Abraham Lincoln's famous July 4, 1861, speech. When Lincoln looked into the emergency, he did

not imagine that the nation he aimed to protect existed outside
of its laws. Instead, he put the problem as one arising exclusively within a matrix of law. Are all the laws but one to fall, he
asked, so that one might be upheld? Here was a republic constructed entirely by laws. Lincoln's choice in the crisis of the
legally constructed republic was not the simple one of rescuing
some independently existing community that the laws aimed
to protect. His dilemma, as his words captured perfectly, was
precisely that there was nothing outside the law to rescue.

From that fundamental insight, the Liebers developed
a theory of the emergency constitution. What the Liebers offered was a crisis-tested conception of emergency constitutions that threaded the needle between constraint and license.
Theirs was a model of democratic constitutionalism that aspired to be strong enough for the occasion while avoiding the
danger that power would undo the very republic it had promised to defend.

It is in the nature of such a manuscript, of course, that
it does not even pretend to tie up every loose end. New challenges have arisen in the century since its drafting, some of
which the Liebers barely speak to at all. Yet in an age that has
become preoccupied with the Schmittian idea of the exception, in a moment when the terrifying allure of naked power
has seized the legal imagination, the Lieber manuscript carries
critical insights about the persistence of law, even in extremis.

In the aftermath of *Milligan* and Morant Bay, the Lieber manuscript proposed a theory of emergency constitutionalism that
speaks powerfully to debates that have persisted in the century
and more since its authors set the manuscript aside.

Nearly 150 years after the elder Lieber's death, the manuscript he never finished offers a useful perspective for emer-

gencies in the ongoing age of terror. Even now, nearly two decades since the terrorist attacks of September 11, 2001, the law of terror is still evolving. But so far, the Liebers' manuscript has proven farsighted. For the Liebers' Civil War experience helped them see how the constitutional norms of the republic—its basic system of public reason—would shape and condition the ways in which emergencies play out in constitutional democracies.

Consider the military commissions system put in place by the administration of George W. Bush soon after 9/11 and ultimately continued by Bush's successor, Barack Obama. From the outset, many on the American political right argued that when enemy combatants are charged with crimes, they should be dealt with outside the regular court system.[131] Criminal trials, they contended, are too slow. The evidentiary rules of the courts, they insisted, are too inhospitable to classified intelligence. Most of all, criminal trials in the federal courts put at risk information obtained through torture or (as some officials euphemistically put it) "enhanced interrogation." Beyond the legal arguments, many Americans seem to share the widespread intuition that criminal justice, with its due process and jury trial traditions, unduly elevates terrorist suspects.

By contrast, critics of the military commission system have defended the criminal law and advocated terrorism trials in the federal courts. Federal law, they point out, provides many tools for such trials, including tough statutes, long prison terms (and the death penalty), experienced judges, aggressive prosecutors, and established procedures for admitting evidence, including systems for evaluating classified information. Such critics—including civil libertarians and political liberals—point to the long record of federal criminal convictions for foreign terrorism.

Debates like these would have been right at home in the middle of the nineteenth century. The Liebers might have been startled by the technology of the U.S. response to terror: drones and satellites and precision weapons would have been radically unfamiliar. But the Civil War–era jurists would have understood many of the basic legal problems that have come with the age of terror.

The Civil War's military commissions, after all, helped inspire the tribunals of the post-9/11 years. The Civil War experience encouraged a generation of executive branch lawyers to defend commissions as part of the president's inherent, constitutional commander-in-chief authority. Indeed, the fiercest of these lawyers seemed to reject any and all limits on the executive in time of crisis. Architects of the martial law of empire, men such as William Finlason, would have recognized and applauded the uncompromising defense of executive authority to establish military commissions.

Critics of twenty-first-century military commissions have nineteenth-century forerunners, too. When the U.S. Supreme Court overruled the post–Civil War commissions in *Ex parte Milligan* in 1866, it articulated a position on the law of emergencies that is alive and well to this day. "The Constitution of the United States is a law for rulers and people, equally in war and in peace," wrote Justice David Davis. Just so, insist the twenty-first-century civil libertarians. There are, they contend, no legal black holes, no spaces for antiterror efforts beyond the law.[132]

The Liebers articulated a middle view, one that aimed to authorize the power necessary to respond to the emergency, but no more. The Liebers disdained those who shied from the necessary exercise of power by the state in crisis. They rejected the hard-and-fast prohibition set out by *Milligan* on military commissions where the courts are open. (Necessity, not geography, was the Liebers' standard.) Recall, too, that Francis Lieber rejected Justice Taney's 1861 *Merryman* opinion precisely because he believed that President Lincoln had unilateral authority when necessary to suspend habeas corpus. The Liebers would thus very likely have rejected the views of today's civil libertarian critics of military commissions. They would likely have maintained that President Bush had the authority to try accused terrorists in military commissions, though only when necessity reasonably so required. In each case the question for them would have been (as it was in *Milligan*) one of necessity and reason, not one of bright-line rules.

But the Liebers would also have rejected the path of Finlason. They rejected unlimited state power in the emergency as a road to the same kinds of terror that the state aimed to hold off. They rejected the idea of a limitless authority in the executive branch. They insisted instead that the president was constrained by the principle of necessity, even if he was also licensed by it.

In one sense, this middle path has been forgotten, in part because of limits internal to the Liebers' framework (more on this below), and in part because the polarizing controversies of the twenty-first century's age of terror have overlooked it.

In another sense, however, the Liebers predicted with uncanny accuracy the basic landscape of the law of emergencies a century and a half after the end of the Civil War. The Liebers insisted that the power of the state in the moment of emergency does not exist independently of the public reason of the society: its most basic norms and commitments. And a century and a half later, the persistent influence of those basic norms has shaped and conditioned the strongest claims of the executive branch.

The post-9/11 story of the U.S. policy on torture illustrates both the power and the limits of constitutional norms.
In a television interview less than a week after the September
11 attacks, Vice President Dick Cheney infamously announced
that the Bush administration would not hesitate to go beyond
existing law with regard to intelligence collection. The United
States, Cheney notoriously said, had to work the "dark side"
and "spend time in the shadows"; the conflict, he insisted,
was with "barbarians" and was, he later added, an "existential" battle. More directly, in 2002 then–White House counsel
(and later attorney general) Alberto Gonzales stated that this
conflict "renders obsolete Geneva's strict limitations on ques-
tioning of enemy prisoners and renders quaint some of its provisions." John Yoo at the Justice Department's Office of Legal
Counsel argued that with respect to "any terrorist threat," the
president possessed unchecked authority over "the amount of
military force to be used in response, or the method, timing,
and nature of the response."[133]

Slowly but surely, however, these assertions of state authority with regard to interrogation were ratcheted back by
the norms of the constitutional order. A range of public and
private institutions and individuals, including investigative
journalists, judge advocates, and private lawyers, combined to
check the executive branch. Through their efforts, the public
norms of the constitutional order turned out to have real bite.
In June 2004 the Bush administration formally withdrew a key
opinion and substituted one that rejected torture and recognized limits on the executive branch. On the eve of the fifth
anniversary of 9/11, President Bush sounded a new note when
he stated that "the United States does not torture. It's against
our laws, and it's against our values."[134]

As one inside observer puts it, the pattern of the post-
9/11 years has been one of power *and* constraint.[135] Think of

the United States' approach to the detention of suspected terrorists. The months following 9/11 saw bold assertions of virtually unfettered presidential power to capture and detain suspected enemies. Justice Department attorneys argued that the president "enjoy[ed] complete discretion" in exercising the commander-in-chief authority vested in him.[136] This theory ran aground in a series of landmark Supreme Court cases—starting with the Court's 2004 decision in *Rasul v. Bush*, which held that U.S. courts had jurisdiction under the federal habeas corpus statute. After Congress attempted to remove the habeas privilege, the Court reasserted the viability of the habeas procedure for detainees not once but twice.[137]

White House efforts to exclude captured enemy combatants from protections of the laws of war foundered as well when the Supreme Court held that U.S. treaty obligations to adhere to Common Article 3 of the Geneva Conventions applied to the conflict with al Qaeda.[138] Yet it was not only the courts that pushed back against the executive branch authority. Once again, judge advocates, private legal organizations like the Center for Constitutional Rights, and the press played important roles in upholding basic norms of the republic. As David Cole has pointed out, many of the most significant changes to presidential policy were not compelled by the Supreme Court. The pressures that worked to recalibrate executive authority were the result of what Cole calls "civil society constitutionalism"—and what the Liebers might have called the reason of the republic.[139]

The history of the military commissions offers a similar lesson about the power of the republic's basic norms. As we write this, the commissions have ground nearly to a halt. For more than a decade, the commissions have struggled to function in the absence of well-settled rules of evidence, without the strictures of attorney-client confidentiality, and lacking any number of other procedures that are so well-established in civilian courts. Substantial questions of unlawful command influence remain unresolved. (President Donald Trump has praised the Guantánamo detention camp and called for harsh verdicts.) Defense lawyers have quit and been held in contempt as the process unravels. The appeals process is complex and untested.[140]

In this and other areas, the public reason of the republic—the constitutive body of law that contains norms about jury trials, the federal courts, and basic criminal procedure—has shaped and reshaped the legal response to terrorism.

None of this is to say that the Liebers' manuscript delivers answers to the legal challenges of the age of terror. The Liebers offer us a vantage for seeing what is at stake in those challenges. The two nineteenth-century jurists help us see the long history of such challenges, stretching back a century and a half and more. But they deliver few specific prescriptions. Indeed, at a deeper level, their manuscript leaves the reader not only with new insights but also with unanswered questions.

It is striking, for example, that the Liebers offer little by way of an institutional account of how to allocate the authority to decide on the necessity. They powerfully insist that decisions about necessity and what it requires are conditioned by an obligation of reasonableness rooted in the basic norms and culture of the regime. But it is surprising that they have so little to say about how to arrange final authority on those decisions. Such an omission is all the more striking because of how much ink American political theory has spilled on precisely those institutional questions. Going back to *The Federalist*, it is fair to say that the American literature on emergency has been preoccupied by institutional questions such as the allocation of authority among the three branches of government.

Yet for a theory resting principally upon the power and integrity of a republic's basic commitments, the Liebers tell their readers very little about what those basic commitments are or ought to be. To be sure, they set torture out of bounds. The reader can glean something about the identity of the regime from that fact. In his other writings, especially during the Civil War, the elder Lieber articulated a powerful vision of a republic organized around virtue. Francis Lieber held strong ideas about the value of a stern civilization and martial rectitude, some (but not all) of which were very attractive. But the Liebers' vision is maddeningly vague. They offer little by way of an account of the identity of the republic or of its principal commitments. And even more worrisome, their accounts seem to have evolved substantially during the older Lieber's adult lifetime. As a young public intellectual in the 1830s, Lieber championed a libertarianism of sorts, one that promoted civil liberty above all. As a more mature jurist during the war he gave voice to a far more robust role for the state. In the 1830s he denied that a president could unilaterally suspend the writ of habeas corpus. In the 1860s he reversed course. Which republic, one wonders, would supply the basic principles and reason of the regime? The libertarian republic of the elder Lieber's antebellum years? Or the martial republic of his mature phase?

No example better captures the problem for the theory than the example of slavery and emancipation. In the years of the elder Lieber's youth, it was precisely the defenders of slavery who worried about the dangerous and transformative risks of martial law. Wartime emancipations, they warned, would allow security emergencies to remake the basic constitutional arrangements of the republic. Emancipation, in their view, would be a transformative event, undoing the identity of a slave society. The defenders of the slaveocracy contended that

if the laws of war could undo slavery, then emergency powers were unlimited. Protecting slavery, they insisted, was one
of the basic commitments of the republic. If the state could
undo that commitment in the name of emergency or martial
law, then the republic's principles seemed not to condition and
constrain the operation of emergency powers. In their view,
the Emancipation Proclamation itself was a culminating example of the abuse of emergency powers: in the name of crisis,
Abraham Lincoln fundamentally altered the identity of the republic. How could the Liebers' theory of martial law answer
such a powerful critique?[141]

This critique was not unanswerable. An entire generation
of antislavery jurists and political figures had argued that the
Constitution was actually an antislavery document, and that
protecting slavery was not one of the republic's basic commitments. The Liebers never offered such an answer to the limits
of their theory. The unexpected and untimely death of the elder
Lieber cut off the inquiry, and the younger man was not as the-
oretically inclined as the father. Nonetheless, the manuscript
left by the two Liebers offers a vantage on crises a century and
a half ago as well as today. The Liebers' theory reaches out like
a bridge to a constitutional world simultaneously very different from, and powerfully similar to, our own.

Notes

1. E.g., Bruce Ackerman, *Before the Next Attack* (New Haven: Yale University Press, 2006); Giorgio Agamben, *State of Exception* (Chicago: University of Chicago Press, 2004); Giorgio Agamben, *Homo Sacer* (Palo Alto,
CA: Stanford University Press, 1998); David Dyzenhaus, *Legality and Legitimacy: Carl Schmitt, Hans Kelsen, and Hermann Heller in Weimar* (Oxford:
Clarendon Press, 1997); David Dyzenhaus, *The Constitution of Law: Legality
in a Time of Emergency* (Cambridge: Cambridge University Press, 2006);
Samuel Issacharoff and Richard Pildes, "Between Civil Libertarianism and

Executive Unilateralism," in *The Constitution in Wartime*, ed. Mark Tushnet (Durham, NC: Duke University Press, 2005), 161–97; Nomi Lazar, *States of Emergency in Liberal Democracies* (Cambridge: Cambridge University Press, 2009); Karin Loevy, *Emergencies in Public Law: The Legal Politics of Containment* (Cambridge: Cambridge University Press, 2016); Eric A. Posner and Adrian Vermeule, *The Executive Unbound* (Oxford: Oxford University Press, 2011); Clinton Rossiter, *Constitutional Dictatorship* (Abingdon: Routledge, 2002); Carl Schmitt, *Political Theology: Four Chapters on the Concept of Sovereignty*, trans. George Schwab (Chicago: University of Chicago Press, 2006); Carl Schmitt, *Dictatorship* (Malden, MA: Polity Press, 2014); Trevor Morrison, "Suspension and the Extra Judicial Constitution," *Columbia Law Review* 107, no. 7 (2007): 1533–616; Stephen I. Vladeck, "The *Field* Theory: Martial Law, the Suspension Power, and the Insurrection Act," *Temple Law Review* 80, no. 2 (2007): 391–439; Stephen I. Vladeck, "Emergency Power and the Militia Acts," *Yale Law Journal* 114, no. 1 (2004): 149–94; Saikrishna Prakash, "The Imbecilic Executive," *Virginia Law Review* 99, no. 7 (2013): 1361–433; Michael Stokes Paulsen, "The Constitution of Necessity," *Notre Dame Law Review* 79, no. 4 (2004): 1257–97; Kim Lane Scheppele, "North American Emergencies," *International Journal of Constitutional Law* 4, no. 2 (April 2006): 213–43.

2. John Fabian Witt, *Lincoln's Code: The Laws of War in American History* (New York: Free Press, 2012); Frank Freidel, *Francis Lieber: Nineteenth-Century Liberal* (Baton Rouge: Louisiana State University Press, 1947); Stephen Neff, *Justice in Blue and Gray* (Cambridge, MA: Harvard University Press, 2010); Charles Mack and Henry Lesesne, eds., *Francis Lieber and the Life of the Mind* (Columbia: University of South Carolina Press, 2005); James F. Childress, "Francis Lieber's Interpretation of the Laws of War: General Orders No. 100 in the Context of His Life and Thought," *American Journal of Jurisprudence* 21 (1976): 34–70; Michael Herz, "Rediscovering Francis Lieber," *Cardozo Law Review* 16 (1995): 2107–34; Paul Finkelman, "Francis Lieber and the Modern Law of War," *University of Chicago Law Review* 80 (2013): 2071–132; David Bosco, "Moral Principle vs. Military Necessity," *The American Scholar*, Winter 2008, https://theamericanscholar.org/moral-principle-vs-military-necessity/.

3. Francis Lieber to Henry Halleck, May 30, 1863, Francis Lieber Papers, Huntington Library, San Marino, California (hereinafter Lieber Huntington Papers); Francis Lieber to Henry Halleck, March 10, 1864, Lieber Huntington Papers.

4. Francis Lieber to Henry Halleck, May 28, 1866, Lieber Huntington Papers; *Ex parte* Milligan 71 U.S. (4 Wall.) 2 (1866).

5. *Ex parte* Merryman, 17 F. Cas. 144 (C.C. D. Md. 1861); *Milligan*, 71 U.S. 2.

6. On the handoff of Lieber's disorganized papers to Johns Hopkins, the Huntington Library, and the judge advocate general, see Freidel, *Francis Lieber*, 418–20; Bonnie G. Smith, "Gender and the Practices of Scientific History: The Seminar and Archival Research in the Nineteenth Century," *American Historical Review* 100 (1995): 1150–76. On Lieber's books, which went to the new University of California at Berkeley, see "The Late Dr. Lieber," *Daily Evening Bulletin* (San Francisco), March 24, 1873.

7. See G. Norman Lieber, *Meaning of the Term Martial Law as Used in the Petition of Right and the Preamble to the Mutiny Act* (n.p., 1877), 2–3 & n.; G. Norman Lieber, "Martial Law during the Revolution," *Magazine of American History with Notes and Queries* 1 (1877): 538–41; G. Norman Lieber, "What Is the Justification of Martial Law," *North American Review* 163, no. 480 (1896): 549–63.

8. "Message to Congress in Special Session, July 4, 1861," in *Collected Works of Abraham Lincoln*, ed. Roy Basler (New Brunswick, NJ: Rutgers University Press, 1953), 4:421, 430.

9. Terminiello v. Chicago, 337 U.S. 1, 36 (1949) (Jackson, J., dissenting); Roger Daniels, *Prisoners without Trial* (New York: Hill and Wang, 2004); Greg Robinson, *By Order of the President* (Cambridge, MA: Harvard University Press, 2003).

10. See, e.g., Jane Mayer, "The Hidden Power," *The New Yorker*, July 3, 2006, https://www.newyorker.com/magazine/2006/07/03/the-hidden-power; Philippe Sands, *Lawless World: Making and Breaking Global Rules* (London: Penguin Books, 2006); Bruce Ackerman, *The Decline and Fall of the American Republic* (Cambridge, MA: Belknap Press, 2013); Robert J. Delahunty and John C. Yoo, "Dream On: The Obama Administration's Nonenforcement of Immigration Laws, the DREAM Act, and the Take Care Clause," *Texas Law Review* 91 (2013): 781–857.

11. See, e.g., Sally Q. Yates, "Sally Yates: Protect the Justice Department from President Trump," *The New York Times*, July 28, 2017, https://www.nytimes.com/2017/07/28/opinion/sally-yates-protect-the-justice-department-from-president-trump.html; Adam Liptak, "Donald Trump Could Threaten U.S. Rule of Law, Scholars Say," *The New York Times*, June 3, 2016, https://www.nytimes.com/2016/06/04/us/politics/donald-trump-constitution-power.html.

12. Schmitt, *Political Theology*, 5.

13. Schmitt, *Dictatorship*, Ch. 4.

14. Witt, *Lincoln's Code*, 173–86.

15. Francis Lieber, *Guerrilla Parties Considered with Reference to the Laws and Usages of War* (New York: D. Van Nostrand, 1862), https://www.loc.gov/rr/frd/Military_Law/Lieber_Collection/pdf/Guerrilla-Parties.pdf.

16. For the most accurate copy of the full text of the Lieber Code, see Witt, *Lincoln's Code*, 375–94. [Hereinafter "Lieber Code."]

17. Ibid., 342–53.

18. Ibid., 328.

19. William Blackstone, *Commentaries on the Laws of England*, 5th ed. (Oxford: Clarendon, 1773), 412–13; Matthew Hale, *The History of the Common Law of England* (London: E. and R. Nutt and R. Gosling, 1739), 41. For modern examples, see Charles Fairman, *The Law of Martial Rule*, 2nd ed. (Chicago: Callaghan, 1943); Kim Lane Scheppele, "Legal and Extralegal Emergencies," in *The Oxford Handbook of Law and Politics*, ed. Gregory A. Caldeira et al. (Oxford: Oxford University Press, 2008), 167–69. For a review of the long history, see John M. Collins, *Martial Law and English Laws, c. 1500–c. 1700* (New York: Cambridge University Press, 2016).

20. Emmerich de Vattel, *The Law of Nations*, ed. Béla Kapossy and Richard Whatmore (Indianapolis: Liberty Fund, 2008), 489.

21. Stephen Neff, *War and the Law of Nations* (Cambridge: Cambridge University Press, 2005); Witt, *Lincoln's Code*, 18; John Fabian Witt, "Two Conceptions of Suffering in War," in *Knowing the Suffering of Others: Legal Perspectives on Pain and Its Meanings*, ed. Austin Sarat (Tuscaloosa: University of Alabama Press, 2014).

22. Lieber Code art. 30. For the influence of Clausewitz, see Witt, *Lincoln's Code*, 179–96.

23. Lieber Code arts. 14, 15; Witt, *Lincoln's Code*, 234–37.

24. Lieber Code art. 5.

25. "Dr. Lieber on the Writ of Habeas Corpus," *New York Times*, April 6, 1862; see also Richard Salomon, "The Unsuspected Francis Lieber," M.A. thesis, City University of New York, 2018, 14–15.

26. GNL MS, Ch. I.

27. Ibid., Ch. *VIII (quoting a lecture by Francis Lieber at Columbia Law School); THE FEDERALIST NO. 28 (Alexander Hamilton).

28. Norman Lieber drew this tripartite division directly from Chief Justice Salmon P. Chase's concurring opinion in *Milligan*, 71 U.S. (4 Wall.) at 141–42; GNL MS, Ch. I.

29. GNL MS, Ch. I. Francis noted that he would have preferred the term "Martial Rule" to avoid confusion with domestic martial law ("Martial Law Proper"), but he deferred to Chase's terms. Today, this is called the international law of belligerent occupation, codified in the 1899 and 1907 Hague Conventions and the 1949 Fourth Geneva Convention.

30. Lieber Code arts. 1–6; FL MS.

31. GNL MS, Ch. I. The term, again, is borrowed from Justice Chase's concurrence in *Milligan*.

32. Daniel J. Hulsebosch, *Constituting Empire: New York and the Transformation of Constitutionalism in the Atlantic World* (Chapel Hill: University of North Carolina Press, 2008), 157–69; see also Frederick B. Wiener, *Civilians under Military Justice: The British Practice since 1689, Especially in North America* (Chicago: University of Chicago Press, 1967).

33. FL MS, Note (3).

34. GNL MS, Ch. I.

35. Ibid.

36. Ibid.

37. Ibid.; U.S. CONST. art. 1, §9 cl. 2; U.S. CONST. amend. III; GNL MS, Ch. I.

38. Lazar, *States of Emergency*, 14, 67–77.

39. John Locke, *Two Treatises of Government and a Letter Concerning Toleration*, ed. Ian Shapiro (New Haven: Yale University Press, 2003), 173.

40. Lieber, "Justification of Martial Law," 553.

41. Ibid.

42. Ibid., 554.

43. Mitchell v. Harmony, 54 U.S. (13 How.) 115, 135 (1851); Lieber, "Justification of Martial Law," 554–55, 563.

44. FL MS, Note (3).

45. GNL MS, Ch. I.

46. FL MS, Note (3).

47. GNL MS, Ch. VII.

48. Ibid., Ch. I. See also FL MS, Note (3).

49. This was based on the same necessity that allowed an occupying army in hostile territory to administer ordinary criminal law. See GNL MS, Ch. I; Ch. VII.

50. Ibid., Ch. VII.

51. Ibid., Ch. I (emphasis added).

52. The Liebers made no exception for emergencies such as natural disasters or economic crises. See Vladeck, "*Field* Theory," for an important discussion of such scenarios.

53. This is in the "York" Letter, which the Liebers cite at length in Chapter VIII: York, "Question of Belligerent Rights; A Legal Investigation of the Entire Subject," *The New York Times*, August 27, 1861, available at http://www.nytimes.com/1861/08/27/news/question-of-belligerent-rights-a-legal-investigation-of-the-entire-subject.html?pagewanted=all; see also Witt, *Lincoln's Code*, 181.

54. GNL MS, Ch. VII; see also The Brig Amy Warwick (Prize Cases), 67 U.S. (2 Black) 635 (1863).

55. GNL MS, Ch. VII; see also Shortridge v. Macon, 22 F. Cas. 20 (C.C.D.N.C. 1867) (No. 12,812). The GNL MS misidentifies this case as "*Shortbridge et. al. v. Mason.*"

egated Emergency Powers" (U.S. Sen., 93d Cong., 2nd sess., July 1974), 4–9.

57. Matthew Warshauer, *Andrew Jackson and the Politics of Martial Law* (Knoxville: University of Tennessee Press, 2006); Dennison, "Martial Law," 52, 53–69; Abraham D. Sofaer, "Emergency Power and the Hero of New Orleans," *Cardozo Law Review* 2 (1981): 233, 238–52.

58. See John Fabian Witt, "A Lost Theory of American Emergency Constitutionalism," *Law & History Review* 36, no. 3 (August 2018): 551–91; John Fabian Witt, "To Save the Country: Reason and Necessity in Constitutional Emergencies," in Gary Gerstle and Joel Isaac, eds., *States of Exception in American History* (forthcoming 2020); see also Peter Blanchard, "Slave Soldiers of Spanish South America: From Independence to Abolition," in *Arming Slaves: From Classical Times to the Modern Age*, ed. Christopher Leslie Brown and Philip D. Morgan (New Haven: Yale University Press, 2013), 255–73.

59. This summary of *Milligan* is drawn from William Rehnquist, *All the Laws but One* (New York: Knopf, 1998), 83–137; and Witt, *Lincoln's Code*, 308–13.

60. On the history of military commissions, see Witt, *Lincoln's Code*, 117–32; Erika Myers, "Conquering Peace: Military Commissions as a Lawfare Strategy in the Mexican War," *American Journal of Criminal Law* 35, no. 2 (2008): 201–40; David Glazier, "Precedents Lost: The Neglected History of the Military Commission," *Virginia Journal of International Law* 46, no. 1 (2006): 5–81.

61. Sarah H. Cleveland, "Powers Inherent in Sovereignty: Indians, Aliens, Territories, and the Nineteenth-Century Origins of Plenary Power over Foreign Affairs," *Texas Law Review* 81, no. 1 (2002): 3, n. 1 (quoting McCulloch v. Maryland, 17 U.S. (4 Wheat.) 316, 405 (1819)).

62. *Milligan*, 71 U.S. at 16.

63. Quoted in ibid. at 105.

64. Ibid.

65. Abraham Lincoln, "Letter to Erastus Corning and Others," June 12, 1863, available at http://www.abrahamlincolnonline.org/lincoln/speeches/corning.htm.

66. *Milligan*, 71 U.S. at 92.

67. Ibid. at 36–37.

68. Ibid. at 57–58.

69. Ibid. at 79.

70. Ibid.

71. Ibid. at 121.

72. Rehnquist, *All the Laws but One*, 123 (quoting Garfield).

73. GNL MS, Ch. I; see also Ch. *VIII.

74. Quoted in *Milligan*, 71 U.S. at 104.

75. Clement Fatovic, *Outside the Law: Emergency and Executive Power* (Baltimore, MD: Johns Hopkins University Press, 2009), 11–37.

76. E.g., Issacharoff and Pildes, "Between Civil Libertarianism and Executive Unilateralism."

77. Lieber, "Justification of Martial Law," 554. This was, in fact, Chase's objective; he feared that if the Court held that Congress had not had power to authorize Milligan's trial, then it would also be powerless to indemnify the military officers on the commission that tried Milligan, which he saw as desirable. *Milligan*, 71 U.S. at 136 (Chase, C.J., concurring).

78. In this, they agreed with Milligan's lawyers, though they did not accept that necessity could justify the violation of law. See *Milligan*, 71 U.S. at 81.

79. Ibid. at 85.

80. Ibid. at 17.

81. GNL MS, Ch. *VIII.

82. See Shakespeare, *Henry V*; Theodor Meron, *Henry's Wars and Shakespeare's Laws* (Oxford: Oxford University Press, 1994).

83. Witt, *Lincoln's Code*, 311–13.

84. Ibid., 307.

85. *Ex parte* Yerger, 75 U.S. (8 Wall.) 85 (1868); see also Witt, *Lincoln's Code*, 315–16; Aziz Rana, "Freedom Struggles and the Limits of Constitutional Continuity," *Maryland Law Review* 71, no. 4 (2012): 1037–45.

86. Cleveland, "Powers Inherent in Sovereignty," 4; Sarah H. Cleveland, "The Plenary Power Background of *Curtiss-Wright*," *University of Colorado Law Review* 70 (1999): 1127; United States v. Curtiss-Wright Exp. Corp., 299 U.S. 304, 318 (1936).

87. See Lauren Benton and Lisa Ford, *A Rage for Order: The British Empire and the Origins of International Law, 1800–1850* (Cambridge, MA: Harvard University Press, 2016).

88. Thomas Holt, *The Problem of Freedom: Race, Labor, and Politics in Jamaica and Britain, 1832–1938* (Baltimore, MD: Johns Hopkins University Press, 1991); Frederick Cooper, Thomas C. Holt, and Rebecca J. Scott, *Beyond Slavery: Explorations in Race, Labor, and Citizenship in Postemancipation Societies* (Chapel Hill: University of North Carolina Press, 2000); Gad

Heuman, *The Killing Time: The Morant Bay Rebellion in Jamaica* (Knoxville: University of Tennessee Press, 1994).

89. See generally Rande Kostal, *A Jurisprudence of Power: Victorian Empire and the Rule of Law* (Oxford: Oxford University Press, 2008).

90. Ibid., 258–60.

91. See generally Kostal, *Jurisprudence of Power*; Thomas Poole, *Reason of State: Law, Prerogative, and Empire* (Cambridge: Cambridge University Press, 2015); Lauren A. Benton, *A Search for Sovereignty: Law and Geography in European Empires, 1400–1900* (Cambridge: Cambridge University Press, 2009).

92. See Nasser Hussain, *The Jurisprudence of Emergency: Colonialism and the Rule of Law* (Ann Arbor: University of Michigan Press, 2003).

93. See Mark Condos, "Licence to Kill: The Murderous Outrages Act and the Rule of Law in Colonial India, 1867–1925," *Modern Asian Studies* 50, no. 2 (2016): 479–517. For the broader phenomenon of white impunity in colonial India, see Elizabeth Kolsky, *Colonial Justice in British India: White Violence and the Rule of Law* (Cambridge: Cambridge University Press, 2010). States of emergency were still a part of the Anglo-imperial playbook a century later in Africa and in South Asia. See David Anderson, *Histories of the Hanged: The Dirty War in Kenya and the End of Empire* (New York: W. W. Norton & Co., 2005); Caroline Elkins, *Britain's Gulag: The Brutal End of Empire in Kenya* (London: Jonathan Cape, 2005), 33–61; T. N. Harper, *The End of Empire and the Making of Malaya* (New York: Cambridge University Press, 1999); Richard Stubbs, *Hearts and Minds in Guerrilla Warfare: The Malayan Emergency, 1948–1960* (New York: Oxford University Press, 1989).

94. See Benton, *Search for Sovereignty*, 162–221.

95. Ibid., 221.

96. Ibid., 166.

97. See, e.g., W. F. Finlason, *Commentaries upon Martial Law, with Special Reference to Its Regulation and Restraint* (London: Stevens & Sons, 1867); W. F. Finlason, *A Treatise on Martial Law: As Allowed by the Law of England, In Time of Rebellion* (London: Stevens & Sons, 1866). For the figure of five books, see Kostal, *Jurisprudence of Power*, 243.

98. Kostal, *Jurisprudence of Power*, 231.

99. Finlason, *Treatise on Martial Law*, xxxi; see also David Dyzenhaus, "The Puzzle of Martial Law," *University of Toronto Law Journal* 59 (2009): 1, 17–19.

100. Finlason, *Treatise on Martial Law*, xxxii; see also Kostal, *Jurisprudence of Power*, 231–32.

101. Kostal, *Jurisprudence of Power*, 229.

102. Finlason, *Treatise on Martial Law*, xxxi–xxxii.

103. Kostal, *Jurisprudence of Power*, 228.

104. Ibid., 229.

105. Finlason, *Treatise on Martial Law*, 71. Quoted in Kostal, *Jurisprudence of Power*, 236.

106. Kostal, *Jurisprudence of Power*, 229.

107. Lieber Code art. 5.

108. Kostal, *Jurisprudence of Power*, 234.

109. See, e.g., GNL MS, Chs. I–IV, Ch. VI.

110. This is not to say that his own thinking proceeded in this order. Kostal argues convincingly that Finlason wrote the treatise and constructed his arguments largely because his political views led him to believe that Governor Eyre should be vindicated.

111. Kostal, *Jurisprudence of Power*, 230 (quoting a February 1868 letter from Finlason to Gladstone).

112. Finlason, *Treatise on Martial Law*, 41. He later clarified that what martial law did was to apply "irregular military law" to civilians, rather than pure military law. See Kostal, *Jurisprudence of Power*, 347–48.

113. Hansard HL Deb., vol. 115, col. 880–881 (April 1, 1851).

114. GNL MS, Ch. I.

115. Ibid.

116. Lieber, *Meaning of the Term Martial Law*.

117. GNL MS, Ch. III.

118. Ibid.

119. Ibid., Ch. V.

120. Ibid., Ch. VI. For discussions of Demerara and Ceylon, see Kostal, *Jurisprudence of Power*, 201–4.

121. GNL MS, Ch. VI. For Cockburn's long and somewhat confused grand jury charge, see Kostal, *Jurisprudence of Power*, 320–41.

122. Finlason, *Treatise on Martial Law*, 107.

123. *Mitchell*, 54 U.S. at 135.

124. Quoted in GNL MS, Ch. VI.

125. See Witt, "Lost Theory of American Emergency Constitutionalism"; Witt, "To Save the Country"; William Lee Miller, *Arguing about Slavery: John Quincy Adams and the Great Battle in the United States Congress* (New York: Vintage, 1998); James Oakes, *Scorpion's Sting: Antislavery and the Coming of the Civil War* (New York: W. W. Norton and Company, 2015); Witt, *Lincoln's Code*.

126. Benjamin Straumann, *Crisis and Constitutionalism: Roman Political Thought from the Fall of the Republic to the Age of Revolution* (Oxford: Oxford University Press, 2016), 42–43; David Dyzenhaus, "The Safety of the People Is the Supreme Law," *The New Rambler*, October 25, 2016.

127. Poole, *Reason of State*; Philip Bobbitt, *The Shield of Achilles: War, Peace, and the Course of History* (New York: Anchor Books, 2002); Lazar, *States of Emergency*, 5.

128. Locke, "The Second Treatise of Government," in *Two Treatises of Government*, ed. Peter Laslett (Cambridge: Cambridge University Press, 1960), 375, ¶ 159.

129. Francis Lieber to Henry Halleck, April 19, 1864, Lieber Huntington Papers; *Congressional Globe*, 39th Cong., 2d Sess. 382 (January 24, 1865). For the elder Lieber, torture was the paradigm example of conduct set outside the pale by the standard of reason in Anglo-American constitutional community. See Witt, "To Save the Country."

130. On the way in which the standard of reason invokes the values of the relevant community, see Robert C. Post, "The Social Foundations of Privacy," *California Law Review* 77 (1989): 957; Robert C. Post, "Federalism, Positive Law, and the Emergence of the American Administrative State: Prohibition in the Taft Court Era," *William & Mary Law Review* 48 (2006): 1; see also Robert C. Post, "The Concept of Public Discourse," *Harvard Law Review* 103 (1990): 601–86.

131. For the arguments on both sides, see, e.g., Fionnuala ni Aoláin and Oren Gross, eds., *Guantánamo and Beyond: Exceptional Courts and Military Commissions in Comparative Perspective* (Cambridge: Cambridge University Press, 2013); John Yoo, *War by Other Means: An Insider's Account of the War on Terror* (New York: Atlantic Monthly Press, 2006); Oona Hathaway, Samuel Adelsberg, Spencer Amdur, Philip Levitz, Freya Pitts, and Sirine Shebaya, "The Power to Detain: Detention of Terrorism Suspects after 9/11," *Yale Journal of International Law* 38:1 (2013): 123–77; Marc. A. Thiessen, "Why Is Trump Treating Accused Terrorists the Way Obama Did?," *The Washington Post* (Nov. 2, 2017), https://www.washingtonpost.com/opinions/why-is-trump-treating-acccused-terrorists-the-way-obama-did/2017/11/02/63a12322-bfc6-11e7-8444-a0d4f04b89eb_story.html.

132. *Milligan*, 71 U.S. at 120–21. For the position that there are no legal "black holes," see, for example, Dyzenhaus, *Constitution of Law*, 196–220.

133. Dick Cheney, "The Vice President Appears on Meet the Press with Tim Russert," September 16, 2001, online by the White House, http://georgewbush-whitehouse.archives.gov/vicepresident/news-speeches/speeches/vp20010916.html; Dick Cheney, "Transcript: Vice President Cheney on 'FOX News Sunday,'" FoxNews.com, January 14, 2007, http://www.foxnews.com/story/2007/01/14/transcript-vice-president-cheney-on-fox-news-sunday.html; Alberto R. Gonzales, "Memorandum for the President. Subject: Decision re Application of the Geneva Convention on Prisoners of War to the Conflict with al Qaeda and the Taliban," January 25, 2002, in Karen J. Greenberg and Joshua L. Dratel, *The Torture Papers: The Road to Abu Ghraib* (Cambridge: Cambridge University Press, 2005), 119; John C. Yoo, "Memorandum Opinion for Timothy Flanagan, the Deputy Counsel to the President: The President's Constitutional Authority to Conduct Military

Operations against Terrorists and Nations Supporting Them," September 25, 2001, in Greenberg and Dratel, *Torture Papers*, 24. Similarly, Jay Bybee (the assistant attorney general at the Office of Legal Counsel (OLC)) argued in an August 1, 2002, memorandum that even if an interrogation method violated federal law—Section 2340A, in particular—this "statute would be unconstitutional if it impermissibly encroached on the President's constitutional power to conduct a military campaign," which includes the "constitutional authority to order interrogations." Jay S. Bybee, "Memorandum for Alberto R. Gonzales Counsel to the President re: Standards of Conduct for Interrogation Under 18 U.S.C. §§ 2340–2340A," August 1, 2002, in *The Torture Papers: The Road to Abu Ghraib*, 200. Under these conceptions, President Bush could—without regard for existing law—solely determine the proper conduct and actions taken in the War on Terror, including allowing "enhanced interrogation" or torture techniques such as "waterboarding, wall-slamming, forced nudity, stress positions, and extended sleep deprivation." David Cole, "The Torture Memos: The Case Against the Lawyers," *The New York Review of Books*, October 8, 2009, http://www.nybooks.com/articles/archives/2009/oct/08/the-torture-memos-the-case-against-the-lawyers/.

134. Daniel Levin, "Memorandum for James B. Comey Deputy Attorney General re: Legal Standards Applicable under 18 U.S.C. §§ 2340–2340A," December 30, 2004, https://www.aclu.org/files/torturefoia/released/082409/olcremand/2004olc96.pdf; George W. Bush, "President Bush Delivers Remarks on Terrorism," *The Washington Post*, September 6, 2006, sec. Politics, http://www.washingtonpost.com/wp-dyn/content/article/2006/09/06/AR2006090601425.html.

135. Jack Goldsmith, *Power and Constraint: The Accountable Presidency after 9/11* (New York: W. W. Norton, 2012).

136. OLC Memorandum Opinion for the Deputy Counsel to the President, "The President's Constitutional Authority to Conduct Military Operations Against Terrorists and Nations Supporting Them," September 25, 2001; OLC Memorandum for Alberto Gonzales, Counsel to the President, "Standards of Conduct for Interrogation," August 1, 2002, at 34, 38 n. 21. In November 2001, President Bush ordered that detainees at Guántanamo "shall not be privileged to seek any remedy or maintain any proceeding . . . in any court of the United States." Military Order of November 13, 2001, "Detention, Treatment, and Trial of Non-Citizens in the War Against Terrorism," sec. 7(2). *Federal Register* 66, no. 222, at 57833. The Justice Department concluded that "the great weight of legal authority" prevented federal courts from exercising habeas jurisdiction over foreign nationals held there. OLC Memorandum for William Haynes, General Counsel of the Department of

Defense, "Possible Habeas Jurisdiction over Aliens Held in Guantanamo Bay, Cuba," December 28, 2001, at 1, 3.

137. *Rasul v. Bush*, 542 U.S. 466 (2004); *Hamdan v. Rumsfeld*, 548 U.S. 557 (2006); *Boumediene v. Bush*, 553 U.S. 723 (2008). The Constitution, Justice Kennedy observed in his *Boumediene* opinion, was "designed to survive, and remain in force, in extraordinary times." Id. The executive's detention authority was also checked in a related case, *Hamdi v. Rumsfeld*, 542 U.S. 507 (2004), in which the Court found that due process required U.S. citizens held at Guantanamo to receive "a meaningful opportunity to contest the factual basis for [their] detention before a neutral decision-maker." Justice O'Connor, writing for the majority, noted that "a state of war is not a blank check for the President when it comes to the rights of the Nation's citizens."

138. *Hamdan*, 548 U.S. at 557. President Bush determined that "[n]one of the provisions of Geneva apply to our conflict with al Qaeda," and that "common Article 3 of Geneva does not apply to al Qaeda or Taliban detainees." The armed forces would follow Geneva principles only when consistent with "military necessity." President Bush Memorandum, "Humane Treatment of al Qaeda and Taliban Detainees," February 7, 2002 (referring to the four Geneva Conventions of 1949, ratified by the United States in 1955, and in particular to Common Article 3, prescribing minimum standards of humane treatment for detainees who do not qualify for POW status under Article 4 of the Third Convention). This conclusion was supported by legal analysis provided in OLC Memorandum for William Haynes, "Application of Treaties and Laws to al Qaeda and Taliban Detainees," January 9, 2002.

139. David Cole, "Where Liberty Lies: Civil Society and Individual Rights after 9/11," *Wayne Law Review* 57 (2012): 1203, 1222–23 (listing executive policy shifts not directly required by the courts or by Congress); see also David Cole, *Engines of Liberty: The Power of Citizen Activists to Make Constitutional Law* (New York: Basic Books, 2016), 249; Goldsmith, *Power and Constraint*, xvi (noting that "in the most unusual and challenging war in American history, and at a time when the President exercises unfathomable powers, we have witnessed the rise and operation of purposeful forms of democratic (and judicial) control over the Commander in Chief, and have indeed established strong legal and constitutional constraints on the presidency").

140. See Scott R. Anderson, "Something Is Rotten with the State of the Military Commissions," *Lawfare: Hard National Security Choices*, March 2, 2018, https://www.lawfareblog.com/something-rotten-state-military-commissions; Robert Chesney, "Military Commissions Compared to Civilian Prosecution in Federal Court: A Revealing Snapshot," *Lawfare: Hard National Security Choices*, February 26, 2018, https://www.lawfareblog.com/military

-commissions-compared-civilian-prosecution-federal-court-revealing
-snapshot; Amy Davidson Sorkin, "At Guantánamo, Are Even the Judges Giving Up?" *The New Yorker*, February 20, 2018, https://www.newyorker.com/
news/daily-comment/at-guantanamo-are-even-the-judges-giving-up.

141. For the proslavery critique of emergency powers, see Witt, "Lost
Theory"; Witt, "Reason and Necessity."

The Liebers' Manuscript

CHAPTER I

Military and Martial Law
Distinguished

There are two kinds of military jurisdiction. The first may, in general terms, be said to be that which relates to the government of the army, both in peace and in war, and is called *Military Law*. The second is an exercise of military power in time of war, insurrection or rebellion, under the Law of War, which for the time being suprecedes or takes precedence of the civil power. This we call *Martial Law*. Martial Law, in the wider signification of the term, therefore embraces both the Martial Law of hostile occupation—the *occupation bellica* of the jurists, and Martial Law applied at home.

To be more precise—Military Law is that branch of the law of the land which relates to the government of the army.[1] It derives its existence from statutes,[2] military regulations and

1. Decisions—Pres & Sec. War 2d Comptroller Auditors Heads of Depts. Atty. Gen. J.A.G.

2. Congress has power, by virtue of Cl. 14, Sec. 8, Art. I of the Constitution, "to make Rules for the Government and Regulation of the land and naval Forces."

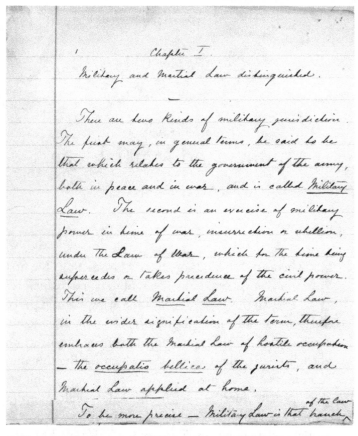

Chapter I.

Military and Martial Law distinguished.

There are two Kinds of military jurisdiction. The first may, in general terms, be said to be that which relates to the government of the army, both in peace and in war, and is called <u>Military Law</u>. The second is an exercise of military power in time of war, insurrection or rebellion, under the <u>Law</u> of War, which for the time being supercedes or takes precedence of the civil power. This we call <u>Martial Law</u>. Martial Law, in the wider signification of the term, therefore embraces both the Martial Law of hostile occupation — the <u>occupatio bellica</u> of the jurists, and Martial Law applied at home.

To be more precise — Military Law is that branch of the law

Figure 2. The first page of Chapter I in the Liebers' manuscript
(GNL manuscript). Source: National Archives.

orders, and from the customs of war.[3] Its jurisdiction extends, under the laws of the United States, not only to the regular forces, but to the militia and other troops when employed in

3. The customs of war are distinctly referred to as a source of military law in the 69th Article of War which prescribes the oath to be taken by members

the service of the United States,[4] and to civilians serving with the armies in the field.[5] Its object is the maintenance of military discipline.

The sources of military law are thus given by Clode:*

The Law which he [the officer or soldier] has to obey may be divided into two branches, thus:—
I. The "*lex scripta*" which . . . may be stated according to this order of obedience is comprised in:—
a. The Mutiny Act, as the Law expressly sanctioned by Parliament.[†]

---

* **Charles Matthew Clode** (1818–1893) was a British lawyer and author who served as the solicitor to the War Office (1858–1876). His publications included *The Administration of Justice under Military and Martial Law* (1872) and *The Military Forces of the Crown, Their Administration and Government* (1869).

† The **Mutiny Act** was first passed in 1689 as legislation to constrain the Crown's ability to use martial law. During the Revolution of 1688, after some of the new King William's forces mutinied in support of his rival James, the British Crown sought to put the administration of its standing army on a more secure legal footing. Civil courts, at the time, could not try soldiers who mutinied against their commanders, and the monarchy could conduct trials in *military* courts only outside the country. Only Parliament could authorize military trials within England, and it did so through the Mutiny Act of 1689. This act was renewed every year through 1879, but lapsed between 1698 and 1701. The original act laid out the crimes of treason and put the military under the direct control of the state for the first time, too. See Charles M. Clode, *The Military Forces of the Crown: Their Administration and Government* (John Murray: London, 1869), 142–44; David Glazier, "Precedents

---

of courts martial. In cases of doubt they are required to administer justice according to their consciences, the best of their understanding, and the *customs of war* in like cases.

4. 97th Article of War.
5. 60th Article of War.

b. The Articles of War, as the Law made by the Crown under Statutory Authority and in accordance with the Mutiny Act.

c. The Regulations or Orders made by the Crown without Statutory Authority (a, b, and c, relating to the whole Army).

d. The District or Garrison Orders made by the General of the District or Governor of the Garrison, for the several Regiments under his Command.

e. The Standing Orders of the Colonel for the Officers and Men of his Regiment. . . .

II. The *"Lex non scripta"*—those lawful orders which, *viva voce* or otherwise, the Commanding Officer may from time to time issue, bidding a subordinate to do or refrain from doing, as a Soldier, certain acts till then undisclosed to him.[6]

But he forgets to mention the most important branch of the *lex non scripta*—the customs of war, which in England as with us are recognized as forming part of the military law of the land by the oath prescribed for the members of courts martial.

Referring to the U.S. Army Regulations, General Holt, Judge Advocate General,* says:

Lost: The Neglected History of the Military Commission, *Virginia Journal of International Law* 46 (2005–2006): 11–12; Ridley McLean, "Historical Sketch of Military Law," *Journal of Criminal Law and Criminology* 8 (1917): 27–32. The first Mutiny Act is reprinted in Clode, *Military Forces*, 499–501.

  * **Joseph Holt** (1807–1894) served as judge advocate general from 1862 to 1875. Holt was a Kentucky lawyer who took a staunch pro-Union position

6. Charles M. Clode, *The Administration of Justice under Military and Martial Law* (London: John Murray, 1872), 74–76.

This part of the written law of the army, well described by Cushing (VIII *Opinions of Attorneys General*, 343)* as being "in aid or complement of statutes," like the Articles of War, derives its original authority from the constitutional provision by which Congress is empowered to "make rules for the government of the land (and naval) forces." As early as in 1813, Congress, in the exercise of this power, authorized the Secretary of War, (by sec. 5, ch 52, of the Act of March 3 of that year) "*to prepare general regulations, better defining and prescribing the respective duties and powers" of the officers of the several staff corps, "and, generally, of the general and regimental staff*"; with the further provision that such regulations, when prepared and approved by the President, should be "laid before Congress" at its next session. A body of regulations, prepared and published (on May 1, 1813) by virtue of this authority, was, in sec. 9. ch. 69. of the act of April 24,

---

during the secession crisis of 1860–1861. He served briefly as secretary of war at the close of James Buchanan's presidency. In 1862 Lincoln appointed him judge advocate general of the Union Army, where he took aggressive and sometimes controversial legal positions on behalf of the president's assertions of legal authority with respect to habeas corpus, military commissions, and more. See generally Elizabeth D. Leonard, *Lincoln's Forgotten Ally: Judge Advocate General Joseph Holt of Kentucky* (Chapel Hill: University of North Carolina Press, 2011); John Fabian Witt, *Lincoln's Code: The Laws of War in American History* (New York: Free Press, 2012), chs. 9–10.

* **Caleb Cushing** (1800–1879) was a Massachusetts politician and lawyer who served as attorney general under President Franklin Pierce. On February 3, 1857, Attorney General Cushing published an opinion concluding that "the power to suspend the laws, and to substitute the military in the place of the civil authority, is not a power within the legal attributes of a governor of one of the Territories of the United States" (374).

1816, formally "recognized" by Congress, "subject, however,"—as it was added—"to such alterations as the Secretary [of War] may adopt with the approbation of the President." Down to the date of the recent act of July 28, 1866,* reorganizing the Army at the close of actual hostilities, these two statutes of 1813 and 1816, contained all the authority vested by Congress in the Secretary of War (as representing the President in the administration of the military department) for making or altering general regulations for the army; the latter statute comprising the entire legislative *sanction* of such regulations as issued; except only that a second issue of regulations (that of September, 1816) was, by an act of March 2, 1821, ch. 13, sec. 14, "approved and adopted for the government of the army of the United States."† But this special act was "repealed" by chapter 88 of the act of May 7 of the next year;‡ and from that date till the recent legislation referred to, no action whatever was taken by Congress in formal approval or disapproval of the regulations, although some six revisions (each with important additions and modifications) were meanwhile—(there had previously been a *third* edition of July, 1821)—issued

---

* An Act to Increase and Fix the Military Peace Establishment of the United States, 14 Stat. 332 (1866).

† An Act to Reduce and Fix the Military Peace Establishment of the United States, 3 Stat. 615, 616 (1821) ("And be it further enacted, That the system of 'General regulations for the army,' compiled by Major General Scott, shall be . . . approved and adopted . . .").

‡ An Act to repeal the fourteenth section of "An Act to Reduce and Fix the Military Peace Establishment," 3 Stat. 686 (1822).

by the War Department. But at length, by section 37, ch 299, of July 28, 1866, it was enacted: "That the Secretary of War be, and he is hereby, directed to have prepared, and to report to Congress, at its next session, a code of regulations for the government of the army, and of the militia in actual service, which shall embrace all necessary orders and forms of a general character for the performance of all duties incumbent on officers and men in the military service, including rules for the government of courts-martial; the existing regulations to remain in force until Congress shall have acted on said report." This statute, comprehensive and ample in its provision for a code not limited in scope, but "for the government of the army" generally, in ratifying, at the same time, the body of regulations now in use (for the new issue has not at this date—July 1, 1868—been adopted), sets at rest any question which might have been raised in regard to the legal effect of any existing regulation not relating to the *powers or duties of staff officers*, as not being authorized under the original Acts of 1813 and 1816.*

---

* The Liebers attribute this passage to Holt, and they may be correct, but the published version appears in William Winthrop, ed., *Digest of Opinions of the Judge Advocate General of the Army*, 3rd ed. (Washington, D.C.: Government Printing Office, 1868), 56 n. In their draft the Liebers further observed that the Act of July 15, 1870, supplied additional congressional authority not mentioned in Winthrop's 1868 *Digest* for executive branch regulations governing the army. See An Act Making Appropriations for the Support of the Army for the Year ending June Thirty, Eighteen Hundred and Seventy-One, and for other Purposes, 16 Stat. 311, 319 (1870).

The President has also, by virtue of his authority as commander-in-chief, power to establish rules for the government of the army, and the Secretary of War is his regular organ to administer the military establishment of the nation, and rules and orders promulgated through him must be received as the acts of the executive, and, as such, are binding on all within the sphere of his authority.[7] But this power is limited, and does not extend to the repeal or contradiction of existing statutes, nor to the making of provisions of a legislative nature.[8]

The 9th of the Rules and Articles of War recognizes the legal effect of all lawful military orders, and makes disobedience an offense punishable with death.

Such is Military Law. What Martial Law is, the "Instructions for the Government of Armies of the United States in the Field" thus explain:[9]

> 1. A place, district, or country occupied by an enemy stands, in consequence of the occupation, under the Martial Law of the invading or occupying army, whether any proclamation declaring Martial Law, or any public warning to the inhabitants, has been issued or not. Martial Law is the immediate

7. United States v. Eliason, 41 U.S. 291 (1842). [Eds. note: In *Eliason* the Supreme Court ruled that regulations promulgated by the secretary of war disallowing extra compensation for officers in the U.S. Army were "binding upon all within the sphere of his legal and constitutional authority."]

8. Power of the President to Create a Militia Bureau in the War Department, 10 U.S. Op. Atty. Gen. 11 (1861); George W. Paschal, *The Constitution of the United States: Defined and Carefully Annotated* (Washington, D.C.: W. H. & O. H. Morrison, 1868), 171.

9. These "Instructions" were prepared by Francis Lieber, L.L.D., approved by President Lincoln, and published by the War Department in General Orders No. 100 of 1863.

and direct effect and consequence of occupation or conquest.

The presence of a hostile army proclaims its Martial Law.

2. Martial Law does not cease during the hostile occupation, except by special proclamation, ordered by the commander-in-chief; or by special mention in the treaty of peace concluding the war, when the occupation of a place or territory continues beyond the conclusion of peace as one of the conditions of the same.

3. Martial Law in a hostile country consists in the suspension, by the occupying military authority, of the criminal and civil law, and of the domestic administration and government in the occupied place or territory, and in the substitution of military rule and force for the same, as well as in the dictation of general laws, as far as military necessity requires this suspension, substitution or dictation.

The commander of the forces may proclaim that the administration of all civil and penal law shall continue, either wholly or in part, as in times of peace, unless otherwise ordered by the military authority.

4. Martial Law is simply military authority exercised in accordance with the laws and usages of war. Military oppression is not Martial Law; it is the abuse of the power which that law confers. As Martial Law is executed by military force, it is incumbent upon those who administer it to be strictly guided by the principles of justice, honor, and humanity, virtues adorning a soldier even more than

other men, for the very reason that he possesses the power of his arms against the unarmed.

5. Martial Law should be less stringent in places and countries fully occupied and fairly conquered. Much greater severity may be exercised in places or regions where actual hostilities exist, or are expected and must be prepared for. Its most complete sway is allowed—even in the commander's own country—when face to face with the enemy, because of the absolute necessities of the case, and of the paramount duty to defend the country against invasion.

To save the country is paramount to all other considerations.[10]

---

10. Martial Law, says Judge Parker, "is that military rule and authority which exists in time of war, and is conferred by the laws of war in relation to persons and things under and within the scope of active military operations in carrying on the war, and which extinguishes or suspends civil rights, and the remedies founded upon them, for the time being, so far as it may appear to be necessary in order to the full accomplishment of the purposes of the war; the party who exercises it being liable in an action for any abuse of the authority thus conferred. It is the application of military government—the government of force—to persons and property within the scope of it, according to the laws and usages of war, to the exclusion of the municipal government, in all respects where the latter would impair the efficiency of military rule and military action." Joel Parker, *Habeas Corpus and Martial Law: A Review of the Opinion of Chief Justice Taney in the Case of John Merryman* (Cambridge: Welch, Bigelow, & Co., 1861), 38. [Eds. note: **Joel Parker** (1795–1875) served on the Massachusetts Supreme Judicial Court and as a professor of law at Harvard. He was an outspoken critic of President Lincoln's expansive use of the war powers during the Civil War. See "Joel Parker," *American Law Review* 10, no. 2 (January 1876): 235–69; Mark Neely, *Lincoln and the Triumph of the Nation: Constitutional Conflict in the American Civil War* (Chapel Hill: University of North Carolina Press, 2011).]

"Military Law," and "Martial Law," as the terms are here used, are therefore entirely distinct, but the distinction is one of comparatively recent days. Formerly the term "Martial Law" alone was used—generally in the sense of all law executed by military authority, but sometimes in the narrower one of what we call "Military Law." For its exact signification in each case we must refer to the circumstances under which it was used. So far as the earlier periods of English history are concerned it is, however, safe to say that in no case was "Martial Law" spoken of—whether in statutes, or by the authorities—in the technical sense which we now attach to it.

Clode calls attention to the confusion which still exists upon this subject—a confusion to which the action of Parliament and of the Crown contributes, for year after year an annual vote has been sanctioned by Parliament for the "Administration" not of Military but "of Martial Law," and each succeeding Government has appointed a "Judge Martial" paid out of this vote, who wholly disclaims having anything whatever to do with any other than "Military Law."[11]

The distinction was thus drawn by Sir D. Dundas, Judge Advocate General,* in 1850: "It is necessary to distinguish between Military and Martial Law. 'Military Law' is to be found in the Mutiny Act and Articles of War. Those, and those alone, it is which are properly called the Military Code, and by which the Land Forces of Her Majesty are regulated. 'Martial Law' is not a written law: it arises on a necessity, to be judged of by

---

* **Sir David Dundas** (1799–1877) was a Scottish politician, lawyer, and Member of Parliament who served as solicitor-general (1846–1848) and as judge advocate general (1849–1852).

11. Clode, *Under Military and Martial Law*, 178.

the Executive, and ceases the instant it can possibly be allowed
to cease. 'Military Law' has to do *only* with the Land Forces
mentioned in the 2^d Section of the Mutiny Act. 'Martial Law'
comprises *all* persons, whether Civil or Military."[12] "It is clear,
therefore," adds Clode, "if anything be so, that Martial and
Military Law are not the same, though out of this confusion of
thought innocent lives may hereafter be, if already they have
not been sacrificed, by an indefinite and undefined responsibility resulting from it."[13]

But that Military Law has to do *only* with the persons
specified in the statutory provisions for the government of
the military forces seems to have been lost sight of by those
who maintain that Martial Law is sometimes an application
of Military Law to persons not ordinarily subject to it. Thus
Finlason,* referring to the proclamation of martial law, says
that its effect is "to extend to all persons in the district proclaimed, and which is thus declared to be in a state of rebellion
or of war,—not merely the regular authority of military law as
exercised in peace, but also all that military power which is
exercised towards an enemy or armed rebel in time of war."[14]
And Simmons remarks that, "it is only in comparatively recent
times—dating them from not long, if at all, before the beginning of the present century—that it (martial law) came to be

---

* **William Finlason** (1818–1895) was a British lawyer turned journalist
who covered the legal issues of the day for publications like the *Times*, *Dub-
lin Review*, and *The Rambler*. He wrote at length about martial law.

12. Clode, *Under Military and Martial Law*, 178.
13. Ibid., 178–79.
14. W. F. Finlason, *A Treatise on Martial Law as Allowed by the Law of
England in Time of Rebellion* (London: Stevens & Sons, 1866), 41. The same
author has written several other works upon the same subject which will be
hereafter referred to.

generally used for the extraordinary exercise of martial or military law—when extended to persons not ordinarily subject to the articles of war in times of actual war or dangerous intestine commotion—as contrasted with military law and the statutory exercise of martial law in the army and navy."[15]

Now, according to the view which, in this country at least, seems to have been definitely accepted, Military Law as it exists in times of war is the same Military Law which is administered in times of peace. The statutory laws creating it may and do recognize the necessity of affixing severer punishment to certain offenses when committed in time of war,—as, for instance, to desertion, which, under the Military Law of the United States, is then only punishable with death. So Military Law is during war extended by statute to certain persons, not subject to it in times of peace. But, it is, nevertheless, the same law, emanating from the same sources, administered by the same tribunals, governed by the same rules, and applying to specified classes of persons. Martial Law is not the application of Military Law *as such* to persons not ordinarily subject to it. If such persons are for the time being made subject to any rules or orders similar to those enforced by Military Law, it does not follow that they are amenable to the military code. The rules and orders may be the same, and yet represent two jurisdictions, united in the same person, but existing side by side entirely independent of each other. Those subject to Military Law are also subject to Martial Law when the latter is in force, and they are within the territorial limits of its jurisdiction, but

15. Thomas Frederick Simmons, *The Constitution and Practice of Courts Martial* (London: John Murray, 1873), § 100, 49 n. [Eds. note: In the margin of the manuscript, the Liebers refer to Joel Prentiss Bishop, *Commentaries on the Criminal Law*, 3rd ed. (Boston: Little, Brown, & Co., 1865), 1: 20 ff.]

non courtat [it does not follow] that all persons subject to Martial Law are also subject to Military Law.

It was said by Lord Brougham*—and others have adopted the dictum—that Martial Law renders every man liable to be treated as a soldier.[16] Were we to understand by this that the *extent* of Martial Law is to render every man so liable we would form a very erroneous conception of its scope. How is a soldier liable to be treated? Under ordinary circumstances only in accordance with Military Law—there being no question here of his civil responsibility—but, as has been already remarked, it is clearly wrong to say that by Martial Law every man is made amenable to Military Law. In Extraordinary cases the soldier may become subject to Martial Law,—not because he is a soldier, but in common with and under the same rule with the rest of the community. He does not stand in this respect in a position peculiar to himself, and which would, therefore, help to explain the similar position of others. It does not, then, throw any light upon the subject to say that Martial Law renders every man liable to be treated as a soldier, for there is nothing in this connection characteristic of the status of the soldier except his subjection to Military Law which is, and under all circumstances remains, distinct from Martial Law, and possesses no fundamental principles in common with it.

---

* **Henry Peter Brougham** (1778–1868) served as a parliamentarian and Lord Chancellor and participated in the Demerara debate (discussed in Ch. VI). See Robert Stewart, *Henry Brougham, 1778–1868: His Public Career* (London: Bodley Head, 1986); Gelien Matthews, *Caribbean Slave Revolts and the British Abolitionist Movement* (Baton Rouge: Louisiana State University Press, 2006).

16. Speech of Lord Brougham in the House of Commons, on the trial of Rev. John Smith of Demerara. June 1, 1824. Hansard's Parl. Debates, 2d Series, p. 976. See Simmons on Courts Martial, p. 97.

Having thus distinguished Martial Law from Military Law, it is necessary that we should direct our attention to another distinction.

The Martial Law of hostile occupation—*occupatio bellica*—is recognized by the Law of nations as a necessary element of the *jus belli*. It springs from the necessity of substituting in the occupied territory some government and authority for those displaced. That hostile occupation carries with it the authority to put in force the military power of the invader for the protection of his own interest, and the safety of the people, cannot be doubted. It is an unquestionable and necessary attribute of the supreme power, with which the invader has become vested. He may exercise it to a greater or less extent, according to circumstances, but he is not limited in his authority by the constitution or laws of the invaded country.

This was the Martial Law which Wellington* enforced in the South of France, and to which he referred, when he said: "That martial law was neither more nor less than the will of the general who commands the army. In fact, martial law was no law at all. Therefore the general, who declared martial law, and commanded that it should be carried into effect, was bound to lay down distinctly the rules, and regulations, and limits, according to which his will was to be carried out. Now, he had in another country carried on martial law: that was to say, he had governed a large part of the population of a country by his own will. But then what did he do? He declared that the country should be governed according to its own national

---

* **Arthur Wellesley** (1769–1852), the first Duke of Wellington, was a celebrated army officer and prime minister of Britain. Wellington served in the Peninsular War, invaded southern France, defeated Napoleon's forces at Waterloo, and oversaw a fraught occupation of France for three years. See Thomas Dwight Veve, *The Duke of Wellington and the British Army of Occupation in France, 1815–1818* (Westport, CT: Greenwood Press, 1992).

laws, and he carried into execution that will. He governed the country strictly by the laws of the country, and he governed it with such moderation, he must say, that political servants and judges, who had at first fled, or had been expelled, afterwards consented to act under his direction. The judges sat in the courts of law, conducting their judicial business, and administering the law by his authority."[17]

General Scott's celebrated order issued in the City of Mexico* is another instance of the exercise of this power, conferred upon him by the Law of Nations as the victorious occupant of a hostile country.

"But," says Attorney General Cushing, "these are examples of martial law administered by a foreign army in the enemy's country, and do not enlighten us in regard to the question of martial law in one's own country, and as administered by its military commanders. That is a case, which the law of nations does not reach. Its regulation is of the domestic resort of the organic laws of the country itself, and regarding which, as it happens, there is no definite or explicit legislation in the United States, as there is none in England."[18]

In the same opinion from which the above is quoted Mr. Cushing draws a distinction between Martial Law as a *foreign* or *international* fact, and Martial Law as a *domestic* or *municipal* fact—the latter corresponding to the state of Siege of the French law:

---

* During the Mexican-American War (1846–1848), General Winfield Scott issued General Orders No. 20 on February 19, 1847, establishing martial law and authorizing military commissions for a wide array of offenses by inhabitants of Mexico.

17. These remarks were made during the discussion on the Ceylon rebellion, when that subject came up in the House of Lords on the 1st of April, 1851. Hansard HL Deb., vol. 115, col. 880–881 (April 1, 1851).

18. Martial Law, 8 U.S. Opp. Atty. Gen. 365, 370 (1857).

In France, the law carefully defines three conditions of things applicable, in this relation, to a city or a given district of the country, namely,—the state of peace,—the state of war,—and the state of siege.

1. The state of peace.—This condition exists at all times, in a city, or other place, not declared to be in the state of war or in the state of siege by the supreme political authority, nor placed in either of these states by circumstances. In the state of peace, all military men are subject to the law-military, leaving the civil authority untouched in its own sphere to govern all persons, whether civil or military in class.

2. The state of war.—This exists in regard to vulnerable points of the sea-coast threatened from the sea, or in regard to the land frontier and other interior points, occupied or threatened by the camp or the march of the enemy. This state may lawfully exist either in virtue of an act of the supreme political authority, or by force of circumstances. When it exists, the military authority may have to take precedence of the civil authority, which, nevertheless, is not deprived of its ordinary attributes, but in order to exercise them must of necessity enter into concert with the military commander.

3. The state of siege.—This may have a lawful origin, like the state of war, either in an act of political sovereignty, or in the necessity of circumstances. When it exists, all the local authority passes to the military commander, who exercises it in his own person, or delegates it if he please to the civil magistrates to be exercised by them under his orders. The civil law is suspended for the time being, or

at least made subordinate, and its place is taken by martial law, under the supreme, if not the direct, administration of the military power.

The state of siege may exist, in a city or in a district of country, either by reason of the same being actually besieged or invested by a hostile force, or by reason of domestic insurrection. In either case, it is the precise fact with which we are now concerned. The state of siege of the continental jurists is the proclamation of martial law of England and the United States,—only we are without law on the subject, while in other countries it is regulated by known limitations. (Maurice Block, s. voc. See also Escriche, s. voc. for similar legal provisions in Spain.)[19]

Under the ministry of Narvaez,* a law was promulgated in Spain, distinguishing between three states of society—the

---

* **Ramón María Narváez** (1800–1868) was the Duke of Valencia and prime minister of Spain intermittently from 1844 to 1866. In his third ministry, Narváez was tasked with quelling a regional revolt among the Carlists who claimed a right to the Spanish crown, and he responded with extrajudicial imprisonment of his rivals. In 1866–1867, Narváez again pressed for legal reforms giving the government more power, including in the areas of crime and public order. See Guy Thompson, *The Birth of Modern Politics in Spain: Democracy, Association, and Revolution, 1854–75* (Basingstoke: Palgrave, 2010); Rhea Marsh Smith, *Spain: A Modern History* (Ann Arbor: University of Michigan Press, 1965), 327, 334, 338; Raymond Carr, "Liberalism and Reaction, 1833–1931," in Raymond Carr, ed., *Spain: A History* (New York: Oxford University Press, 2001), 211–12.

19. Martial Law, 8 U.S. Opp. Atty. Gen. 365, 370–71 (1857). Cushing refers the reader to Maurice Block, probably *Dictionairre de L'Administration Francais* (Paris: Libraire Administrative, 1856), 798, and Joaquin Escriche,

normal state, the state of alarm, and the state of war. The state of alarm could be declared upon suspicion, and either that, or the state of war might be proclaimed by the local authorities of a town in case of emergency, only giving information of it to the central government. Until the restoration of the normal state, the government might arrest, imprison, exile or put to death those whom it might judge to be rebels. This was, in fact, a despotic application of martial law.

Under this classification Martial Law enforced in time of rebellion within the states or districts occupied by rebels treated as belligerents must be regarded as an international fact. Wars are—so far as relates to this inquiry—of two kinds, viz: international and civil. In a civil war or rebellion the government has the right to treat its rebellious citizens both as belligerents and as subjects. As subjects they may be held accountable for their political crime. As belligerents they are entitled to the protection, as they are subject to the consequences of an enforcement of, the laws of war. Rebellion is a state of war, and rebels in their belligerent character are public enemies. The Law of War is, therefore, applicable to such a condition the same as in a war *inter gentes*.[20]

The division of the subject by Chief Justice Chase presents it in a clearer light.* "There are," he said,

* **Salmon P. Chase** (1808–1873) was Lincoln's secretary of the treasury and then, beginning in 1864, the sixth Chief Justice of the Supreme Court of the United States. The Liebers here quote from his concurring opinion in *Ex parte Milligan*, in which Chase contended that while Congress had

probably *Diccionario Razonado de Legislacio Civil, Penal, Commercial y Forense* (Caracas: Valentin Espinal, 1840). The Liebers included Cushing's references.

20. See William Whiting, *War Powers under the Constitution of the United States* (Boston: Lee & Shepard, 43d ed., 1871), 44–46, and cases cited.

under the Constitution three kinds of military jurisdiction: one to be exercised both in peace and
war; another to be exercised in time of foreign war
without the boundaries of the United States, or
in time of rebellion and civil war within states or
districts occupied by rebels treated as belligerents;
and a third to be exercised in time of invasion or
insurrection within the limits of the United States,
or during rebellion within the limits of states maintaining adhesion to the national government, when
the public danger requires its exercise. The first of
these may be called jurisdiction under *Military
Law*, and is found in acts of Congress prescribing
rules and articles of war, or otherwise providing
for the government of the national forces; the second may be distinguished as *Military Government*,
superseding, as far as may be deemed expedient,
the local law, and exercised by the military commander under the direction of the President, with
the express or implied sanction of Congress; while
the third may be denominated *Martial Law Proper*,
and is called into action by Congress, or temporarily, when the action of Congress cannot be invited,
and in the case of justifying or excusing peril, by
the President, in times of insurrection or invasion,
or of civil or foreign war, within districts or locali-

---

not authorized military courts like the one that tried Lambdin Milligan, an
Indiana resident who participated in pro-Confederacy intrigue and plotting,
Congress could have done so under the Constitution's war powers. For more
on Chase, see John Niven, *Salmon P. Chase: A Biography* (Oxford: Oxford
University Press, 1995).

ties where ordinary law no longer adequately se-
cures public safety and private rights.[21]

Martial Rule,[22] or Military Government, relates to the occupied territory of an enemy; Martial Law Proper, strictly speaking, to the inhabitants of a district, belonging, and maintaining allegiance to, the country by whose military authority it is
enforced. There is one application of the Law of War, however,
which is not included under this classification. When civil war
assumes such magnitude that it becomes necessary for the
opponents to treat each other as belligerents, the contest assumes—so far as regards their reciprocal relations under the
law of war—the character of an international war. It has until
recently been held and such is the ruling of the Supreme Court
that all the subjects of the one state are enemies to the other
and its subjects, but the soundness of the rule is no longer universally admitted.* However this may be—we have virtually
two opposing states belligerent. In civil, as well as in foreign
wars, therefore, both the armed enemy and the unarmed citizen are required to observe the laws of war towards the hostile
state, and, if captured, can be punished for a violation of these
laws. Whenever war exists this power is necessarily conferred.
No war could, without it, be confined within the limits prescribed by the rules of warfare amongst civilized nations. No

* The Liebers' citation is to "Bluntschli's International Law," written by
the elder Lieber's longtime correspondent, the German international lawyer
Johann Caspar Bluntschli. See J. C. Bluntschli, *Das modern Völkerrecht der
civilizierten Staten* (Nordlingen: Drud & Berlag, 1868).

21. *Ex parte Milligan*, 71 U.S. 2, 142 (1866) (Chase, C.J., concurring). [Eds.
note: The Liebers mischaracterize Chase's opinion as a dissent, but he disagreed only with the majority's rationale, not with the outcome.]

22. A term suggested by Dr. Lieber.

matter where the offense be committed, or where the capture be effected (except, of course, on neutral territory), this jurisdiction of necessity attaches.

The principles which underlie the Martial Law of hostile occupation—the Military Government of Chief Justice Chase—are the same, whether it be enforced within the territory of a foreign, or of a rebellious enemy. It is a simple application of that branch of the Law of Nations known as the Law of War. Whether it be over the territory of a foreign enemy, or of subjects treated as belligerents, is immaterial. Martial Law Proper,[23] however, springs from a different source, and, at the first glance, appears to be irreconcilable with the Anglican guarantees of life, liberty, and property. It is based upon the right of national self-preservation. "To save the country," say the Instructions already cited, "is paramount to all other considerations."[24] "With governments as with individuals" says Bishop* "self-preservation is the first duty, taking precedence

* **Joel Prentiss Bishop** (1814–1901) was a leading American legal thinker in the nineteenth century whose writings covered numerous legal topics, including marriage and divorce, criminal law, and statutory interpretation. In his influential *Commentaries on the Criminal Law* (Boston: Little, Brown and Company, 1856), Bishop wrote that the first duty of a nation is "self-preservation"—a principle that undergirds Lieber's theory of martial law as well. For more, see Stephen A. Siegel, "Joel Bishop's Orthodoxy," *Law & History Review* 13, no. 2 (Autumn 1995): 215–59.

23. The term "Martial Law Proper" has, for the purposes of this work, been adopted by the author. Dr. Lieber had, however, previously suggested that it would have been well to designate the martial law enforced in an enemy's country as Martial Rule, and martial law enforced at home in the government's own country simply as Martial Law—if indeed, he says, that can be called Law which is rather a negation of rights and legal protection. But in order to avoid any possible confounding of the two, the latter will hereafter be referred to as Martial Law Proper.

24. Instructions for the Government of Armies of the U.S. in the Field, art. 5.

of all other duties."[25] This is no new doctrine. It is a principle inherent in all politics. Says Hamilton:

> That there may happen cases in which the national government may be under the necessity of resorting to force, cannot be denied. Our own experience has corroborated the lessons taught by the examples of other nations; that emergencies of this sort will sometimes arise in all societies, however constituted; that seditions and insurrections are, unhappily, maladies as inseparable from the body politic, as tumours and eruptions from the natural body; that the idea of governing at all times by the simple force of law (which we have been told is the only admissible principle of republican government), has no place but in the reveries of those political doctors whose sagacity disdains the admonitions of experimental instruction.[26]

With the necessity of resorting to force comes also the necessity of employing the means which will render the resort to force effective. Martial Law is one of these means. When, and where, by whom, and over what, the power may be exercised are questions concerning which opinions differ widely, but that there may be some circumstances which will justify recourse to it is not disputed. The Supreme Court in *Ex parte Milligan* at least recognized so much.[27] Yet the exercise of this

25. Bishop, *Commentaries on the Criminal Law*, 1:506.

26. *The Federalist*, No. 28, and in Luther v. Borden, 48 U.S. 1, 45–46 (1849).

27. And see dissenting opinion of Justice Woodbury in *Luther v. Borden*, 48 U.S. 1, 75 (1849) (Woodbury, J., dissenting). [Eds. note: This was an action of trespass brought by a supporter of the Dorr Rebellion, an 1842 uprising aiming to broaden democracy in Rhode Island, against representatives of the ruling "charter government" who attempted to arrest him. In *Luther v. Borden*, Justice Woodbury thought it "very doubtful" that the charter government

power is apparently forbidden by the Constitution. There are some who, finding an insurmountable obstacle in this fact, say that Martial Law (Proper) is a violation of the Constitution—justifiable on the ground of necessity.[28] With reference to this view the Supreme Court say:

> The Constitution of the U.S. is a law for rulers and people, equally in war and in peace, and covers with the shield of its protection all classes of men, at all times and under all circumstances. No doctrine, involving more pernicious consequences, was ever invented by the wit of man, than that any of its provisions can be suspended during any of the great exigencies of government. Such a doc-

---

of Rhode Island had possessed the authority to declare martial law, at least under the circumstances at issue, but he conceded that the federal government possessed such authority when necessity so required. See 48 U.S. at 83.]

28. Mr. Horace Binney, in his treatise on "The Privilege of the Writ of Habeas Corpus under the Constitution," referring to the fourth Amendment says:—"Either the language of the amendment, though general, speaks in reference to the normal condition of the country only, when there is no rebellion or invasion and consequent war, foreign or civil; or under such circumstances, rebellion or invasion supersedes the amendment for the time. The former seems to be the preferable conclusion." Horace Binney, *The Privilege of the Writ of Habeas Corpus under the Constitution* (Philadelphia: C. Sherman & Son, 1862), 55. These remarks, says the Judge Advocate General, apply equally to the first six articles of the Amendments to the Constitution. [Eds. note: This was an important point for the Liebers. They put great weight on the principle of necessity, but they insisted that this principle lay inside the U.S. Constitution, not outside of it. Bishop's idea of self-preservation, to them, did not interrupt the Constitution's internal logic, but instead was already incorporated within it. For the judge advocate general's extension of Binney's idea to the first six articles of the Bill of Rights, see William Winthrop, *Digest of Opinions of the Judge Advocate General of the Army* (Washington: Government Printing Office, 3d ed., 1868), 230 n.†]

trine leads directly to anarchy or despotism, but the theory of necessity upon which it is based is false: for the government, within the Constitution, has all the powers granted to it which are necessary to preserve its existence; as has been happily proved by the result of the great effort to throw off its just authority.[29]

That the constitution as a whole is equally applicable to peace and to war is a proposition which seems to be unimpeachable. That each of its provisions applies equally to those two conditions is, however, one which that instrument itself refutes. The privilege of the writ of *habeas corpus* may be suspended when, in cases of Rebellion or Invasion—i.e. in time of war—the public safety may require it, but it could not be done in time of peace. Soldiers may, in time of war, be quartered upon the inhabitants against their consent, but not in time of peace. Thus the Constitution itself expressly recognizes a different law as applicable to these two conditions. The law thus recognized is, in fact, the law of necessity as applied to a time of war, and this law of necessity the Supreme Court (in *Ex parte Milligan*) acknowledged, although attempting to confine it within impossible bounds, viz: the theatre of active military operations, where the courts are closed, criminal justice cannot be administered according to law. The Court speak, indeed, as if the trial of offenders were the sole object of

29. *Ex parte Milligan*, 71 U.S. (4 Wall.) at 106. [Eds. note: The Liebers' disagreement with *Milligan* was thus not about the question whether the necessity authority of the government was internal to the Constitution. The justices and the Liebers agreed that it was. As the passage that follows indicates, however, the Liebers insisted that the justices in *Milligan* badly misunderstood the logic of the necessity power.]

Martial Law; whereas it is but one of the ways in which it may be exercised.

Martial Law Proper is not built upon a violation of the Constitution, for the Constitution, in some of its provisions, recognizes the law of necessity as qualifying those of otherwise general application. Were it not so, the war power here spoken of as Martial Law Proper would none the less exist, for the law of necessity cannot be controlled. Statutes cannot be framed, nor can human ingenuity devise the means, to evade it. But it rests upon this ground alone. To say—as has in effect been said—that the time of war calls forth, and sets up as the supreme law of the land, a new system of law, applicable to this exceptional condition irrespective of necessity, is a doctrine which the student of Anglican civil liberty must at once reject. Whatever is done by virtue of this power must be connected with the necessity which is looked to for its justification. That which would justify one *act* might be totally inapplicable to another. This necessity, however, cannot always be determined by the facts of individual instances of its enforcement; it may be necessary to extend martial law over a whole class of cases, and it then becomes justifiable because of the necessity of giving it such extended application.

But, if Martial Law Proper is a law of necessity its jurisdiction must extend wherever the necessity exists. It cannot be restrained within territorial limits. Martial rule, said the Supreme Court in *Ex parte Milligan*, must be confined to the locality of actual war. Beyond that there can be no necessity for its exercise. But, this would be a question of fact, and not of law.[30] The law of necessity can be limited neither by statute, nor by judicial decision.

30. "Martial Law," 8 U.S. Op. Atty. Gen. 365, 368–70 (1857).

Necessity is a fact, and yet there is often no little difficulty in determining whether the fact exists. The State is never
exposed to instantaneous destruction, as the individual may
be. The danger lies not so much in individual attempts at its
overthrow, as in the collective effect of a number of such attempts. Consequently the remedy is in anticipating, and preventing the spread of disaffection, by administering prompt
punishment in individual cases. When an army is face to face
with the enemy, and private property is seized, or destroyed,
for military purposes, the necessity for such a measure is an
easily determinable fact. When, however, it becomes a question of a resort to Martial Law Proper for the trial of offenders, under the common law of war, the necessity is more re-
mote, and not so easily determined. It has been claimed—as
already remarked—that, when war exists, a war power springs
up which assumes supreme and exclusive jurisdiction over
all acts, wherever committed, which are calculated to interfere with the prosecution of the war. If this be so, it entirely
does away with the ordinary trial for treason, for it is impossible to imagine a treasonable act which would not, directly or
remotely, have this effect. Yet the laws relative to treason are
expressly made to meet such cases, and, so long as they furnish the adequate remedy, there can be no necessity and consequently no justification for setting them aside.[31] But, if in any
case, the statute law should furnish no adequate remedy—no
means of suppressing an evil by which the military defense of
the country is impaired—in such a case that necessity would
arise, which is the justification of Martial Law Proper. From
the nature of the case, however, the necessity cannot be limited
to an absolute and immediate necessity involved in each act.

31. See *Milligan.*

When in the early days of the Civil War the courts granted writs of *habeas corpus* in favor of volunteer soldiers to such an extent as seriously to threaten the military movements and strength,* it became an imperative necessity to interpose the war power for the protection of the army, and the defense of the country. The action of the courts in each case, considered singly, did not perceptibly affect the conduct of the war. It was the frequency of the proceedings that gave them importance, and which gave rise to the necessity of adopting a general rule to counteract them, viz: the suspension of the privileges of the writ.

As the different provisions of the Constitution cannot apply equally to peace and to war, we must look beyond the express guarantees to see where is lodged the power of taking measures necessary in time of war to the natural common defense—to the right of self-preservation—an attribute of sovereignty inherent in all polities, and one of the express objects of our Union. Because this power is not expressly defined, is

* The literature on Lincoln's suspensions of habeas corpus typically focuses on the detention of Confederate sympathizers engaged in acts of rebellion, not on the point about volunteers that the Liebers raise here. Leading work in the literature on habeas in the Civil War includes Mark Neely, *Lincoln and the Triumph of the Nation: Constitutional Conflict in the American Civil War* (Chapel Hill: University of North Carolina Press, 2011); Daniel Farber, *Lincoln's Constitution* (Chicago: University of Chicago Press, 2003); and James G. Randall, *Constitutional Problems under Lincoln* (Urbana: University of Illinois Press, 1951). For habeas and the volunteer problem, see Mark Neely, "Legalities in Wartime: The Myth of the Writ of Habeas Corpus," in Stephen D. Engle, ed., *The War Worth Fighting: Abraham Lincoln's Presidency and Civil War America* (Gainesville: University Press of Florida, 2015), 110–24; Frances M. Clarke and Rebecca Jo Plant, "No Minor Matter: Underage Soldiers, Parents, and the Nationalization of Habeas Corpus in Civil War America," *Law & History Review* 35, no. 4 (November 2017): 881–927; see also "Affairs in Illinois," *New York Times*, November 20, 1861.

no proof that it does not exist. The right of self-defense being a necessary attribute of sovereignty, recognized by our Constitution, and Martial Law Proper a necessary means of self-defense, its rightful exercise must rest somewhere, although not mentioned amongst the enumerated powers.

"The Powers," says the Constitution (Amendment X), "not delegated to the United States by the Constitution, nor prohibited by it to the States, are reserved to the States respectively or to the people." The corresponding article of the Articles of Confederation is: "Each state retains its sovereignty, freedom and independence, and every Power, Jurisdiction and right, which is not by this confederation expressly delegated to the united states, in congress assembled." The Articles of Confederation say "*expressly* delegated." In the Constitution the word "expressly" is omitted. When the amendment was before Congress it was moved to insert the word expressly, but the proposition was rejected on the ground that it was impossible to confine a government to the exercise of express powers.[32] That the Confederation did so, was, as Chief Justice Story remarks,[33] one of its great defects. There are, therefore, powers tacitly delegated, and among them must be reckoned the power so to apply general powers expressly delegated as to attain the end contemplated by the Constitution. They are a means of accomplishing a lawful object. Says the Supreme Court in the opinion above cited: "The government, within the Constitution, has all the powers granted to it which are necessary to preserve its existence; as has been happily proved by the result of the great effort to throw off its just

32. Thomas Lloyd, ed., *The Congressional Register* (New York: Hodge, Allen, & Campbell, 1790), 2: 234 ff.

33. Joseph Story, *Commentaries on the Constitution of the United States* (Boston: Hilliard, Gray, & Co., 1833), 2: 752, §1900.

authority."[34] And, we might add, one of the most effective weapons in our hands, without which the others would have been blunt indeed, was an exercise of the power of Martial Law Proper.

Martial Law Proper then is an enforcement by a country of the law of war with reference to its own subjects. It is the law of necessity applied at home in a time of war. It is an exercise of military authority, over persons, property, or rights, not ordinarily subject to such jurisdiction. It for the time being suspends the administration of the ordinary law whenever, and in so far as, it is necessary to the national defense. And it extends to all parts of the country, not treated as belligerent, (to which the martial law of hostile occupation would apply) where such necessity exists.[35] It springs from the principle *salus populi suprema lex*—a rule which Locke speaks of as "so just and fundamental a Rule, that he, who sincerely follows it, cannot dangerously err." Wherefore, he says: "Whatsoever cannot but be acknowledged to be of advantage to the Society, and People in general, upon just and lasting measures, will always, when done, justifie itself."[36, *]

* It is possible that as many as four pages of the original manuscript are missing beginning at this point.

34. *Milligan*, 71 U.S. at 106.

35. See H. W. Halleck, *International Law; or, Rules Regulating the Intercourse of States in Peace and War* (San Francisco: H. H. Bancroft & Co., 1861), 373, §§ 25 *et seq.*; Bishop, *Commentaries on the Criminal Law*, 20–34; James Kent, *Commentaries on American Law*, 6th ed. (New York: William Kent, 1848), 1: 341 n.; Whiting, *War Powers under the Constitution*, 51.

36. John Locke, *Two Treatises of Government*, 2: ch. 13, § 158. *The Quarterly Review* (vol. 83) contains an article on the Ceylon Rebellion, in 1848, from which the following is an extract:

We shall define martial law to be the law of necessity, or defense. The right which a Governor of a colony has to proclaim martial law over

The following order of General Schenck* is given to show how far, in the opinion of an American commanding general, Martial Law ought to extend in a district endangered by the propinquity of actual hostilities, and the well known existence of treasonable persons within the district:

HEADQUARTERS MIDDLE DEPARTMENT,
Eighth Army Corps, Baltimore, June 30, 1863.
The immediate presence of a rebel army within this department, and in the State of Maryland, requires, as a military necessity, a resort to all the proper and usual means of defence and security. This security is to be provided against known

---

* **General Robert C. Schenck** (1809–1890) was a Republican politician, academic, and Union Army general. As commander of the Middle Department of the Army in Baltimore, Schenck suspended publication of unsympathetic newspapers and took a hard line against Confederate sympathizers. See Barbara J. Fields, *Slavery and Freedom on the Middle Ground: Maryland during the Nineteenth Century* (New Haven: Yale University Press, 1985), 105–28.

---

subjects, may be said to bear a close analogy to the right which an individual, in absence of legal protection, has to slay an assailant. In both cases, the evil must be grave. In both cases, all regular means of defense must be exhausted, or beyond reach, before the aggrieved party resorts to extremities. In both cases, the burden of proof lies on him who has ventured on such an expedient; and if he fails to vindicate himself, he is liable to severe punishment.

[Eds. note: The article referred to is "The Mysteries of Ceylon," *Quarterly Review*, American ed., vol. 88, no. 175 (January 1851): 66. However, the Liebers' phrasing and punctuation differ from the journal's; instead they follow that of the judge advocate general in Lambdin Milligan's military commission trial—who also cited volume 83 of the *Quarterly Review*, rather than volume 88. See Benn Pittman, ed., *The Trials for Treason at Indianapolis* (Cincinnati: Moore, Wilstach & Baldwin, 1865), 257.]

hostilities and opposition to the lawful and National Government from every quarter and in every form. Traitors and disaffected persons within must be restrained and made to contribute to the common safety, while the enemy in front is to be met and punished for this bold invasion.

Martial law is therefore declared, and hereby established in the city and county of Baltimore, and in all the counties of the Western Shore of Maryland. The Commanding General gives assurance that this suspension of the civil government within the limits defined shall not extend beyond the necessities of the occasion.

All the civil courts, tribunals, and political functionaries of State, county, or city authority, are to continue in the discharge of their duties, as in times of peace, only in no way interfering with the exercise of the predominant power assumed and asserted by the military authority.

All peaceful citizens are requested to remain quietly at their homes and in pursuit of their ordinary vocations, except as they may be possibly subject to calls for personal services, or other necessary requisitions for military purposes or uses hereafter.

All seditious language or mischievous practices tending to the encouragement of rebellion are especially prohibited, and will promptly be made the subject of observation and treatment. Traitorous and dangerous persons must expect to be dealt with as the public safety may seem to require.

To save the country is paramount to all other considerations. When the occasion for this proclamation passes by, no one will be more rejoiced than the Commanding General that he can revoke his order and return to the normal condition of a country at peace, and a Government sustained by a united and loyal people.

                    Robt. C. Schenck,
                    Major-General Commanding

We must, therefore, keep constantly in mind these important points:

1. The distinction between Martial Law and Military Law.
2. The fact that this distinction was not recognized in former times; that the term *Martial* Law was used to designate all kinds of military jurisdiction; that it was never limited to the meaning which we now attach to it; but that it was often used in speaking of what we call Military Law.
3. The distinction between the Martial Law of hostile occupation, (whether of foreign or rebellious territory), and Martial Law Proper.

We will then be prepared to consider the following questions:

Can Martial Law Proper be under any circumstances lawfully enforced?
Does it exist in England by virtue of the prerogative, or must it be authorized by act of Parliament? And, if not authorized by act of Parliament, must its exercise be followed by an act of indemnity?

> Has it any place in this country? If so, does it ex-
> ist by virtue of any provision of the Constitu-
> tion, or by virtue of any principles reconcilable
> with its provisions; or, is it a setting aside of the
> Constitution?
> What will justify the enforcement of Martial Law?
> To what acts and over whom may it be extended?
> When and where may it be enforced?

Before, however, we proceed to the direct examination of the subject from the various points of view suggested by these questions, it will be necessary for us to turn our attention to the great field of English history, so often searched for precedents and authorities, and afterwards to the newer field of American history. In both it is interwoven with constitutional questions of the greatest importance; but, in English history it is so intimately connected with the history of the administration and government of the army that a sketch of the latter will, it is believed, materially assist us in forming a true conception of the subject. It will certainly enable us the better to understand the authorities. The consideration of the subject from this historical point of view seems, therefore, properly to precede that of the principles upon which it is based, and of the rules by which it is governed.

Looking to English history we will find many instances of the irregular exercise of military authority which have been referred to as precedents in Martial Law. They were in a majority of cases unjustifiable on the ground of necessity, and even indefensible upon the extreme theories of the advocates of a supreme war power. Martial Law as a necessary, and therefore justifiable, means of self-defence, submerged under this abuse of prerogative. The legal, and the illegal, exercise of the prerogative were not separated and distinguished. Through many generations the people submitted to these abuses, but in time the evil worked its own cure. During the period, however, when resistance to them was making itself heard and felt, we cannot expect to find an acknowledgment of a principle apparently conflicting with the rights which the people were endeavoring to place upon a more secure footing. Several of the early authorities speak of "Martial Law," but in general they use that term in a different sense from that which we now give it. To understand them as using it in the same sense would entirely, mislead us as to their meaning, and it is, therefore, of great importance to ascertain what kind of military jurisdiction they were speaking of. The same is true of the statutes, and notably so of the Petition of Right, and the Mutiny Act. There is one case—that of the Earl of Lancaster*—which stands forth as a case of great importance, both because it seems to show that, in the days of Edward II, Martial Law was, to a certain extent, a recognized substitute for the ordinary law in time of rebellion, and because it is cited as a precedent by Coke, Hale and Blackstone. If the conclusions arrived at in these pages are correct, however, it was not cited with reference to that kind of

---

* **Thomas of Lancaster** (c. 1278–1322), the second Earl of Lancaster, was executed in 1322 after leading a failed insurrection against Edward II. His sham trial, sometimes said to have been under authority of martial law, became an important marker in the history of Anglo-American constitutionalism. As William Blackstone put it some centuries later, the execution of Lancaster was posthumously reversed (to the benefit of his heirs) "because it was done in time of peace" when to "execute any man by colour of martial law" was simple murder because "against *magna carta*." William Blackstone, *Commentaries on the Laws of England*, 5th ed. (Oxford: Clarendon, 1773), 1:410. For more on Lancaster, see John Maddicott, *Thomas of Lancaster, 1307–1322: A Study in the Reign of Edward II* (London: Oxford University Press, 1970).

military authority which we designate as Martial Law Proper.
This power did not receive any definite recognition in England
until towards the close of last century. Its recognition then was
precipitated by the Irish Rebellion, but the principle has been
confirmed on many subsequent occasions, and is now an acknowledged element of the prerogative. The power of *Parliament* to call martial law into action has never been questioned.

CHAPTER II

The Mutiny Act. Military Law

The Mutiny Act of I William & Mary marks an important era in the history of the government and administration of the British army.* The Mutiny Act, and the Articles of War, form the basis of the Military Law of England. The first Mutiny Act was passed the 3d of April, 1689, and went into effect the 12th of April. Since then it has been, with a few exceptions, and with certain amendments introduced from time to time, annually renewed. The reason for this yearly renewal is to be found in the fundamental constitutional principle that a standing army in time of peace, without the consent of Parliament, is against the law of England. Consequently the yearly consent of Parliament was deemed necessary. In the reign of William III the Mutiny Act was on several occasions allowed to expire. Thus, the Mutiny Act, passed in 1697, expired in the spring of 1698. Speaking of this time Macaulay† says: "As yet, no such act had been passed

* See note on the Mutiny Act in Chapter I above.

† **Thomas Babington Macaulay** (1800–1859) was a prominent English historian best known for his five-volume *History of England*, written in a literary style and intended for popular reading. The *History* begins in 1685

except in time of war, and the temper of the Parliament and of the nation was such that the ministers did not venture to ask, in time of peace, for a renewal of powers unknown to the Constitution. For the present, therefore, the soldier was again, as in times which preceded the Revolution, subject to exactly the same law which governed the citizen."[1] It has, indeed, been said that the army was, during the intervals, governed by Articles of War based upon the royal prerogative,[2] but it is not correct to say that the prerogative was recognized as extending to the adoption of a code for the government of the army in time of peace, within the realm.

Articles of War had been put forth during the preceding reigns of Charles I, Charles II, and James II.* These codes were

---

with the accession of James II and concludes in the final, unfinished volume with the death of William III. The *History* sold tens of thousands of copies during Macaulay's lifetime, though it faced varied criticism from clergy for its treatment of religion. For an introduction, see J. W. Burrow, *A Liberal Descent: Victorian Historians and the English Past* (Cambridge: Cambridge University Press, 1981), part I.

* The Crown used Articles of War to control, direct, and discipline troops. This ability was a recognized part of the sovereign's prerogative dating to the Conquest. In 1629 and 1639, Charles I issued Articles of War governing his army; in 1666 and 1672, Charles II issued Articles of War in response to wars with the French and the Dutch, respectively; and in 1685, James II issued Articles of War in response to Monmouth's Rebellion. These articles often laid out punishments for various acts. Charles II's Articles of War in 1666, for instance, punished robbery and desertion with death. As the Liebers note, Articles of War could be issued in response to conflicts both abroad and domestically, but could not operate during peacetime. A brief summary of the use of Articles of War can be found in W. S. Holdsworth, "Martial Law Historically Considered," in *Essays in Law and History* (Oxford: Clarendon Press, 1946), 1–19 (especially 3–8).

1. Lord Macaulay, *History of England* (New York: Harper & Brothers, 1861), 20.

2. Thomas Frederick Simmons, *The Constitution and Practice of Courts Martial*, 6th ed. (London: John Murray, 1873), § 91 (p. 46).

royal orders to enforce military obligations. They generally related to the government of the army when on service in time of war and beyond the realm, but this was not the case with all. That the prerogative extended to the adoption of Articles of War for the government of the Army abroad is well established. So, also, in time of war within the realm. But, it was not recognized as extending to the enforcement of military discipline at home in time of peace.

Upon this latter point military writers have in general expressed a different view, and there are not wanting authorities to sustain them. Thus, Sir Matthew Hale says:[3]

> If in the time of peace a commission issue to exercise martial law, and such commissioners condemn any of the king's subjects (not being listed under the military power), this is without all question a great misprision, and an erroneous proceeding. . . .
>
> But suppose they be listed under a general or lieutenant of the king's appointment under the great seal, and modelled into the form and discipline of an army, either in garrison or without, yet as long as it is *tempus pacis* in this kingdom, they cannot be proceeded against as to loss of life by martial law. . . .
>
> It must therefore be a time of war, that must give exercise to their jurisdictions, at least in cases of life.

This is certainly not a very positive statement of the law, but it would seem that Sir Matthew Hale was willing to

---

3. Matthew Hale, *The History of the Pleas of the Crown* (London: E. Rider, 1800), 1: 499–500.

concede that the jurisdiction might be lawfully exercised in cases not extending to loss of life. The view thus expressed is believed not to accord with a liberal construction of the Petition of Right, and is clearly inconsistent with the preambles to the first Mutiny Acts. The exercise of the prerogative in this respect was, indeed, in conflict with the principle that the law of England did not admit of a standing army in time of peace without the consent of Parliament. It was not recognized as a permanent part of the national system, and the law did not, therefore, recognize the legality of codes put forth by the crown for its government within the realm in time of peace.

Accordingly, we nowhere met during this period with any recognition by Parliament of such a prerogative. No Mutiny Act until the first of Queen Anne's reign* took any notice of the power of the crown to adopt Articles of War.[4] This act

---

* After Queen Anne took the throne in 1702, the annual Mutiny Act for the first time referred to monarchical authority to exert special legal authority over the military, when *outside* of England. See 1 Anne c. 16; Clode, *Military Forces*, 146. For the text of the Mutiny Act and its changes between 1689 and 1717, see Charles M. Clode, *The Administration of Justice under Military and Martial Law* (London: John Murray, 1874), 209.

4. I am unable to account for a statement made by Finlason, in his *Review of the Authorities as to the Repression of Riot or Rebellion*. He says:

> After the Revolution, when the Bill of Rights declared the illegality of a standing army in time of peace without the consent of Parliament, it became necessary to give that authority annually, and at the same time it was natural that Parliament should provide for the permanent regulation of a standing army in time of peace. But it is a great error to suppose that the *authority of the Crown* over the army rests merely on the Mutiny Act. The Mutiny Act is founded on the Bill of Rights, which, ever since 1689, has recited—

> > That the keeping or raising a standing army within the Kingdom in time of peace without the consent of Parliament is illegal, and that no

and successive others provided that nothing in them should be held to abridge the Majesty's power to establish Articles of War, erect Courts-Martial, and inflict penalties thereunder, as might have been done beyond the seas in time of war before the act was passed. But it was not until 1717 that it was made lawful for the crown to adopt Articles for the government of the army within the realm in time of peace.* The Mutiny Act of that year provides:

* The key words here are "within the realm," as previous Mutiny Acts, of course, had recognized this authority outside England. The modifications to the Mutiny Act which the Liebers quote are shown, in the context of other contemporary changes to the Act, in Clode, *Administration of Justice*, 209.

> man can be forejudged of life or limb, or subjected in *time of peace* within the realm to any kind of punishment by martial law, or in any other manner than according to the known laws of the realm; and that it is requisite that soldiers, who shall mutiny or stir up sedition, or be guilty of crimes or offences to the *prejudice of good order* and military discipline, be brought to more exemplary and speedy punishment than the usual forms of law will allow; and there it enacts that the sovereign may make articles of war for the better government of the army, which shall be judicially taken notice of; and that no person *within the United Kingdom or the British Isles* shall by such articles be subject to any punishment extending to life and limb, except for crimes by the Acts made punishable. And it proceeded to enact that all the provisions of the Act shall apply to persons *enlisted or in pay as soldiers*, or all persons who shall be serving with any part of the army at home or abroad.

William Finlason, *A Review of the Authorities as to the Repression of Riot or Rebellion* (London: Stevens & Sons, 1868), 57–58. The Bill of Rights contains absolutely no provision of this nature. As Clode remarks, when speaking of the Mutiny Act of 1712: "Neither had any reference whatever been made in prior Acts to the power which the Crown had exercised of issuing Articles of War, though it must have been within the cognizance of Parliament that such had been issued, and that the army was in fact governed by them" (Clode, *Administration of Justice*, 25).

That it shall be lawful for His Majesty to form, make, and establish Articles of War, and erect and constitute Courts-martial with power to try, hear, and determine any crime or offence by such Articles of War, and inflict penalties by sentence or judgment of the same as well within the Kingdoms of Great Britain and Ireland as in any of His Majesty's Dominions beyond the sea.[5]

The difference in language is noticeable. By the first mutiny act of Queen Anne's reign it was declared that nothing in it should be held to abridge an existing power. By that of 1717 it was declared that "it shall be lawful" for the King to establish and enforce Articles of War within the Kingdoms of Great Britain and Ireland, and his dominions beyond the sea. It made that lawful which was not lawful before. One was declaratory; the other enacting. One related to a prerogative power; the other to a statutory power.[6]

At the time of the Restoration the law recognized no army except the militia.[7] Charles II, however, soon began to

5. Six of the lords signed a protest against this bill, (March 23d, 1717, 3 George I): "Because the Bill doth establish martial law, extending to the life of the offender, in time of peace, which we conceive is contrary to the ancient laws of this Kingdom; and the soldiers are obliged to obey the military orders of their superior officers, under the penalty of being condemned by a court-martial to suffer death for their disobedience, &c." William Cobbett, ed., *Cobbett's Parliamentary History* (London: T. C. Hansard, 1811), 7: 429–30.

6. Note here referring to Clode's views. [Eds. note: As far as we can tell, Norman never wrote such a note summarizing Clode's views on the Mutiny Act of 1717.]

7. Lord Macaulay, *History of England* (New York: Harper & Brothers), 1: 270–71.

form a standing army, paying it out of his own revenues.[8] In 1685 the regular army consisted of about nine thousand men. "The discipline," says Macaulay,

> was lax, and, indeed, could not be otherwise. The common law of England knew nothing of courts-martial, and made no distinction, in time of peace, between a soldier and any other subject; nor could the government then venture to ask even the most loyal parliament for a Mutiny Bill. A soldier, therefore, by knocking down his colonel, incurred only the ordinary penalties of assault and battery, and, by refusing to obey orders, by sleeping on guard, or by deserting his colours, incurred no legal penalty at all. Military punishments were doubtless inflicted during the reign of Charles the Second, but they were inflicted very sparingly, and in such a manner as not to attract public notice, or to produce an appeal to the courts of Westminster Hall.[9]

James II soon increased the number of the regular forces to twenty thousand, and towards the close of his reign to forty thousand. The condition of affairs in 1687 is best illustrated by the steps taken by James to secure the punishment of certain soldiers. They are thus described by Macaulay:

> The king had scarcely formed that army on which he chiefly depended for the accomplishing of his

8. Previous to this time there had never been a standing army in England, unless we care to consider the four thousand archers raised in Cheshire by Richard II, and Henry the Seventh's Yeomen of the Guard.

9. Macaulay, *History of England*, 1: 276.

designs when he found that he could not himself
control it. When war was actually raging in the
kingdom, a mutineer or a deserter might be tried
by a military tribunal, and executed by the provost
marshal. But there was now profound peace. The
common law of England, having sprung up in an age
when all men bore arms occasionally and none constantly, recognised no distinction, in time of peace,
between a soldier and any other subject; nor was
there any act resembling that by which the authority necessary for the government of regular troops
is now annually confided to the sovereign. Some old
statutes, indeed, made desertion felony in certain
specified cases. But those statutes were applicable
only to soldiers serving the king in actual war, and
could not without the grossest disingenuousness be
so strained as to include the case of a man who, in
a time of profound tranquillity at home and abroad,
should become tired of the camp at Hounslow and
should go back to his native village. The government
appears to have had no hold on such a man, except
the hold which master bakers and master tailors
have on their journeymen. He and his officers were,
in the eye of the law, on a level. If he swore at them
he might be fined for an oath. If he struck them he
might be prosecuted for assault and battery. In truth
the regular army was under less restraint than the
militia. For the militia was a body established by an
act of parliament, and it had been provided by that
act that slight punishments might be summarily inflicted for breaches of discipline.

It does not appear that, during the reign of Charles the Second, the practical inconvenience arising from this state of the law had been much felt. The explanation may perhaps be that, till the last year of his reign, the force which he maintained in England consisted chiefly of household troops, whose pay was so high that dismission from the service would have been felt by most of them as a great calamity. The stipend of a private in the Life Guards was a provision for the younger son of a gentleman. Even the Foot Guards were in a situation which the great body of the labouring population might regard with envy. The return of the garrison of Tangier and the raising of the new regiments had made a great change. There were now in England many thousands of soldiers, each of whom received only eightpence a day. The dread of punishment was therefore necessary to keep them to their duty; and such punishments their officers could not legally inflict. James had therefore one plain choice before him, to let his army disolve itself, or to induce the judges to pronounce that the law was what every barrister in the Temple knew that it was not.[10]

Having accordingly dismissed from the King's Bench and Old Bailey the judges upon whom he could not rely, and replaced them with more subservient tools, several deserters were brought to trial before these courts, and were convicted

10. Ibid., 2: 255–56.

and received sentence "in the face of the letter and of the spirit of the law."[11]

Such being the state of the law when William of Orange was called to the throne, it became evident that some change must be introduced, if the regular forces, which it was necessary to maintain, were to be kept under any sort of discipline. Yet, the aversion of the English people to a standing army was so great that there would probably have been much difficulty in securing the passage of a bill for this government, had it not been for the mutiny of a regiment—now the first of the line. "This event," says Macaulay,[12]

> facilitated an important change in our polity, a change which, it is true, could not have been long delayed, but which would not have been easily accomplished except at a moment of extreme danger. The time had at length arrived at which it was necessary to make a legal distinction between the soldier and the citizen. Under the Plantagenets and the Tudors there had been no standing army. The standing army which had existed under the last kings of the House of Stuart had been regarded by every party in the state with strong and not unreasonable aversion. The common law gave the Sovereign no power to control his troops. The Parliament, regarding them as mere tools of tyranny, had not been disposed to give such power by statute.

11. Ibid.

12. Ibid., 8: chap. XI. I have quoted so fully from Macaulay because I believe certain important words in the Mutiny Act have been misinterpreted by recent English writers, and because it is desirable to expose the error, if error it is, by the words of one of their own most eminent historians.

James, indeed, had induced his corrupt and servile
judges to put on some obsolete law a construction
which enabled him to punish desertion capitally.
But this construction was considered by all respectable jurists as unsound, and, had it been sound,
would have been far from effecting all that was
necessary for the purpose of maintaining military
discipline. Even James did not venture to inflict
death by sentence of a court-martial. The deserter
was treated as an ordinary felon, was tried at the assizes by a petty jury on a bill found by a grand jury,
and was at liberty to avail himself of any technical
flaw which might be discovered in the indictment.

The Revolution, by altering the relative position of the prince and the Parliament, had altered
also the relative position of the army and the nation. The King and the Commons were now at
unity; and both were alike menaced by the greatest
military power which had existed in Europe since
the downfall of the Roman empire. In a few weeks
thirty thousand veterans, accustomed to conquer,
and led by able and experienced captains, might
cross from the ports of Normandy and Brittany to
our shores. That such a force would with little difficulty scatter three times that number of militia, no
man well acquainted with war could doubt. There
must then be regular soldiers; and, if there were
to be regular soldiers, it must be indispensable,
both to their efficiency, and to the security of every
other class, that they should be kept under a strict
discipline. An ill disciplined army has ever been a
more costly and a more licentious militia, impotent

against a foreign enemy, and formidable only to the country which it is paid to defend. A strong line of demarkation must therefore be drawn between the soldiers and the rest of the community. For the sake of public freedom, they must, in the midst of freedom, be placed under a despotic rule. They must be subject to a sharper penal code, and to a more stringent code of procedure, than are administered by the ordinary tribunals. Some acts which in the citizen are innocent, must in the soldier be crimes. Some acts which in the citizen are punished with fine or imprisonment, must in the soldier be punished with death. The machinery by which courts of law ascertain the guilt or innocence of an accused citizen is too slow and too intricate to be applied to an accused soldier. For, of all the maladies incident to the body politic, military insubordination is that which requires the most prompt and drastic remedies. If the evil be not stopped as soon as it appears, it is certain to spread; and it can not spread far without danger to the very vitals of the commonwealth. For the general safety, therefore, a summary jurisdiction of terrible extent must, in camps, be intrusted to rude tribunals composed of men of the sword.

But, though it was certain that the country could not at that moment be secure without professional soldiers, and equally certain that professional soldiers must be worse than useless unless they were placed under a rule more arbitrary and severe than that to which other men were subject, it was not without great misgivings that a House

of Commons could venture to recognise the existence, and to make provision for the government of
a standing army. There was scarcely a public man
of note who had not often avowed his conviction
that our polity and a standing army could not exist
together. The Whigs had been in the constant habit
of repeating that standing armies had destroyed
the inhibitions of the neighboring nations. The
Tories had repeated as constantly that, in our own
island, a standing army had subverted the Church,
oppressed the gentry, and murdered the King. No
leader of either party could, without laying himself
open to the charge of gross inconsistency, propose
that such an army should henceforth be one of the
permanent establishments of the realm. The mutiny at Ipswich, and the panic which that mutiny
produced, made it easy to effect what would otherwise have been in the highest degree difficult. A
short bill was brought in which began by declaring,
in explicit terms, that standing armies and courts
martial were unknown to the law of England. It was
then enacted that, on account of the extreme perils
impending at that moment over the state, no man
mustered on pay in the service of the crown should,
on pain of death, or of such lighter punishment as
a court martial should deem sufficient, desert his
colours or mutiny against his commanding officers. This statute was to be in force only six months,
and many of those who voted for it probably believed that it would, at the close of that period, be
suffered to expire. The bill passed rapidly and easily. Not a single division was taken upon it in the

House of Commons. A mitigating clause, indeed, which illustrates somewhat curiously the manners of that age, was added by way of rider after the third reading. This clause provided that no court martial should pass sentence of death except between the hours of six in the morning and one in the afternoon. The dinner-hour was then early, and it was but too probable that a gentleman who had dined would be in a state in which he could not safely be trusted with the lives of his fellow creatures. With this amendment, the first and most concise of our many Mutiny Bills was sent up to the Lords, and was, in a few hours, hurried by them through all its steps and passed by the King.[13]

Thus was made, without one dissentient voice in Parliament, without one murmur in the nation, the first step toward a change which had become necessary to the safety of the state, yet which every party in the state then regarded with extreme dread and aversion. Six months passed; and still the public danger continued. The power necessary to the maintenance of military discipline was a second time intrusted to the crown for a short term. The trust again expired, and was again renewed. By slow degrees, familiarity reconciled the public mind to the names, once so odious, of standing army and court-martial. It was proved by experience that, in a well-constituted society, professional soldiers may be terrible to a foreign enemy, and yet submissive to the civil power. What had been at first tol-

13. Stat. 1 W. & M., Sess. 1, c. 5; Common's Journals, March 28, 1689.

erated as the exception began to be considered as
the rule. Not a session passed without a Military
Bill. When at length it became evident that a political change of the highest importance was taking
place in such a manner as almost to escape notice,
a clamour was raised by some factious men desirous to weaken the hands of the government, and
by some respectable men who felt an honest but
injudicious reverence for every old constitutional
tradition, and who were unable to understand that
what at one stage in the progress of society is per-
nicious, may at another stage be indispensable.
This clamour however, as years rolled on, became
fainter and fainter. The debate which recurred every spring on the Mutiny Bill came to be regarded
merely as an occasion on which hopeful young
orators fresh from Christchurch were to deliver
maiden speeches, setting forth how the guards of
Pisistratus seized the citadel of Athens, and how
the Praetorian cohorts sold the Roman empire to
Didius. At length these declamations became too
ridiculous to be repeated. The most oldfashioned,
the most eccentric politician could hardly, in the
reign of George the Third, contend that there ought
to be no regular Soldiers, or that the ordinary law,
administered by the ordinary courts, would effec-
tually maintain discipline among such soldiers.

All parties being agreed as to the general
principle, a long succession of Mutiny Bills passed
without any discussion, except when some particular article of the military code required amendment. It is perhaps because the army became thus

gradually and almost imperceptibly one of the institutions of England that it has acted in such perfect harmony with all the other institutions, has
never once, during a hundred and sixty years, been
untrue to the throne or disobedient to the law, has
never once defied the tribunals, or overawed the
constituent bodies. To this day, however, the Estates
of the Realm continue to set up periodically, with
laudable jealousy, a landmark on the frontier which
was traced at the time of the Revolution. They sol-
emnly reassert every year the doctrine laid down
in the Declaration of Rights; and they then grant to
the Sovereign an extraordinary power to govern a
certain number of soldiers acceding to certain rules
during twelve months more.[14]

Such was the state of the law, and such the events which
led to the passage of the first mutiny act. The preamble of that
act was in the following words:

Whereas, the raising or keeping a standing Army
within this kingdome in time of peace unlesse it
be with consent of Parlyament is against law. And
whereas it is judged necessary, by their Majestyes
and this present Parlyament That dureing this time
of Danger severall of the Forces which are now on
foote should be continued and others raised for the
Safety of the Kingdome for the common defence
of the Protestant Religion and for the reduceing of
Ireland.

14. Macaulay, *History of England*, 3: 42–47.

> And whereas noe man may be forejudged of
> Life or Limbe, or subjected to any kinde of punish-
> ment by Martiall Law, or in any other manner than
> by the judgement of his Peeres, and according to
> the Knowne and Established Laws of this Realme.
> Yet neverthelesse, it being requisite for retaineing
> such Forces as are or shall be raised during this exi-
> gence of Affaires in their Duty an exact Discipline
> be observed. And that Soldiers who shall Mutiny
> or Stirr up Sedition, or shall desert Their Maj-
> estyes Service be brought to a more exemplary and
> speedy Punishment than the usuall Forms of Law
> will allow.[15, *]

An explanation here suggests itself which I believe to be
worthy of consideration. We have seen that in the preamble to
the earlier Mutiny Acts the law was stated thus: "Whereas no
man can be prejudged of life or limb, or subjected to any Kinde
of punishment by martiall law, or in any other manner than
by the judgment of his peeres, and according to the Knowne
and established laws of this realm." This is in substance but a
repetition of the recital in the Petition of Right: "Whereas by
authority of Parliament in the 25th year of Edward III, it is
enacted that no man shall be forejudged of life or limb against
the form of the Great Charter, and the laws of the land; and
by the said Great Charter and other laws of the realm no man

---

* Eds. note: Two pages may be missing here.

15. Charles M. Clode, *The Military Forces of the Crown: Their Administration and Government* (London: John Murray, 1869), 1: 499 (quoting the First
Mutiny Act, 1 Wm. & M. c. 5).

ought to be adjudged to death but by the laws established in this realm."*

The above language of the Mutiny Act goes no further than that of the Petition of Right. It is in the one as comprehensive as in the other, and it cannot be doubted that the Parliament of 1689 intended to announce the same principles as had been proclaimed by that of 1628. If, therefore, we can ascertain what was understood and intended to be the effect of the Petition of Right, we will have a guide to assist us in constructing the preamble to the Mutiny Act. Fortunately, we are here not left to conjecture. There has come down to us, in Rushworth's Historical Collections,[16] a report of the debate in the committee of the whole House of Commons, which resulted in the adoption of the Petition, and which leaves no room for doubt as to the intention of the legislators. As will be seen more fully hereafter, that part of the Petition which relates to Martial Law was aimed at, and intended to correct, an existing abuse of power. This abuse was the issuing of commissions whereby soldiers, mariners and others who should join with them were subjected in time of peace to trial and punishment by military jurisdiction. The fact that it was a time of peace was throughout the debate constantly advoked to, and it was on this account that the commissions were declared illegal. It was admitted

* A central document in English legal history, the Petition of Right took advantage of King Charles I's (r. 1625–1649) desperate need for finances to extract concessions, including (most notably in this context) a ban on martial law. See Petition of Right (1628), Art. VII, available at http://www .nationalarchives.gov.uk/pathways/citizenship/rise_parliament/transcripts/ petition_right.htm.

16. John Rushworth, ed., *Historical Collections of Private Passages of State* (London: M. Wotton, 1686), 2: 76–90.

that commissions for the trial of soldiers in time of war would be legal; but, this being a time of peace, they were declared illegal. It was not the intention of Parliament to place any restriction upon an existing legal power, but simply of declaring the law as thus understood. The Petition was declaratory of the law of peace—not of the law of war. It being a time of peace, these commissions were illegal, whether directed against the soldier or the citizen, and Parliament did not stop to distinguish between the power which might, and that which might not have been lawfully exercised, had it been a time of peace.

It is fair to presume, therefore, that in apparently announcing the same principle in language no more comprehensive, Parliament intended that such should be the effect of the Mutiny Act. It was passed at a time when there was peace within the realm, and, the prerogative not extending to the adoption of a penal code for the government of the army within the realm in time of peace, its object was to supply this want.[17] The history of the Act proves this. But, the preamble was included as a recital of law, and its comprehensive terms would seem to exclude the construction that it had reference only to a time of peace. We are not, however, bound to accept this recital as a conclusive statement of law. "A mere recital in an Act of Parliament, either of fact or law," said Lord Campbell, "is not conclusive; and we are at liberty to consider the fact or the law to be different from the statement in the recital."[18] We may therefore go behind it to see what the law was.

17. "The Mutiny Acts are only necessary to authorize the Crown to apply, in time of peace, those regulations which the Crown may, by prerogative, apply in time of war; and of rebellion, which amounts to war." William F. Finlason, *Treatise on Martial Law* (London: Stevens & Sons, 1866), iii.

18. Queen v. Inhabitants of Haughton, 1 Ellis & Blackburn Rep. 514 (1879).

The effect of the Amendment of the preamble to the Mutiny Act by the inclusion of the words, "in time of peace," and "within the realm," was apparently indirectly to recognize the existence of some kind of military jurisdiction in time of war within the realm, and in time both of war and peace without the realm. If any such jurisdiction or power existed these words removed the apparent repugnancy of the preamble to the prior acts. Was there such a power, and, if so, what was it? By some, these words are looked upon as a recognition of the right of the crown to resort to martial law in time of rebellion, but there is reason to doubt the correctness of this conclusion. It is not probable that Parliament in the year 1703 intended to recognize any principle which had not been previously recognized as part of the political system. Its intention must have been to reconcile the preamble of the earlier acts with some recognized principle, and the trial and punishment by martial law for treason of those engaged in rebellion does not appear to have been generally so regarded. There is some conflict of opinion upon this point, but the debate on the Petition of Right clearly shows that at that day at least this was not generally admitted to be a legal exercise of the prerogative.

On the other hand there was an undisputed prerogative with the exercise of which the preamble of the earlier acts seemed to conflict, and with which it was reconciled by the amendment. The words inserted fully and exactly covered this prerogative power. The sovereign had the right by Articles of War to provide for the government of his troops beyond the realm, or in time of war within the realm. No one disputed the legality of such an exercise of the prerogative; yet it had been ignored in previous acts. Is it not possible that the preamble was remodeled so as to reconcile it with this power, which was universally recognized as belonging to the crown? If such was the object, the words used were precisely adapted to it.

Moreover, the very first act, the preamble to which was adopted in this new form, contained a proviso that nothing in it should be held to abridge his Majesty's power to establish Articles of War, erect Courts-Martial, and inflict penalties thereunder, as might have been done beyond the seas in time of war before the Act was passed. Here there was a recognition in the Mutiny Act of a prerogative, with which the preamble to former acts were in conflict. That this recognition, and the altered preamble appear for the first time in the same act would, under these circumstances, appear to be a good reason for regarding them as having some bearing upon each other.

And, further, the language of the amended preambles recites that no man may be "subjected *in time of peace* to any kind of punishment *within this Realm* by martial Law, &c." Now, if this recital relates to Martial Law alone, the words "within this Realm" might have been omitted, for Martial Law can *nowhere* be enforced, except where there is a state of war. It has, indeed, been held that the Petition of Right only applies to England, within the four seas;[19] but see Charge of Ch. J. Cockburn in *Queen v. Nelson and Brand* * that there must be a state of war to justify its declaration, but that in all other parts of the British dominions Martial Law may be resorted to for the purpose of preventing the outbreak of rebellion.[20]

---

* This case, which arose out of an 1865 revolt in Jamaica, will be discussed further in Chapter VI.

19. Finlason, *Treatise on Martial Law*, 18.
20. Frederick Cockburn, ed., *Charge of the Lord Chief Justice of England to the Grand Jury at the Central Criminal Court in the Case of the Queen against Nelson and Brand* (London: William Ridgway, 1867), 65–66.

This view is an extreme one, and is not sustained by the best authorities—certainly not to the extent of justifying a resort to Martial Law for the trial and punishment of those who in time of peace conspire to levy war. If we follow these, the question suggests itself—why were the words "within the Realm" inserted? By virtue of what power might any one be subjected to punishment in time of peace beyond the Realm—outside of England? May these words not have been introduced for the purpose of embracing the prerogative, by virtue of which the crown might put forth Articles of War for the government of the army at such time, in such places?

However this may be, it at least appears that there was something, besides the power of executing martial law, to which the disputed words *might* have applied. There was no necessary connection between them and Martial Law—in the modern acceptation of the term, and we must look elsewhere to see whether the power existed. Returning to the amended preamble Clode says: "The Crown, therefore, was no longer restricted by *Statute* from exercising the power (if otherwise valid) of declaring Martial Law in times other than those of Peace, or in places other than within the Realm."[21] It would seem to be more correct to say that the effect of the amendment was to reconcile the preamble with the power vested in the crown of adopting and enforcing Articles of War for the government of the army beyond the realm, or within the realm in time of war, and also with the power of enforcing Martial Law in time of war, or rebellion, *if such a power existed.*

21. Clode, *Administration of Justice*, 48.

CHAPTER III
Martial Law in English History

The Great Charter, as it stands at the head of the English statute book, is in the form in which it was promulgated in the ninth year of the reign of Henry III.* Its 29th chapter is in these words: "Nullus liber homo capiatur, vel imprisonetur, aut disseisietur de aliquo libero tenemento suo vel libertatibus vel liberis consuetudinibus suis, aut utlagetur, aut exulet, aut aliquo alio modo destruatur, nec super eum ibimus, nec super eum mittemus nisi per legale judicium parium suorum vel per legem terrae. Nulli vendemus, nulli negabimus, aut differemus rectum aut justitiam."

---

* The Great Charter (Magna Carta) enshrined a set of royal concessions to a group of barons dissatisfied with King John's military and tax policy. John agreed to the charter at Runnymede in 1215, but Henry III issued the definitive version in 1225. Magna Carta came to be seen as a fundamental statement of English liberties. Opponents of the Crown often invoked Magna Carta in the political crises of the early-modern period. Chapter 29, the provision that the Liebers discuss, is its most famous chapter and is the precursor to the Anglo-American concept of due process. For an introduction to Magna Carta, see David Carpenter, *Magna Carta* (London: Penguin Books, 2015).

This chapter is thus translated in the common edition of the English Statutes:* "no freeman shall be taken or imprisoned, or be disseized of his freehold, or liberties, or free customs, or be outlawed or exiled, or any otherwise destroyed, nor will we pass upon him, nor condemn him, but by lawful judgment of his peers, or by the law of the land. We will sell to no man, we will not deny or defer to any man, either justice or right."†

The words "nec super eum ibimus, nec super eum mittemus" have been differently translated—by some, "nor shall we pass upon him, nor condemn him"; by others, "nor will we pass upon him, nor commit him to prison." Coke gives this explanation: "No man shall be condemned at the King's suit, either before the King in his bench, where pleas are *coram rege* (before the King), (and so are the words *nec super ibimus*, to be understood‡), nor before any other commissioner or judge whatsoever, and so are the words '*nec super mittemus*,' to be

---

* The "common edition" of the English Statutes is likely a reference to the English *Statutes at Large*. This collection of all English statutes invariably begins with Magna Carta. See, e.g., *The Statutes at Large of England and of Great-Britain: From Magna Carta to the Union of the Kingdoms of Great Britain and Ireland*, 20 vols. (London: George Eyre and Andrew Strahan, 1811).

† The Liebers borrowed heavily here from a passage in Ohio lawyer Rollin C. Hurd's 1858 treatise on habeas corpus. Hurd's text provides the Latin and the English translation, and then goes on (as the Liebers do) to discuss differing translations of the key terms of the Magna Carta. See Rollin C. Hurd, A *Treatise on the Right of Personal Liberty and on the Writ of Habeas Corpus* (Albany, NY: W. C. Little & Co., 1858), 81–82.

‡ It seems virtually certain that the Liebers are borrowing from Hurd here. In quoting Coke, Hurd, like the Liebers, renders it as "*nec super ibimus*," while the actual passage from Coke says "nec super eum ibimus" (Edward Coke, *The Second Part of the Institutes of the Laws of England* [London: M. Flesher, 1642], 46).

understood, but by the judgment of his peers, that is equals, or according to the law of the land."[1]

Spooner, in his *Essay on the Trial by Jury*,* continues the passage thus: "no freeman shall be arrested, or imprisoned, or deprived of his freehold, or his liberties, or free customs, or be outlawed or exiled, or in any manner destroyed (harmed), nor will we (the King) proceed against him, nor send any one against him, by force or arms, unless according to (that is, in execution of) the sentence of his peers, *and* (or, *or* as the case may require) the Common Law of England (as it was at the time of Magna Carta, in 1215)."[2]

After defending this translation with much learning, Spooner adds:

It is evident that the difference between the true and false translations of the words, *nec super eum ibimus, nec super eum mittemus*, is of the highest

---

* **Lysander Spooner** (1808–1887), an American anarchist and abolitionist, practiced law in Boston and published several pamphlets on slavery. His *Essay on the Trial by Jury* (1852) is most famous for supporting the view that juries could assess both the facts of a case and the validity of the governing law (a view known today as jury nullification). For more on Spooner, see A. John Alexander, "The Ideas of Lysander Spooner," *New England Quarterly* 23, no. 2 (June 1950): 200–217; Helen J. Knowles, "Seeing the Light: Lysander Spooner's Increasingly Popular Constitutionalism," *Law & History Review* 31, no. 3 (August 2013): 531–58; and Randy Barnett, "Was Slavery Unconstitutional Before the Thirteenth Amendment? Lysander Spooner's Theory of Interpretation," *Pacific Law Journal* 28, no. 4 (Summer 1997): 977–1014.

1. Coke, *Second Part*, 46. Again, Hurd is the source here; he too says "*nec super mittemus*," while the actual passage from Coke says "super eum mittemus." (Coke, *Second Part*, 46.)

2. Lysander Spooner, *An Essay on the Trial by Jury* (Boston: Jewett and Company, 1852), 49–50. [Eds. note: This passage is also quoted verbatim in Hurd, *Treatise*, 83.]

legal importance, inasmuch as the true translation, *nor will we (the King) proceed against him, nor send (any one) against him by force or arms*, represents the King only in an *executive* character, *carrying the judgment of the peers and 'the law of the land' into execution*; whereas the false translation, *nor will we pass upon him, nor condemn him*, gives color for the exercise of a *judicial* power, on the part of the king, to which the king had no right, but which, according to the true translation, belongs wholly to the jury.[3]

The "Articles of the Great Charter of Liberties," to which the King gave his assent a few days before the date of the Charter,* contained these words: "Ne corpus liberi hominis capiatur nec imprisonetur nec disseisetur nec utlagetur nec exuletur nec aliquo modo destruatur *nec rex eat vel mittat super eum vi* nisi per judicium parium suorum vel per legem terrae."

Which Spooner thus renders: "The body of a freeman shall not be arrested, nor imprisoned, nor disseized, nor outlawed, nor exiled, nor in any manner destroyed, *nor shall the*

---

* Known today as the "Articles of the Barons," the "Articles of the Great Charter of Liberties" were likely drawn up on June 10, 1215, five days before Magna Carta was issued. While historians disagree over whether the Articles were written separately or in consultation with King John, all of the chapters in the Articles are present in some form in Magna Carta. Magna Carta also contained twelve additional provisions. For the full text of the Articles of the Barons, see J. C. Holt, *Magna Carta*, 3d ed. (Cambridge: Cambridge University Press, 2015), Appendix 5.

3. Spooner, *Essay on the Trial by Jury*, 29–30. [Eds. note: This passage does not appear in Hurd.]

King proceed or send (any one) against him <u>with force</u>, unless by the judgment of his peers, or the law of the land."[4]

The real meaning of these words of the Charter may, says Lingard, "be learned from John himself, who the next year promised by his letters patent . . . nec super eos *per vim vel per arma* ibimus, nisi per legem regni nostri, vel per judicium parium suorum in curia nostra" (nor will we go upon them *by force or by arms,* unless by the law of our kingdom, on the judgment of their peers in our own court). "He had hitherto been in the habit of *going* with an armed force, or *sending* an armed force on the lands, and against the castles, of all whom he knew or suspected to be his secret enemies, without observing any form of law."[5]

The phrase *nisi per legem terrae* being properly construed, as Coke says,[6] "*unless by due process of law,*" the word *vel,* continues Spooner, must in cases of *judgment* be rendered by "*and,*" so as to require the concurrence both of "the judgment of the peers *and* the law of the land," but in cases of arrest and imprisonment, simply for the purpose of bringing a man to trial, by "*or,*" because there can have been no judgment of a jury in such a case, and "the law of the land" must therefore necessarily be the only guide to, and restraint upon, the King.

Such are the provisions of Magna Carta. What bearing have they upon the right, claimed as existing in the Crown, of enforcing Martial Law in times of rebellion? Rebellion may

4. Spooner, *Essay on the Trial by Jury*, 29.

5. John Lingard, *History of England* (London: Charles Dolman, 1855), 47. [Eds. note: In this passage, the Liebers seem to have been leaning hard on Spooner's *Essay on the Trial by Jury*. Spooner quotes the same Lingard passage and offers virtually the same translation provided by the Liebers. See Spooner, *Essay on the Trial by Jury*, 29 n.]

6. Coke, *Second Part*, 50.

create a state of war,[7] but what is the test by which we are to determine whether the state of war exists or not? "According to
the authorities," says Lord Cockburn,* "the criterion is whether
the courts are open, and the course of justice uninterrupted."[8]

The question then is whether when such is not the case
the provisions of Magna Carta nevertheless forbid the execution of Martial Law.

---

* **Sir Alexander James Edmund Cockburn** (1802–1880) was a lawyer
and Liberal MP for Southampton prior to his appointment as Chief Justice of Queen's Bench in 1859. As Chief Justice, Cockburn gave his six-hour
charge to the grand jury in the case of Colonel Nelson and Lieutenant Brand
in April 1867. Nelson and Brand were accused of murder because they executed George William Gordon under martial law in Jamaica. Cockburn
argued that the common law only permitted martial law insofar as it was
used to respond quickly in times of emergency. Because Gordon's execution
took place after the violence had ended, Cockburn urged the jury to find
Nelson and Brand culpable. The grand jury, however, refused to indict them.
Cockburn's *Charge to the Grand Jury* is a central source for the Liebers in this
chapter. For more on Cockburn, see Van Vechten Veeder, "Sir Alexander
Cockburn," *Harvard Law Review* 14, no. 2 (June 1900): 79–97.

7. Traitorously to levy war against the government is rebellion, but it is
also treason. It is therefore not claimed that every act of rebellion will justify
a recourse to martial law. It is only when the rebellion has assumed so formidable a character that it can no longer be suppressed by ordinary means that,
it is said, martial law may be enforced. Then arises that paramount necessity
upon which it is based. Whether it has attained such magnitude is a question of fact—to be determined either by the executive or legislative branch
of the government. The views upon the latter point are in violent conflict.
They will be considered in the appropriate place. But, whenever rebellion is
here spoken of, the word will be used in the sense of such a violent armed
traitorous resistance to the government of such magnitude that the ordinary
laws of the land are helpless to suppress it.

8. Frederick Cockburn, ed., *Charge of the Lord Chief Justice of England
. . . in the Case of the Queen Against Nelson and Brand* (London: William
Ridgway, 1867), 69 [hereinafter Cockburn, ed., *Nelson and Brand Charge*].

The trial of the Earl of Lancaster, in the reign of Edward II, is generally referred to as the first authoritative instance of the application of Martial Law to be met with in English history and as furnishing the earliest construction with reference to it of the provisions of Magna Carta. Lancaster had been engaged in rebellion against the King, and was apprehended and tried for high treason by an irregular Tribunal consisting of the King and certain peers. He was not arraigned, but they made a record of his crimes, upon which he was convicted, sentenced to death, and executed. This trial is spoken of by both historians and legal authorities—among the latter Coke and Hale—as a trial by martial law.[9] "I very much doubt its having been so," says Lord Cockburn, "for I have read the whole record of the proceedings, as set out at length in Rymer's 'Foedera,' and they do not appear to have any reference to martial law at all. The Earl, it seems, was tried by the King and certain of his peers, instead of being tried, as he ought to have been, by his peers in Parliament. It was an irregular trial, undoubtedly, but I question very much whether it was a case of martial law, though, as the trial did not take place before the proper Tribunal, it has been treated as such."[10]

"But" says Finlason "an irregular execution of a civilian in rebellion, by officers of the Crown, is the very definition of martial law." And again, "This is the proper definition of martial law, that is, executions under the authority of the Crown without due course of law."[11] These definitions are, indeed,

9. Edward Coke, *The Third Part of the Institutes of the Laws of England* (London: M. Flesher, 1644), 52. [Eds. note: Coke wrote that "Thom. Countee de Lancaster being taken in an open insurrertion, was by judgement of mar-shall law put to death."]

10. Cockburn, ed., *Nelson and Brand Charge*, 26.

11. William F. Finlason, *Commentaries upon Martial Law* (London: Stevens and Sons, 1867), 76, 77.

open to much criticism. The very essence of martial law, *i.e.* *military authority*, is entirely ignored. "Martial Law," say the American "Instructions" already quoted, "is simply military authority exercised in accordance with the laws and usages of war."[12] Trials by martial law, therefore, are military trials, conducted by officers, acting in a military capacity. Without these elements, whatever the trial may be, it is not a trial by martial law, for it is not based upon military authority.

Lancaster was taken in open rebellion. He was tried by the King, six earls, and the royal barons, and was condemned and executed. In the reign of Edward III his attainder was annulled, because he had not been arraigned in the King's court, nor tried by his peers, "though it was in time of peace." How, it was asked, could that be, when with a large force he had besieged the castle of Tickill, and taken the town of Burton: The answer was, that "the chancery and courts of justice were still open, and the King had not displayed his banner."[13] Or, as Coke says: "Quod non fuit araniatus et an responsionem positus tempore pacis, eo quod curiae Regis fuerent apertae in quibus lex fiebat unicuique prout fieri consuevit. . . . Quod contra cartam de libertatibus, [. . .] tempore pacis, absque araniamento se[u] responsione se[u] legali judicio."[14]

12. Instructions for Armies in the Field, art. 4.

13. Lingard, *History of England*, 3: 43 n.

14. Coke quoted in Finlason, *Commentaries upon Martial Law*, 75. [Translated, the passage reads as follows: "Because in a time of peace he was not arraigned or made to answer, and because the courts of the King were then open, in each of which the law was carried out. . . . And because [he was executed] contrary to the charter of freedoms . . . in time of peace and without arraignment, answer, or lawful adjudication." See also Sir Edward Coke, *The Selected Writings and Speeches of Sir Edward Coke,* ed. Steve Sheppard (Indianapolis: Liberty Fund, 2003), 2: 516. Note that Finlason took liberties with Coke's text, including omitting an ellipsis between "libertatibus" and "tempore" and erroneously transcribing "seu" as "sen."]

Lord Hale, remarking upon this case in his *History of the Common Law of England*, says:

And accordingly was that famous case of Edmond earl of Kent; who being taken at Pomfret, 15 Edw. 2., the King and divers Lords proceeded to give Sentence of Death against him, as in a kind of Military Court, by a Summary Proceeding; which Judgement was afterwards in 1 Edw. 3, revers'd in parliament.[15] And the reason of that reversal serving to the purpose in hand, I shall here insert it as entered in the record, viz.: "Quod cum quicung; homo ligeus domini regis pro seditionibus, &c tempore pacis captus & in quacunque curia domini regis ductus fuerit de ejusmodi seditionibus & aliis feloniis sibi impositis per legem & consuetudine regni arrestari debet & ad responsionem adduci, et inde per communem legem, antequam fuerit morti adjudicand (triari) &c. Unde cum notorium sit & manifestum quod totum tempus quo impositum fuit eidem comiti propter mala & facinora fecisse, ad tempus in quo captus fuit & in quo morti adjudicatus fuit, fuit tempus pacis maximae, cum per totum tempus praedictum & cancellaria & aliae plac. Curiae domini regis apertae fuer in quibus cuilibet lex fiebatur sicut fieri consuevit, nec idem dominus rex unquam tempore illo cum vexillis explicatis equitabat &c." And accordingly the

---

15. It is to be noticed that Hale here speaks of the trial and execution of Edmond Earl of Kent. He evidently referred to Thomas of Lancaster. Edmond, Earl of Kent, brother of Edward II, was not executed until after his nephew Edward III had ascended the throne. The two cases should not be confounded.

judgment was reversed; for Martial Law, which is
rather indulg'd than allow'd, and that only in Cases
of Necessity, in Time of open War, is not permitted in Time of Peace, when the ordinary courts of
justice are open.[16]

So Coke says: "The time of peace is when the courts are open.
For, where they are, you may have a commission of Oyer and
Terminer," and where the common law can determine a thing,
the martial law ought not." And again: "when the courts are
open martial law cannot be executed."[17] And Lord Hale says:
"The exercise of martial law, whereby any person shall lose
his life, or members, or liberty, may not be permitted in time
of peace when the King's courts are open."[18] But, "it is to be

16. Sir Matthew Hale, *The History of the Common Law of England* (London: E. & R. Nutt, 1739), 41–42. [J. W. Gordon renders the long Latin passage
thusly: "Whenever the subject of the Lord the King, shall be arrested for
sedition in time of peace, before he can be adjudged to death, according to
the common law, he must be taken into some court of the King, and held to
answer for such seditions and other felonies; whence it follows, that when it
is made known and manifest, that all the time during which it is alleged that
the crimes were done, on account of which he was arrested, to the time in
which he was taken and adjudged to death, was a time of profound peace,
and during all the time aforesaid, the Chancery and other courts of the King
were open, in which any law could be executed, as it was the custom to have
done, the same Lord the King had no power, during that time, to exercise
military control." Gordon, *An Argument Against the Jurisdiction of Military Commissions to Try Citizens of the United States* (Indianapolis: Hall &
Hutchinson, 1865), 22.]

17. Quoted in Rushworth, *Historical Collections*, 3: app. 81. [See also Coke,
Selected Writings and Speeches (Sheppard, ed.), 3: 1263 (citing Robert Johnson et al., eds., *Commons Debates 1628* {New Haven: Yale University Press,
1977}, 2: 545–46).]

18. Hale, *History of the Common Law*, 39–40.

observed," adds Chief Justice Cockburn in a note to his charge
to the Grand Jury in the case of *Queen v. Nelson and Brand*
that both these writers "are speaking of martial law, not with
reference to its exercise for the purpose of suppressing a rebellion, but as a rude substitute for the law of the land when, in
time of war, justice cannot be administered by the ordinary
tribunals."[19] "A rebel," said Coke, "may be slain in the rebellion.
But if he be taken, he cannot be put to death by the martial
law." And Rolle, afterwards Chief Justice, in the course of the
same debate—in Committee of the whole House, on the Petition of Right—remarked: "If a subject be taken in rebellion,
and be not slain at the time of the rebellion, he is to be tried
after by the common law."[20]

Lancaster's judgment was reversed because given in time
of peace, when the King's courts were open. It would seem to
follow, then, that, had the courts been closed in consequence
of the existence of a state of war, there would have been no recognized reason for reversal. The latter fact would, apparently,
have been held to legalize the tribunal, but it could only have
done so upon the ground that it was an exercise of the war
power. An irregular trial and execution, having no connection
with the exercise of this power, would not have been justified
by the fact that a state of war existed; nor would there have
been a reversal, for the reason that it was a time of peace, of a
judgment which, whether in peace or in war, would have been
equally illegal. The question of greatest importance, is—not
whether Lancaster's was actually a case of martial law—but

19. Cockburn, ed., *Nelson and Brand Charge*, 69–70 n.
20. [Eds. note: The Liebers cite Rushworth, *Historical Collections*, 3: app.
79–81, for the Coke quotations, but they appear to have drawn the references
from Cockburn, *Nelson and Brand Charge*, 59.]

whether the reversal of his attainder was based upon the assumption that it was such. If it was—and this seems to be the correct view—it proves that at that early day it was undoubted, that there might be a state of facts to which the provisions of Magna Carta did not apply; that the guarantees of liberty, confirmed by that charter, did not exclude the exercise of an exceptional authority under circumstances which rendered it impossible for them to be carried out; that, in fact, when war existed to such an extent that the courts were closed, and the common law was silent, it might be replaced by martial law; but that, when the courts were open, the law would be administered only through them.

The executions of the followers of Wat Tyler,* in the reign of Richard II, and those which occurred during the war between the houses of York and Lancaster deserve no consideration in a treatise which claims to treat of martial law in its legal aspect. They were irregular executions without form of trial, the arbitrary acts of a rude age, and cannot be looked to as guides in our investigation.

Henry VII, after the battle of Stoke,† made, says Lord Bacon, "a progress from Lincoln to the Northern parts, though it

* **Wat Tyler** (d. 1381) was the leader of the Peasants' Revolt in 1381. The rebellion began when Tyler killed a poll tax collector who had assaulted his daughter. The unrest spread throughout Kent in early June 1381. Eventually, under Tyler's command, the rebels reached London. On June 14, Richard II met with the rebels at Mile End and agreed to make concessions. Even so, Tyler made further demands, including calling for the abolition of villeinage and serfdom. When Tyler and Richard II met again at Smithfield, fighting broke out between Tyler and the King's party. Tyler was injured and later executed. After Tyler's death, the rebellion was quickly subdued. For more on Wat Tyler, see R. H. Hilton and T. H. Aston, eds., *The English Rising of 1381* (Cambridge: Cambridge University Press, 1984), and R. B. Dobson, ed., *The Revolt of 1381*, 2nd ed. (London: Macmillan, 1983).

† The Battle of Stoke Field, on June 16, 1487, was the final battle of the War of the Roses. Edward IV's sister, Margaret of Burgundy, attempted to

were indeed rather an itinerary circuit of justice than a progress. For all along as he went, with much severity and much
inquisition, partly by martial law and partly by commission,
were punished the adherents and aiders of the late rebels. Not
all by death, for the field had drawn much blood, but by fines
and ransoms, which spared life and raised treasure."[21] The latter was indeed the principal object.

This so-called "circuit of justice" was held after the insurrection had been entirely suppressed. If therefore we are
to give the term "martial law" as used by Bacon the same signification that we attach to it now, the question arises, was it
then legally enforced: But, it is by no means certain that Bacon used it in this sense. And, whatever the proceedings were,
they were, thinks Lord Cockburn, utterly illegal. "If it be true"
he says,

> that you can apply martial law for the purpose of
> suppressing rebellion, it is equally certain that you
> cannot bring men to trial for treason under mar-
> tial law, after a rebellion has been suppressed. It
> is well established, according to the admission of
> everybody, even of those who go the farthest in

---

restore the House of York by funding a rebel force of Irish troops and German mercenaries. Under the command of the Earl of Lincoln, the rebels put
forward the imposter Lambert Simnel as the true Earl of Warwick and heir
to the throne. Henry VII's forces, commanded by the Earl of Oxford and the
Duke of Bedford, emerged victorious. All told, there were seven thousand
casualties at the Battle of Stoke Field, including the Earl of Lincoln. Simnel was captured and put to work in the King's kitchens. For more on the
Battle of Stoke, see Michael Bennet, *Lambert Simnel and the Battle of Stoke*
(Gloucester: St. Martin's Press, 1987).

21. Cockburn, ed., *Nelson and Brand Charge*, 28.

upholding martial law, that the only justification
of it is founded on the assumption of an absolute
necessity—a necessity paramount to all law, and
which, lest the commonwealth should perish, authorises this arbitrary and despotic mode of proceeding; but it never has been said or thought, except perhaps by King Henry VII, that martial law
could be resorted to when all the evil of rebellion
had passed away, and order and tranquillity, had
been restored, for the mere purpose of trying and
punishing persons whom there was no longer any
sufficient cause for withdrawing from the ordinary
tribunals and the ordinary laws.[22]

During the reign of Edward VI, there were two instances
of the application of what was called martial law, both of which
were, however, illegal assumptions of arbitrary power. This
reign was characterized by the turbulent state of the populace
in different parts of England, culminating in frequent riots and
disorders. It was during this reign that the great insurrection
in the West occurred where 10,000 men laid siege to Exeter.*
In that year a proclamation was issued in the following words:

---

* The Western Rebellion began in 1549 with Cornish opposition to Edward VI's religious policies. The unrest soon spread to Oxfordshire and
Buckinghamshire. On July 2, 1549, a group of Cornish and Devon rebels
laid siege to Exeter. The King dispatched Lord Russell and later Lord Grey
to put down the rebellion. Lord Grey was eventually able to defeat the rebels
at Enslow Hill, which allowed Lord Russell to end the siege after thirty-five
days. Shortly thereafter, the insurgents were soundly defeated at Sampford
Courtenay. For more on the Western Rebellion, see Andy Wood, *The 1549
Rebellions and the Making of Early Modern England* (Cambridge: Cambridge

22. Ibid., 29.

Neither by drum, tabret, pipe, or any other instrument striking or sounding, bell or bells ringing,
opening, crying, poshing, riding, running, or by
any news, rumours or tales, divulging or spreading, or by any other device or token whatsoever
to call together or muster, or attempt to assemble
or muster, any number of people; either to pluck
down any hedge, pale, fence, wall, or any manner
of enclosures, or to hunt, waste, spoil, desolate,
or deface any park, chase, warren, house, lodge,
pond, waters, or do any other unlawful act which
is forbidden; or to redress any thing which should
or might be by the King's Majesty's commission re-
formed, redressed, or amended: and this upon pain
of death, presently to be executed by the authority and order of law martial: wherein no delay or
deferring of time should be permitted, as in other
causes, being indeed of less importance.[23]

This proclamation was not a resort to martial law for the
suppression of rebellion; it assumed to make law for the prevention of riot. There thus is an important distinction to be
observed between rebellion or insurrection on the one hand,
and riot on the other.

Insurrection is the rising of people in arms against
their government, or a portion of it, or against one

University Press, 2007). The Liebers developed their account of the rebellion
from Cockburn, *Charge to the Grand Jury*, 29–32.

23. Quoted in Cockburn, ed., *Nelson and Brand Charge*, 32.

or more of its laws, or against an officer or officers of the government. It may be confined to mere armed resistance, or it may have greater ends in view.

The term *rebellion* is applied to an insurrection of large extent, and is usually a war between the legitimate government of a country and portions or provinces of the same who seek to throw off their allegiance to it, and set up a government of their own.[24]

A *riot* is simply a tumultuous disturbance of the peace by three or more persons assembled together of their own authority, with the intent, mutually, to assist each other against any one who shall oppose them, and putting their design into execution, in a violent and turbulent manner, to the terror of the people, whether the object was lawful or not. Martial Law does not deal with riot. Riot is suppressed, and the rioters are punished by the ordinary law. The civil power may be aided by the military, but it is only by the military acting as an arm of the civil power. There is no paramount danger lest the commonwealth should perish.

It was also an illegal assumption of legislative powers when the Crown, in the third and subsequent years of this reign, issued commissions creating lord-lieutenants of the counties,* whose duty it was made,

---

* Beginning in the reign of Henry VIII, lords-lieutenant were commissioned in times of emergency and given broad powers to inquire into rebellious activity. These commissions were initially reviewed on a yearly basis, but Edward VI started to establish them on a more permanent basis. By 1600, the lord-lieutenant of a county was in charge of raising a local militia

24. Francis Lieber, Instructions for the Government of Armies of U.S. in the Field, arts. 149 and 151.

To inquire of all treasons, misprisions of treason, insurrections, rebellions, unlawful assemblies and conventicles, unlawful speaking of words, confederacies, conspiracies, false allegations, contempts, falsehoods, negligencies, concealments, oppressions, riots, routs, murders, felonies, and other ill deeds whatsoever; and also accessories of the same: and to appoint certain days and places for the inquiry thereof: and to be the King's lieutenants within the respective counties, for levying of men, and to fight against the King's enemies and rebels, and to execute upon them martial law, and to subdue all invasions, insurrections, &c.[25]

The disturbances, which marked this reign, still continuing, a commission was in 1552 given to John Earl of Bedford, and others "to put in execution all such martial law as shall be thought in their discretion most necessary to be executed."[26] Apparently, this commission was never acted on.

---

and was authorized to appoint local magistrates. For a modern account, see G. S. Thomson, *Lords Lieutenants in the Sixteenth Century: A Study in Tudor Local Administration* (London: Longmans, Green and Co., 1923).

25. Cockburn, ed., *Nelson and Brand Charge*, 33 (quoting Peter Strype, *Ecclesiastical Memorials* (Oxford: Clarendon Press, 1822), 2: 278–79.

26. Cockburn, ed., *Nelson and Brand Charge*, 34 (quoting Strype, *Ecclesiastical Memorials*, 4: 31). [Eds. note: **John Russell**, first Earl of Bedford (c. 1485–1555) was a diplomat and envoy for Henry VIII and a courtier to Edward VI and Mary I. As the Liebers note, there is considerable doubt whether this commission to execute martial law was ever issued. Cockburn, on whom the Liebers rely, observed that he had "not been able to find the commission in question" and that "there is no evidence that this commission ever was acted upon." The underlying source is Strype, *Ecclesiastical*

These instances of arbitrary power in the reign of Edward VI need not be dwelt upon. They were not attended by any of the circumstances upon which martial law can alone rest, nor applied to the object for which it is claimed that martial law may be resorted to. They were, indeed, not strictly speaking instances of martial law at all, but simply of the exercise of an arbitrary and illegal power. The same is true of two proclamations issued by Mary and Elizabeth—The one declaring the introduction into the country of heretical and seditious works, the other bulls from Rome, or traitorous works from abroad punishable by "Martial Law."[27]

The power to resort to summary proceedings for the suppression of insurrection was, however, exercised during the reign of Queen Elizabeth at the time of the rising in the North under the Earls of Westmoreland and Northumberland.*

* The Earls of Westmoreland and Northumberland, with strong Catholic sentiment in the North, revolted in 1569–1570 against Queen Elizabeth in favor of Mary's claim to the throne. Armies loyal to Elizabeth quickly dispersed the rebel forces. Northumberland fled to Scotland but was later returned to England by the Scots and executed. Westmoreland died in exile in the Netherlands. Roughly five hundred rebel fighters were hanged in the aftermath. For a modern account, see Krista J. Kesselring, *The Northern Rebellion of 1569: Faith, Politics, and Protest in Elizabethan England* (New York: Palgrave Macmillan, 2007).

Memorials, 2: 207, which lists "a commission, in [March 1552], to John Earl of Bedford, William Earl of Pembroke, the Lord Darcy, Sir William Petre, Sir John Baker, Sir Philip Hoby, Sir Robert Bows, Sir Thomas Wroth, Edward Griffyth, John Gosnold, or to ten, nine, eight, seven, or six of them, to put in execution all such martial laws as shall thought by their discretions most necessary to be executed."]

27. See James Anthony Froude, *History of England from the Fall of Wolsey to the Death of Elizabeth* (London: Longmans, Green, and Company, 1866), 3: ch. 18; also George Brodie, *A Constitutional History of the British Empire* (London: Longmans, Green, & Co., 1866), 1: 160–64. [Eds. note: Queen

Froude* gives an account of it in his History of England. "After they were defeated," says Mr. Justice Blackburn in his charge to the grand jury in the case of *The Queen v. Edward John Eyre*, "after the army had broken them down, there was a great deal of the process of summary execution done.... [A] great deal of tyranny was, no doubt, exercised; in point of fact, a great deal of summary trial and execution took place in a way which, according to our modern view, was most tyrannical and oppressive, and which would not be sanctioned now."[28]

   In the year 1595 certain riots occurred at London, occasioned by the destitution of a part of the population.† They

---

* **James Anthony Froude** (1818–1894) was an Oxford-educated author of the influential eleven-volume *History of England from the Fall of Wolsey to the Death of Elizabeth*, the first two volumes of which were published in 1856. Froude's description of the Northern Rebellion is given in his *History of England from the Fall of Wolsey to the Death of Elizabeth* (London: Longmans, Green, and Company, 1866), 3: ch. 18, esp. pp. 559–66. For more on Froude, see W. H. Dunn, *James Anthony Froude: A Biography*, 2 vols. (Oxford: Clarendon Press, 1961).

† In the spring and summer of 1595, apprentices in London rioted in response to high food prices. Finding common cause with disbanded soldiers, the apprentices formed plans to murder the Lord Mayor. Fighting broke out after several hundred rebels massed on Tower Hill on June 29, 1595. In response, Queen Elizabeth instituted "martial law." She appointed Sir Thomas Wilford, a lifelong soldier with prior service in the Netherlands and

---

Mary's proclamation of June 6, 1558, threatened that "whoever shall, after the proclaiming hereof, be found to have any of the said and seditious books ... shall in that case be reputed and taken for a rebel and shall without delay be executed for that offence according to the order of marshal law." Queen Elizabeth may have drawn upon Mary's example when she issued a proclamation in 1588 promising capital punishment for those importing bulls from Rome. See, generally, Frederic A. Youngs, *The Proclamations of the Tudor Queens* (Cambridge: Cambridge University Press, 1976).]

   28. W. F. Finlason, *Report of the Case of the Queen v. Edward John Eyre* (London: Chapman & Hall, 1868), 71–72.

were simply riots, but, upon application of the municipal authorities, Queen Elizabeth issued a commission to Sir Thomas Wilford, in these words:

> Forasmuch as we understand that of late there have been sundry great unlawful assemblies of a number of base people in riotous sort, both in our City of London and in the suburbs of the same, and in some other parts near to our said City; for the suppression whereof, although there hath been some proceedings in ordinary manner by the mayor of said City, and sundry offenders have been committed to several prisons, and have also received corporal punishment, by divers orders of our Council in the Star Chamber of Westminster; and for the stay of the like tumults to follow we have also, by our proclamation published the fourth of this month, charged all our justices and other officers having charge for the keeping of peace to have special regard to the inquisition of all that hereafter shall attempt to commit the like offences, and specifically for apprehension of all vagrant persons, and them commit to prison, and punish according to the laws of our realm: yet for that the insolvency of many of the kind of desperate offenders is such as they

---

Normandy, as provost marshal to end the disturbances. Wilford eventually convicted five rioters of high treason, but as the Liebers note, these rebels were not tried under martial law. They were executed on July 24. For more on the riots, see Ian Archer, *The Pursuit of Stability: Social Relations in Elizabethan London* (Cambridge: Cambridge University Press, 1991), and Lindsay Boynton, "The Tudor Provost Marshal," *English Historical Review* 77 (July 1962): 437–55.

care not for any ordinary punishment by imprisonment and other severe punishment inflicted on
them, therefore find it necessary to have some such
notable rebellious and incorrigible persons to be
speedily suppressed by execution of death, according to the justice of our martial law; and therefore
we have made choice of you, upon special trust of
your wisdom, discretion, and other qualities meet
for this purpose, to be our Provost Marshal, giving
you authority, and so we command you, upon signification given to you by our Justices of Peace in
our City of London, or of any place near to our said
City in our Counties of Middlesex, Surrey, Kent,
and Essex, of such notable rebellious and incorrigible offenders worthy to be speedily executed by
martial law, to attack and take the same persons,
and in the presence of the said justices, according to justice of martial law, to execute them upon
the gallows or gibbet openly by or near such place
where the said rebellious and incorrigible offenders shall be found to have committed the said great
offences. And furthermore, we authorise you to repair with a convenient company into all common
highways near to our said City where you shall understand that any vagrant persons do haunt, and
calling to your assistance some convenient number of our justices and constables abiding about
the said places, to apprehend all such vagrant and
suspected persons, and them to deliver to the said
justices, by them to be committed and examined
of the causes of their wandering, and finding them
notoriously culpable in the unlawful manner of life

as incorrigible, and so certified to you by the said
justices, you shall by our law martial cause to be
executed upon the gallows or gibbet some of them
that are so found most incorrigible offenders, and
some such also of them as have manifestly broken
the peace, sithence they have been judged and condemned to death for former offences, and have had
our pardon for the same.[29]

This commission was, indeed, not carried into full effect,
the persons arrested under it being turned over to the civil
tribunals, but it, also—though nominally authorizing the enforcement of martial law—was simply an unlawful exercise of
arbitrary power.

Of a different nature was the commission given by James
I to the Lord Compton, as Lord-Lieutenant of Wales,* directing him—

To fight all enemies, traytors, and rebells from
tyme to tyme, and them to invade, resist, suppress,
subdue, slea, kill, and put to execution of death by

---

* **William Compton, First Earl of Northampton** (d. 1630), was both
the Lord Lieutenant of Warwickshire and the president of Wales (an equivalent position) from 1618 onward. In these roles, he coordinated military
arrangements and had the power to declare "martial law." Compton married the wealthy daughter of Sir John Spencer, a Lord Mayor of London, but
nonetheless mismanaged his estate and had financial difficulties. His son,
Spencer Compton, became Lord Lieutenant of Warwickshire after his father's death and held the position until 1643. For more on Lord Compton,
see Arthur Collins, *The Peerage of England* (London: W. Innys and J. Rich-
ardson, 1756), 2: 212–14.

29. Cockburn, ed., *Nelson and Brand Charge*, 39–40.

all waies and meanes from tyme to tyme by your
discretion. And further to doe, execute, and use
against the said enemies, traytors, rebells, and such
other like offenders, and their adherentes aforementioned from tyme to tyme, as necessiti shall
require, by your discretion, the lawe called the
martiall lawe according to the lawe martiall; and
of such offenders apprehended or being brought in
subjection to save whom you shall think good to be
saved, and to slea, destroie, and put to execution of
death such and as many of them as you shall think
meete by your good discretion to be put to death.

And further, our will and pleasure is, and by
these presents wee doe give unto you full power
and authoritie that in case any invasion of enemies,
insurrection, rebellion, riots, routes, or unlawfull
assemblies, or any like offences shall happen to be
moved in any place of this our realme out of the
limits of lieutenancie as you shall think requisite,
or as shall be directed from us as is aforesaid, shall
repair to the place where any such invasion, rebellion, unlawfull assembly, or insurrection shall happen to be made, to subdue, represse, and reforme
the same, as well by battaile or other kind of force,
as otherwise by the laws of the realm and the lawe
martiall, according to your discretion.[30]

The authorization for the application of martial law as
contained in this commission was not acted upon, because no
emergency arose demanding it. But, leaving out of consideration

30. Quoted in Cockburn, *Nelson and Brand Charge*, 41–42.

the fact that the commission deals also with "riots, routes, or
unlawfull assemblies, or any like offences," to which martial
law cannot be applied, it is the nearest approach with which
we have yet met to a proper understanding of the purposes to
which it may be applied. "*To doe, execute, and use against the
said enemies, traytors, rebells, and such other like offenders, and
their adherentes aforementioned from tyme to tyme, as necessiti
shall require, by your discretion, the lawe called the martiall lawe
according to the lawe martiall*"—that is, according to the Law of
War, were it not for what immediately follows these words, this
would show a singular appreciation of the subject.

With reference to this commission Lord Cockburne says:

Assuming for the present that the Sovereign, or the
governor of a dependency to whom the executive
powers of the Crown are intrusted, has power to
proclaim and exercise martial law in case of rebellion, I know of no authority for saying that, by way
of anticipation, such power can be committed to
the lord-lieutenant of a county in England, where
the Crown can exercise its own power and prerogative, and where the executive government has the
authority in such matters; nor can it be contended
that the Crown can give to a lord-lieutenant of a
county the power, after rebels have been "brought
into subjection," to execute martial law upon any
one to whom he in his discretion shall think it
ought to be applied. For these reasons I think it
clear that the commissions of lieutenancy of Edward VI and James I were both of them illegal.[31]

31. Ibid., 42–43.

The next instance of an attempt to enforce martial law in England—the last, according to Lord Cockburn[32]—occurred in the reign of Charles I. Parliament not having granted this monarch the necessary means to prosecute certain enterprizes abroad, he resorted to an illegal method of supplying the wants. This was done by the means of what was called benevolences or forced loans, and for the purpose of exacting a compliance with these demands soldiers were quartered upon those who refused them.* The consequence was the soldiers committed many excesses, which it was found necessary to punish by military process. It must be remembered that there was not at this time any such thing as a recognized standing army in England, and there was no code having the effect of law for the punishment by military law of soldiers in time of peace. As we have already seen—it was not until the year 1717 that it was lawful for the sovereign, "to form, make, and establish Articles of War, and erect and constitute Courts-martial with power to try, hear, and determine any crime or offense by such Articles of War, and inflict penalties by sentence or judgment of the same as well within the Kingdoms of Great Britain and Ireland as in

* In the mid-1620s, in need of money to pay for wars with France and Spain, Charles I turned to benevolences (also known as "forced loans"). These measures required wealthy subjects to contribute additional funds to the king. Many refused to pay and were imprisoned without trial, a punishment upheld in the Five Knights' Case. Additional grievances stemmed from the practice of quartering soldiers in subjects' homes. The Petition of Right (1628) was a response to these practices. Among other things, it prohibited taxation without the consent of Parliament and forbade the declaration of martial law in times of peace. For an introduction to these issues, see Ann Hughes, *The Causes of the English Civil War*, 2nd ed. (Basingstoke: St. Martin's Press, 1998).

32. Ibid., 43.

any of His Majesty's Dominions beyond the sea."[33] The soldier
was no more subject in time of peace to trial and punishment
in England by military jurisdiction than the civilian. The law
of England, in force at that time, recognized in this respect no
difference between them. Accordingly, the commissions issued
by Charles I were—irrespective of the nature of the charges
brought before them—in violation of the law of England, and
called forth the well-known statement of grievances contained
in the Petition of Right. There is reason to believe, says Lord
Cockburn, that Lord Coke himself drew up at least that part of
it which is applicable to the present question,* and is as follows:

> Whereas of late great companies of soldiers and
> mariners have been dispersed into divers coun-
> tries of the realm; and the inhabitants, against their
> wills, have been compelled to receive them into
> their houses and there to suffer them to sojourn,
> against the laws and customs of this realm, and to
> the great grievance and vexation of the people.
>
> And whereas, by authority of Parliament in
> the 25th year of Edward III, it is enacted that no

---

* Previously Chief Justice of Common Pleas and Chief Justice of King's
Bench, **Edward Coke** (1552–1634) helped draft the 1628 Petition of Right.
For more on Coke's role in the framing of the Petition of Right, see Steven D.
White, *Sir Edward Coke and the Grievances of the Commonwealth* (Man-
chester: Manchester University Press, 1979); and Lindsay Boynton, "Martial
Law and the Petition of Right," *English Historical Review* 79, no. 311 (April
1964): 255–84.

33. Mutiny Act of that year. See *ante*. [Eds. note: The Liebers introduce
the Mutiny Act of 1717 in chapter 2 above. There as here they relied on
Charles M. Clode, *The Administration of Justice under Military and Martial
Law* (London: John Murray, 1872), 209 n.]

man shall be forejudged of life or limb against the form of the Great Charter and the laws of the land; and by the said Great Charter and other laws of this realm no more ought to be adjudged to death but by the laws established in this realm; nevertheless divers commissions under the Great Seal have been issued forth, by which certain persons have been appointed commissioners, with power and authority to proceed within the land according to the justice of martial law against such soldiers or mariners, or other dissolute persons going with them, as should commit any murder, robbery, felony, mutiny, &c., and by such summary course and order as is acceptable to martial law, and as is used in armies in time of war, to proceed to the trial and condemnation of such offenders, and them cause to be executed and put to death according to martial law. By pretext whereof some of your Majesty's subjects have been by some of the said commissioners put to death, when and where, if by the laws and statutes of the land they have deserved death, by the same laws and statutes also they might, and by no other ought, to have been judged and executed. And also sundry grievous offenders, by colour thereof claiming an exemption, have escaped the punishments due to them by the laws and statutes of this realm, by reason that divers officers and ministers of justice have unjustly refused to have forborne to proceed against such offenders according to the same laws and statutes, upon pretence that the said offenders were punishable only by martial law, and by authority of such

commissions as aforesaid, which commissions are
wholly and directly contrary to the laws and statutes of this realm.

They do therefore humbly pray that your
Majesty would be pleased to remove the said soldiers and mariners, and that your people may not
be burdened in time to come, and that the aforesaid
commissions for proceeding by martial law may be
revoked and annulled, and that hereafter no commissions of the like nature may issue forth to any
person whatsoever to be executed as aforesaid, lest
by colour of them any of your Majesty's subjects be
destroyed or put to death contrary to the laws and
franchise of the land.[34]

Charge of the Lord Chief Justice of England to the Grand
Jury in the case of *The Queen v. Nelson and Brand*. London,
1867. p. 45 n.:

An instance certainly occurred during the great
Civil War when a partial application of martial law
was made by authority of an ordinance passed by
the two Houses of Parliament. In 1644, when the
Civil War was going on, the Long Parliament determined to establish martial law to a certain extent,
and an ordinance was passed whereby a commission was granted to the Earl of Essex, Captain-
General of the Parliamentary Forces, together with
twenty-nine others of the nobility, gentry, and
principal officers, "or any twelve of them," with full

34. Cockburn, ed., *Nelson and Brand Charge*, 64–65.

power to hear and determine all such causes as be-
long to military cognizance, according to certain
articles therein set forth.* ('Parliamentary History,'
vol. XIII, p. 299.) These articles related mostly to
offences of military cognizance, but there are one
or two under which civilians might be tried. By the
1st article, for instance, "No person whatever shall
go from London and Westminster, in any part of
the Kingdom under the power of the Parliament, to
hold any communication whatever, either person-
ally, by letters, or messages, with the King, Queen,
or Lords of the Council abiding with them, without consent of both Houses, or their committee for
managing the war, or the Lord General or officer
commanding in chief, on pain of death, or other
corporal punishment at discretion." By Article 3,
"No person whatsoever, not under the power of the
enemy, shall voluntarily relieve any person being in
arms against the Parliament, knowing him to be as:
with money, victuals, or ammunition, on pain of
death, or other corporal punishment at discretion;

* **Robert Devereux, Third Earl of Essex** (1591–1646) commanded parliamentary forces until 1645. Recognizing that these troops were badly in need
of discipline, the Long Parliament passed an ordinance regarding military
behavior that granted Essex and others the power to try all violations of its
provisions. The ordinance may have later served as a model for the Mutiny
Act of 1689. The full text of the ordinance can be found in *Journals of the
House of Commons* (London, 1803), 3: 562. For more on the Earl of Essex's
military career, see Godfrey Davies, "The Parliamentary Army under the
Earl of Essex, 1642–5," *English Historical Review* 49, no. 193 (January 1934):
32–54; John Morrill, "Devereux, Robert, third earl of Essex (1591–1646)," *Oxford Dictionary of National Biography*, Oxford University Press, 2004; available at http://www.oxforddnb.com/view/article/7566.

nor shall voluntarily harbour any such, or pain of
such discretionary punishment." By Article 5, "No
guardian or officer of any prison shall wilfully suffer
any prisoner of war to escape, on pain of death; or
negligently, on pain of imprisonment, and further
punishment at discretion." Several military officers
were tried under the commission. I do not find any
instance of a civilian having been brought to trial
under it, unless it was Roger l'Estrange,* who was
tried for coming to Lynn Regis as a spy, and sentenced to death, though he afterwards escaped; but
then acting as a spy has always been deemed matter
of military cognisance.[35]

It will serve no useful purpose to examine the extent to
which Martial Law was carried under the Protectorate, when
for thirteen years England was under military government,
for our investigation is limited to the question whether the
power could be constitutionally exercised, and the whole sys-

---

* **Roger L'Estrange** (1616–1704) was a royalist during the English Civil
War. He was involved in the defeat of royalist forces at King's Lynn ("Lynn
Regis" in the text). In 1643, he was given a royal warrant to recover the town
using bribery, but was captured and tried as a spy under court-martial.
Though sentenced to death, he was reprieved and eventually fled to Holland.
He returned in August 1653 under Oliver Cromwell's accommodation policy
and served as licensor of the press during the Restoration. A royalist until
his death, he was knighted by James II in 1685. For more on L'Estrange, see
Anne Dunan-Page and Beth Lynch, eds., *Roger L'Estrange and the Making
of Restoration Culture* (Aldershot: Ashgate, 2008), and George Kitchin, *Sir
Roger L'Estrange: A Contribution to the History of the Press in the Seventeenth
Century* (London: K. Paul, 1913).

35. Cockburn, ed., *Nelson and Brand Charge*, 45 n.

tem then in force was unconstitutional.* Nor need one dwell upon the instances of martial law enforced upon the adherents of Monmouth in the reign of James II.† The age which produced its Kirke‡ and Claverhouse,‡‡ produced also its

* The Protectorate refers to the period between December 1653 and the Restoration of 1660. During this period, Oliver Cromwell (and briefly his son, Richard Cromwell) ruled over the English Commonwealth. For more on the Protectorate, see David L. Smith, ed., *Cromwell and the Interregnum* (Malden: Blackwell, 2003), and Barry Coward, *The Cromwellian Protectorate* (Manchester: Manchester University Press, 2002).

† **James Scott, the Duke of Monmouth** (1649–1685), an exiled son of Charles II, led an early attempt to unseat James II in 1685. Monmouth landed at Lyme Regis and found popular support for his cause. But only a few weeks later, the King's forces defeated the rebels at Sedgemoor. Monmouth and his supporters were tried in the Bloody Assizes, and Monmouth was executed on July 15. For more on the Monmouth Rebellion, see Steven Pincus, *1688: The First Modern Revolution* (New Haven: Yale University Press, 2009), ch. 4; Tim Harris, "Scott [Crofts], James, duke of Monmouth and first duke of Buccleuch," *Oxford Dictionary of National Biography*, Oxford University Press, 2004; available at http://www.oxforddnb.com/view/article/24879.

‡ Army officer **Percy Kirke** (d. 1691) was a royal commander in the Battle of Sedgemoor that ended Monmouth's rebellion. His regiment was called "Kirke's Lambs" because of the Paschal Lamb on its crest. In the six weeks after the battle, Kirke rounded up rebels to bring to the Bloody Assizes, notoriously executing several men and extorting pardons for a fee from others. Despite fighting on behalf of the royal army, Kirke was one of the army's major supporters of William III and served under William after the Glorious Revolution. For more on Kirke, see John Childs, *General Percy Kirke and the Later Stuart Army* (London: Bloomsbury, 2014).

‡‡ **John Graham Claverhouse** (1648?–1689), known as Bonnie Dundee, was a Scotsman and a soldier. His military service eventually caught the attention of the Duke of York (later James II). In 1678, he entered into James's service and began to work closely with him. In 1683, he was charged with ensuring that local citizens near Stirling took the oaths of loyalty required by the Test Acts. His brutal actions to maintain order in the face of encroaching rebellion, including at least three executions, soon came to be known as the "killing time." Claverhouse died in battle on July 27, 1689. For more on

Jeffreys,* and we turn almost with a feeling of relief from the murders under semblance of law during the Bloody Assizes to the murders committed by Kirke's Lambs in utter disregard of even its forms. Passing these by, therefore, we now come down to the period which has already been considered in connection with the Mutiny Act. This seems to be a favorable point to pause in our limited investigation, and to examine the views put forward by the great expounders of the law of England of that day. It is to there, indeed, that we must principally look. Much of the historical period over which our investigation has carried us, was an age when the prerogative was at its highest power, or rather, was exercised without regard to law. Its illegal exercise can never be cited as precedent to qualify a repetition of the abuse. Therefore, it is not to the solitary acts of the dark days of English history that we must look, but rather to the judgment (if any there be) pronounced upon these acts by the learned men of that late period, when the English people rose against, and threw off the yokes which had been imposed upon them, and to which they had until then submitted, despite their much-cherished guarantee of liberty.

Finlason, in his *Commentaries upon Martial Law*, refers to other instances of its application; as, for instance, after the

---

Claverhouse, see Magnus Linklater and Christian Hesketh, *Bonnie Dundee: John Graham of Claverhouse* (Edinburgh: Canongate, 1992).

* One of the most infamous figures in English legal history, **George Jeffreys** (1645–1689) was appointed Chief Justice of King's Bench in 1683. Jeffreys was a strong supporter of James II. He was sent west with four other judges to try the rebels involved in Monmouth's Rebellion. In total, the judges tried more than one thousand rebels accused of treason in a series of trials known as the "Bloody Assizes." For more on Jeffreys, see G. W. Keeton, *Lord Chancellor Jeffreys and the Stuart Cause* (London: McDonald, 1965).

Jack Cade insurrection in the reign of Henry VI;* as executed
by Norfolk in the reign of Henry VIII;† in the execution of
Arundel and others under Edward VI;‡ in the commissions to
Empson and Dudley under Henry VII;‡‡ in that to the Count

---

* The Jack Cade Rebellion of 1450 protested the extortions of Henry VI's
tax collectors and the favoritism he displayed toward his advisers. Led by the
Irishman **Jack Cade**, the rebellion began in Kent and culminated in twenty
thousand rebels marching on London. After looting London for three
days, the rebellion dispersed when the Royal Council granted the rebels'
demands. However, a bounty of one thousand marks was issued for Cade
"quick or dead," and Alexander Iden, sometimes described as the Sheriff of
Kent, caught and killed Cade shortly thereafter. In January of the following
year, Henry rode to Kent with his justices and convicted some of the other
leaders of the rebellion, leading to twenty-six executions. For more on the
Jack Cade insurrection, see I. M. W. Harvey, *Jack Cade's Rebellion of 1450*
(Oxford: Clarendon Press, 1991).

† Following Henry VIII's dissolution of the monasteries, there was a large
uprising in the north. The Dukes of Norfolk and Suffolk and the Earl of
Shrewsbury led Henry VIII's forces. Through Norfolk, Henry VIII negoti-
ated a deal with the rebels. However, after they disbanded, he tried many of
the rebel leaders. Finlason quotes Hume for the proposition that "Norfolk
spread the royal banner, and wherever he thought proper executed martial
law, in the punishment of offenders." David Hume, *The History of England*
(London: T. Cadell, 1782), 4: 175. See also G. W. Bernard, *The King's Reforma-
tion: Henry VIII and the Remaking of the English Church* (New Haven: Yale
University Press, 2005).

‡ **Humphrey Arundel (also Arundell)** (1512/13–1550) was one of the
leaders of the Western Rising that was suppressed by Lord Grey and Lord
Russell. Arundell was sent to the Tower and convicted of treason. In January 1550, he and three others were executed at Tyburn, and their heads were
placed on London's city gates. For more on Arundell, see Anthony Fletcher
and Diarmaid MacCulloch, *Tudor Rebellions*, 5th ed. (New York: Pearson
Longman, 2008).

‡‡ **Sir Richard Empson and Edmund Dudley** were two notorious enforc-
ers of Henry VII's oppressive economic policies. Together they acquired a
range of powers to increase revenues. These included the ability to imprison
individuals, grant pardons, declare forfeitures, and dole out appointments,

of Rivers under Edward IV;* in the execution by sentence of drum-head court-martial of mutinous soldiers in the time of Cromwell,† &c.[36] It seems a fruitless lark, however, to examine each individual instance of the illegal application of martial law in the early days of English history. The great point is to ascertain why they were illegal, and this can but be determined by a reference to the opinions of those who have always been looked upon as faithful expounders of the law of England. That the crown exceeded its legal powers, and did so in time of peace, would not prove that it would not have been an illegal exercise of such powers had it been a time of war. We must

---

in all cases to extort fees. The two men were extremely unpopular and just three days after Henry VII's death, Henry VIII had them arrested as symbols of his father's failed economic policies. They were accused of attempting to influence the succession and convicted of the trumped-up charge of treason. They were executed on August 17, 1510. For more on Empson and Dudley, see M. R. Horowitz, "Richard Empson, Minister of Henry VII," *Historical Research* 55, no. 131 (May 1982): 35–49, and C. J. Harrison, "The Petition of Edmund Dudley," *English Historical Review* 87, no. 342 (January 1972): 82–99.

* **Richard Woodville, First Earl Rivers** (d. 1469) helped put down the Jack Cade Rebellion and was later appointed Lord Constable of England in 1467. Initially a Lancastrian, he switched to the Yorkist side. His daughter Elizabeth married Edward IV. Describing the position of Lord Constable, David Hume noted that "the powers are unlimited, perpetual, and remain in force during peace as well as during war and rebellion." David Hume, *The History of England* (London: T. Cadell, 1770), 5: 484. For more on Rivers, see Charles Ross, *Edward IV* (Berkeley: University of California Press, 1974), 85–132.

† A drum-head court-martial was an improvised tribunal meant to hear and try offenses committed during military actions. Cromwell made use of such procedures to summarily shoot the ringleaders of mutinies. For a description of one such instance, see Joel Tyler Headley, *The Life of Oliver Cromwell* (New York: Charles Scribner's Sons, 1888), 187–88.

36. Finlason, *Commentaries upon Martial Law*, 83 n. and 91.

look elsewhere to ascertain whether it was illegal *because* it was a time of peace. The mere fact that it was done in time of *peace* throws no light upon this question. It is believed that the above sketch is a sufficient introduction to a consideration of the authorities of a later period.

CHAPTER IV
Views of Early
English Authorities

Perhaps no words have been more frequently quoted in connection with the subject of Martial Law than those of Sir Mathew Hale, yet he has not been correctly, because not fully, quoted. Thus, we constantly meet with this extract from his writings: "That the exercise of martial law, whereby any person should lose his life, or member, or liberty may not be permitted in time of peace, when the king's courts are open for all persons to receive justice in according to the laws of the land."[1] And it is taken for granted that Hale used the term "martial law" in the same sense in which we use it now. Such was not the case. The passage cited will be found in his *History of the Common Law*. Let us see in what connection.[2]

> "The third court," he says, "wherein the civil law has its use in this Kingdom, is the military court,

---

1. Matthew Hale, *The History of the Common Law of England* (London: E. and R. Nutt and R. Gosling, 1739), 39–40.
   2. Ibid., 36–40.

held before the constable and marshal anciently, as the *judicus ordinarii* in the case; or otherwise before the king's commissioners of that jurisdiction, as *judicus delegati*. . . .

[T]he constable and marshal had also a judicial power, or a court wherein several matters were determinable. As first, appeals of death or murder committed beyond the sea, according to the course of the civil law. Secondly, the right of prisoners taken in war. Thirdly, the offences and miscarriages of soldiers contrary to the laws and rules of the army. For always, preparatory to an actual war, the kings of the realm, by advice of the constable and marshal, were used to compose a book of rules and orders for the due order and discipline of their officers and soldiers, together with certain penalties on the offenders; *and this was called martial law.* We have extant, in the Black Book of the Admiralty and elsewhere, several exemplars of such military laws; and especially that of the ninth Richard 2, composed by the king with the advice of the duke of Lancaster and others.

But touching the business of martial law, three things are to be observed (*t*), viz:

First, that in truth and reality it is not a law, but something indulged, rather than allowed, as a law. The necessity of government, order, and discipline, in an army, is that only which can give these laws a countenance;—quod enim necessitas cogit defendit.

Secondly, this indulged law was only to extend to members of the army, or, to those of the opposite army, and never was so much indulged as intended to be executed or exercised upon others. For others who were not listed under the army, had no colour or reason to be bound by military constitutions, applicable only to the army, whereof they were not parts. But they were to be ordered and governed according to the laws to which they were subject, though it were a time of war.

Thirdly, that the exercise of martial law, whereby any person should lose his life, or member, or liberty, may not be permitted in time of peace, when the king's courts are open for all persons to receive justice according to the laws of the land. This is in substance declared by the Petition of Right, 3 Car. I, whereby such commissions and martial law were repealed, and declared to be contrary to law."

He then refers to Lancaster's case, and after giving the reason for the reversal of his judgment, continues: "And accordingly the judgment was reversed: for martial law, which is rather indulged than allowed, and that only in cases of necessity, in time of open war, is not permitted in time of peace, when the ordinary courts of justice are open."[3]

And, again, after citing the record of the reversal of Lancaster's judgment, he says: "This notable record, even before the statute of 25 E[dward]. 3. gives us an account of these things: 1. That in time of peace no man ought to be adjudged to death for treason, or any other offence without being arraigned and put to answer. 2. That regularly, where the king's

---

3. Ibid., 41.

courts are open, it is a time of peace in judgment of law. 3. That no man ought to be sentenced to death by the record of the king without his legal trial *per pares*. 4. That in this particular case the commons, as well as the king and lords, gave judgment of reversal."[4]

In these remarks we find, apparently the expression of two different views. First, it appears that under the term "Martial Law" Hale included what we now call military law, the Law of war so far as it extended to prisoners of war, or those of the opposite army, and Martial Law as applicable to subjects engaged in rebellion. That he included the latter might be inferred from his remarks with reference to Lancaster's case which he treats as a case of Martial Law. The judgment pronounced against Lancaster was reversed—not because the exercise of such jurisdiction was under *all* circumstances illegal, but because it was in time of peace. And therefore, in referring to this case, and after quoting from the record the reason assigned for the reversal of the judgment, he continues: "[F]or martial law, which is rather indulged than allowed, and that only in cases of necessity, in time of war, is not permitted in time of peace, when the ordinary courts of justice are open."[5] But, secondly, he speaks of this indulged law as extending only to members of the army, or those of the opposite army, and as never being so much indulged as intended to be executed or exercised upon others. Yet Lancaster was tried as a rebel, not as a member of the army, or of the opposite army. Had he been regarded simply as a member of an opposing army,

4. Matthew Hale, *The History of the Pleas of the Crown* (London: E. and R. Nutt and R. Gosling, 1736), 1: 347. [Eds. note: While the Liebers' text implies that they are tracing one argument by Hale, they are in fact citing parts of two different works.]

5. Hale, *Common Law*, 41.

he would have been an enemy entitled under the law of nations to the protection of the Law of War. When captured he
would have been a prisoner of war, and could not under any
circumstances have been put to death simply for the reason
that he had been in arms. An enemy—simply as such—oc-
cupies under the Law of Nations a lawful status; it is lawful for
him to levy war. When it is unlawful, it is not because he is an
enemy but because, in addition to his character as enemy he is
also something else—in this case, a subject unlawfully levying
war against the government to which he owed allegiance, and
thus committing treason. It was for *this* reason that Lancaster
was put to death. He was convicted of treasonably levying war
against the King, and certain acts which were felonies at Common Law were in the record charged against him in going to
make up a case of treason. Now, if it was because it was a time
of peace that the judgment was illegal, or, in other words, if it
would have been legal had it been a time of war, we are to consider what was the character of the act which would in time
of war have brought under the jurisdiction of Martial Law a
person not of the army, nor a prisoner of war, and—looking to
Lancaster's case—the answer would be Rebellion. Yet it is not
clear that this was Hale's view. His remarks considered connectedly rather lead to a different conclusion, and this would
seem to have been his meaning when he said that those who
were not listed under the army were to be governed according
to the laws to which they were subject, though it were a time
of war.

Under the title "Murder" in the third volume of Coke's
Institutes[6] we find the following passage:

6. Coke, *The Third Part of the Institutes of the Laws of England* (London:
M. Flesher, 1644), 52.

"If a lieutenant, or other that hath commission of marshall authority, in time of peace hang, or otherwise execute any man by colour of marshall law, this is murder, for this is against Magna Charta, cap. 29,[7] and is done with such power and strength, as the party cannot defend himself; and here the law implieth malice. Vide Pasch. 14 E. 3. in Scaccario the abbott of Ramseys case in a writ of error in part abridged by Fitzh. tit. Scire fac. 122 for time of peace.

Thom. countee de Lancaster being taken in an open insurrection was by judgment of marshall law put to death, in anno 14. E. 4. This was adjudged to be unlawfull, *eo quod non fuit arrainatur, seu ad responsionem positus tempore pacis, eo quod cancellaria, et* alice curiae regis fuerunt tunc apertae, in quibus lex fibat unicuique, prout fieri consuevit, quod contra cartam de libertatibus cum dieius Thomas fuit unus parium et magnatum regni non imprisenetur, &c. Nec dictus rex super eum ibit, nec super eum mittet, nisi per legale judicium

7. "Magna Carta, 1225," *The National Archives*, available at http://www.nationalarchives.gov.uk/education/resources/magna-carta/magna-carta -1225-westminster/ ("No free man shall in future be arrested or imprisoned or disseised of his freehold, liberties or free customs, or outlawed or exiled or victimised in any other way, neither will we attack him or send anyone to attack him, except by the lawful judgment of his peers or by the law of the land. To no one will we sell, to no one will we refuse or delay right or justice.") [Eds. note: This article, of the 1225 version of the charter, is one of the longest-lived provisions of the charter. It came to be associated with the concept of liberty and due process. See J. C. Holt, *Magna Carta*, 3rd ed., ed. George Garnett and John Hudson (New York: Cambridge University Press, 2015), 33–34.]

parium sucrum, &c. tamen tempore iacis absque
arraniamento, sue responsione, seu legali judicio
parium suorum, &c. adjuaicatus eft morti." *

And elsewhere[8] he thus defines the "time of peace": "And
therefore when the courts of justice be open, and the judges
and ministers of the same may by law protect men from wrong
and violence, and distribute justice to all, it is said to be time of
peace. So, when by invasion, insurrection, rebellions, or such
like, the peaceable course of justice is disturbed and stopped,
so as the courts of justice be as it were shut up, *et silent leges inter arma*, then it is said to be time of war. And the trial hereof
is by the records, and judges of the court of justice, for by them
it will appear, whether Justice had her equal course of proceeding at that time or no, and this shall not be tried by jury."
And again,[9] in constructing the words, "no man destroyed, &c.," as said in Magna Charta, he says: "That is, forejudged of life, or limbe, disinherited, or put to torture, or
death. . . . Thomas earle of Lancaster was destroyed, that is,

---

* The Coke passage translates as: "Because in a time of peace he was not
arraigned or made to answer, and because the Chancery and other courts of
the King were then open, in which the law was being carried out; because,
when the aforementioned Thomas was one of the Peers and Magnates of the
Realm, he should not be imprisoned contrary to the charter of freedoms,
etc. Neither shall the aforementioned King proceed against him, nor issue a
decree about him, unless through the lawful adjudication of his Peers, etc.
Nevertheless, in time of peace and without arraignment, whether by defense
or by lawful adjudication of his Peers, etc., he was condemned to death."

8. Edward Coke, *The First Part of the Institutes of the Lawes of England*
(London: Societie of Stationers, 1628), folio 249 verso.
9. Edward Coke, *The Second Part of the Institutes of the Lawes of England*
(London: M. Flesher & R. Young, 1642), 48.

adjudged to die, as a traitor, and put to death in 14 E. 2, and a record thereof made: and Henry earle of Lancaster his brother, and heire, was restored for two principall errors in the proceeding against the said Thomas Earle," and he then recites the errors as set forth in the preceding extract.

Hale and Coke have been frequently referred to as recognizing the right of the Crown to resort, in time of rebellion, to martial law for the trial and punishment of those engaged in rebellion, but the correctness of this interpretation is questionable. The debate in committee of the whole House of Commons on that part of the Petition of Right which relates to Martial Law, shows that at that time, certainly, no such principle was recognized. This debate has been preserved in Rushworth's *Historical Collections*, and will be found in the appendix to this work.[10] Mr. Noy, afterwards Attorney-General, Mr. Rolls, afterwards Sergeant-at-law, and author of the abridgement, Mr. Bankes, afterwards successively Attorney-General and Lord Chief Justice of the Common Pleas, Mr. Mason, a distinguished lawyer and member of Parliament, and Coke himself participated in it.* In weighing the words then pronounced it

---

* **William Noy** (1577–1634, also known as William Noye) was a lawyer and politician who served as attorney general under Charles I. **Sir John Bankes** (1589–1644) was an Oxford-trained lawyer and judge who succeeded Noy in the office of attorney general. Bankes, a close adviser to Charles I, was appointed chief justice of the court of common pleas in 1641. **Henry Rolle** (circa. 1589–1656) was a judge of the King's Bench in 1645. Three years after his appointment, he became Chief Justice. As a lawyer, Rolle was known for handling issues of habeas corpus and martial law. See J. H. Baker, *An Introduction to English Legal History*, 4th ed. (New York: Oxford University Press, 2002); Kevin Sharpe, *The Personal Rule of Charles I* (New Haven: Yale University Press, 1992).

10. John Rushworth, *Historical Collections of Private Passages of State* (London: J. Wright and R. Chiswell, 1681), 3: 76–90.

is necessary that we should keep in mind the circumstances which led to the debate. The King, it will be remembered, had issued commissions subjecting to trial by what was then called martial law soldiers, mariners, and persons joined with them. He did this in time of peace. Therefore Parliament, by the Petition, declared martial law in time of peace illegal—meaning by martial law, all law administered by the military power.[11] It was to the fact that under the laws of England this power could not be legally exercised in time of peace—though it were for the government of the army—that the debate called attention, but

11. That so much of the Petition of Right as relates to Martial Law was intended to apply to a time of peace only is evident when we consider that otherwise it would have been in conflict with the acknowledged power of the crown to provide for the government of the army in time of war. It is also apparent from the debates. When the Petition was under discussion in Parliament, the House of Lords prepared the following addition: "We humbly present this Petition to your majesty, not only with a care of preserving our own liberties, but with due regard to save entire that sovereign power, wherewith your majesty is trusted, for the protection, safety and happiness of your people." The Commons would hear of no such saving clause, and particularly objected to the expression "Sovereign power." This point was fully discussed in conference of committees of the two houses, and called forth the following remarks from Sir Henry Martyn: "Then this Addition, being joined to our Petition, must produce this construction, viz: 'We pray that no freeman may be compelled, by imprisonment to lend money to his maj., . . . ; nor undergo a commission of martial law for life and member, in time of peace, &c. except his maj. Be pleased to require our moneies, . . . , and execute martial law upon us in time of peace, by virtue of his sovereign power.'" The Lords finally gave up the proposed addition. Thus it is evident that there was no intention of going further than to declare illegal martial law—as the term was then used—in time of peace. What-ever military power belonged to the crown in time of war, the Petition left untouched. Parliament limited its action to, and based its statement of grievances upon, the facts before it. It did not go beyond these to determine to what extent other circumstances might qualify [as] a resort to military power. William Cobbett, *Cobbett's Parliamentary History of England* (London: R. Bagshaw, 1807), 2: 355, 368.

it went beyond this, and touched upon the precise question which we are here considering.

Mr. Lord Chief Justice Bankes made use of these words: "But this Commission for Martial Law alters the Common Law; *for it extends to all that joyn with soldiers.*"[12] Commissions for martial law being in time of peace equally illegal whether declared against those of, or those not of the army, he would not have said that these particular commissions, which were issued in time of peace, were illegal *because* extending to the latter. What he meant by this, and his previous remarks, appears to have been that the commissions were illegal because issued in time of peace, and that they would have been illegal in time of war in as far as they altered the Common Law by subjecting to martial law persons not of the army.

So they said: "If Martial Law may be executed in time of War, but it goes with a restraint only to Soldiers; that it may be in time of War there is no Question."[13] "As for the Earl of Lancaster," he adds, "he drew Forces together and killed many, and was taken and carried to Pomfret, and had a Judgment, and they never called him to answer for himself; but they made a Record of his Rebellion, and the King adjudged he should be executed, forfeit his Lands; and this was reversed, because the King's Court was open, and no Man must spill the blood of War in Peace, but if he had been slain in Battel it had been good, or if he had been *in Exercitu*, and *pro hominibus de Exercitu.*"

"I speak not of prosecution against a Rebel," said Coke; "he may be slain in the Rebellion; but if he be taken, he cannot

---

12. Rushworth, *Historical Collections*, 3: 77.
13. Ibid., 80. [Eds. note: The speaker is William Noy, who continued "but for time of Peace it is a Question."]

be put to death by the Martial Law."[14] And Rolle no doubt
meant the same thing, when he said: "If a Subject be taken in
Rebellion, if he be not slain in the time of his Rebellion, he is
to be tried after by the Common Law."[15] That is, he might be
killed in battle, or whilst attempting to escape, but, if made
prisoner, he could not be put to death by martial law.

It may, indeed, have been the intention of Parliament to
give expression to their view in the Petition of Right in calling attention to the illegality of proceeding (in time of peace)
against soldiers, mariners, and other dissolute persons going
with them "by such summary course and order as is agreeable
to martial law, and *as is used in armies in time of war*."[16] This
would appear to be Lord Cockburn's view, and, according to
him, Hale's.*

The difficulty appears to be this, that, in weighing the
remarks of Hale and Coke upon Lancaster's case, we are apt
to lose sight of the point in illustration of which they cite it. It
must be remembered that they were speaking of Martial Law
in the sense of all lawful military jurisdiction, but they did not
expressly admit that such jurisdiction could legally be extended
over others than soldiers, or those of the opposite army. It has
been said that, because they do not expressly disclaim the existence of such a power, they tacitly admit it. This, however, is

---

* Cockburn quoted directly from the Petition of Right in his Charge to
the Grand Jury in the 1867 case *Queen v. Nelson and Brand*, discussed in subsequent chapters. See Frederick Cockburn, *Charge of the Lord Chief Justice*
(London: William Ridgway, 1867), 64.

14. Ibid., 81.
15. Ibid., 79.
16. Petition of Right (1628), Art. VII, available at http://www.national
archives.gov.uk/pathways/citizenship/rise_parliament/transcripts/petition
_right.htm.

no fair inference. They claimed to treat of the whole body of
the laws of England, and, if they did not expressly include this
power, the fairer inference would be that they did not recognize its existence. To the military jurisdiction of which they
spoke soldiers were subject only in time of war; in peace they
stood upon the same footing with other subjects. Lancaster
was tried and executed by military authority—at least the proceedings were so regarded by Hale and Coke—and the judgment was reversed because, when this was done, it was a time
of peace. Therefore this case was cited to prove that, under
the laws of England, *no man*—and consequently no soldier—
could be thus proceeded against in time of peace. This was
the particular point which they wished to illustrate, and it is
not a fair inference from their remarks—particularly when we
consider them all connectedly—to regard them as sanctioning
an application of Martial Law to such a case as Lancaster's in
time of war.

Looking at the subject from our point of view, with a
strongly marked line of distinction between military and martial law, Lancaster's would not be a case exactly pertinent to
the point which these writers were explaining, but there was
no such distinction, and this example was adduced simply to
show that no military authority could to this extent be exercised in time of peace, no matter who the object. They did not
(as they might have done) go further than this and say that
because Lancaster was not a soldier he was not amenable to
"martial law" either in peace or in war. This would, indeed,
have been to go beyond the record, which assigned as the reason for the reversal that Lancaster had been illegally tried and
executed *in time of peace.*

The original trouble was in the record of reversal. Had
the words "in time of peace" been omitted from this record,

and the reversal thus been based upon the illegality of the
proceedings as being in violation of the constitutional guarantees of Magna Carta, such action would no doubt have better
accorded with Hale's and Coke's conceptions of the scope of
"martial law," as the term is used by them; but Parliament simply accepted the reason upon which the petition for reversal
was based, and that reason was the illegality of the proceedings in time of peace. That was probably regarded as a correct
exposition of the law at that time—a time when, we must re-
member, the prerogative was at a height of power which it did
not retain. Hale and Coke, however, in citing the case, make
use of it as an illustration of the illegality of subjecting to trial
and punishment by military authority in time of peace *any*
persons, even such as were subject to it in time of war by a law
"indulged rather than allowed," i.e. soldiers. They do not seem
to have anticipated that their reference to this case would give
rise to the inference that they recognized martial law as extending in time of rebellion to the trial for treason of persons
not connected with the military service.

That Blackstone, writing more than a century later
(1765), drew no other inference from Lancaster's case than
that, except by virtue of the Mutiny Act, military Law could
not be enforced against the soldier in time of peace, seems to
be beyond question. In treating of the military state, he says:[17]

> When the nation was engaged in war, more veteran
> troops and more regular discipline were esteemed
> to be necessary than could be expected from a
> mere militia. And therefore at such times more

17. William Blackstone, *Commentaries on the Laws of England*, 5th ed.
(Oxford: Clarendon, 1773), 412–13.

rigorous methods were put in use for the raising of armies, and the due regulation and discipline of the soldiery: which are to be looked upon only as temporary excrescences bred out of the distemper of the state, and not as any part of the permanent and perpetual laws of the kingdom. For martial law, which is built upon no settled principles, but is entirely arbitrary in its decisions, is, as Sir Matthew Hale observes, in truth and reality no law, but something indulged rather than allowed as a law. The necessity of order and discipline in an army is the only thing which can give it countenance; and therefore it ought not to be permitted in time of peace, when the king's courts are open for all persons to receive justice according to the laws of the land. Wherefore, Thomas earl of Lancaster being condemned at Pontefract, 15 Edw. II, by martial law, his attainder was reversed 1 Edw. III. because it was done in time of peace. And it is laid down, that if a lieutenant, or other, that hath commission of martial authority, doth in time of peace hang or otherwise execute any man by colour of martial law, this is murder; for it is against *magna carta*.

Thus Blackstone but reproduces Hale and Coke, and he does so in a manner which leaves no room for doubt that he is speaking of military, and not of martial law, as we understand these terms. Lancaster's case is again cited to illustrate the illegality of applying military authority to that extent in time of peace to any subject; but the citation is made with particular reference to that class of citizens who, it is admitted, are subject to "martial law" in time of war—that is, soldiers. What he

lays down is, that no citizen and therefore no soldier can be
thus proceeded against in time of peace. By no fair reasoning
are we permitted to infer that he also meant that because *no*
class of citizens might be thus proceeded against in time of
peace, therefore *all* might be in time of war.

In the case of *Grant v. Gould*[18] Lord Loughborough,* then
(1792) Lord Chief Justice of the court of Common Pleas, and
afterwards Lord Chancellor, made the following observations:

> Martial law such as it is described by Hale, and
> such also as it is marked by Mr. Justice Blackstone,
> does not exist in England at all.[19] Where martial
> law is established and prevails in any country, it
> is of a totally different nature from that which is
> inaccurately called martial law merely because the
> decision is by a court-martial, but which bears no
> affinity to that which was formerly attempted to
> be exercised in this kingdom, which was contrary
> to the constitution, and which has been for a cen-
> tury totally exploded. Where martial law prevails,
> the authority under which it is exercised claims a

* **Alexander Wedderburn** (1733–1805) was a prominent Scottish jurist
who served as lord chancellor under George III. See Alexander Murdoch,
"Alexander Wedderburn, First Earl of Rosslyn (1733–1805)," *Oxford Dictionary of National Biography*, Oxford University Press, 2004; available at
http://www.oxforddnb.com/view/article/28954.

18. 2 H. BL. 69, 98–99, 126 Eng. Rep. 434, 449–50 (1792). [Eds. note: **Samuel George Grant** was tried before a court-martial in 1792 for persuading
two drummers to desert the British army and enlist in that of the East India
Company, but he argued that he had never been a soldier and was therefore
not subject to court-martial.]

19. It would seem that Lord Loughborough was mistaken in ascribing
these statements to Hale and Blackstone.

jurisdiction over all military persons in all circumstances. Even their debts are subject to inquiry by a military authority, every species of offence, committed by any person who appertains to the army, is tried, not by a civil judicature, but by the judicature of the regiment or corps to which he belongs. It extends also to a great variety of cases, not relating to the discipline of the army, in those states which subsist by military power. Plots against the sovereign, intelligence to the enemy, and the like, are all considered as cases within the cognizance of military authority.

In the reign of King William, there was a conspiracy against his person in Holland, and the persons guilty of that conspiracy were tried by a council of officers. There was also a conspiracy against him in England, but the conspirators were tried by the common law.* And, within a very recent period, the incendiaries who attempted to set fire to the Docks at Portsmouth were tried by the common law.† In this country, all the delinquencies of soldiers are not triable, as in most other countries in Europe, by martial law; but where they are ordinary offences against the civil peace, they are tried by the common law courts. Therefore it is

* The Jacobite movement, loyal to the deposed King James II (r. 1685–1688) and often cooperating with the French government, made several attempts to overthrow King William III (r. 1689–1702). See Daniel Szechi, *The Jacobites: Britain and Europe, 1688–1788* (New York: Manchester University Press, 1994), 54–56.

† This may refer to **James Aitken**, "John the Painter," who famously sabotaged the Portsmouth dockyards through arson in the 1770s. See Jessica Warner, *John the Painter: Terrorist of the American Revolution* (New York: Thunder's Mouth Press, 2004).

totally inaccurate to state martial law as having any place whatever within the realm of Great Britain. But there is by the providence and wisdom of the Legislature an army established in this country, of which it is necessary to keep up the establishment.

The army being established by the authority of the Legislature, it is an indispensable requisite of that establishment that there should be order and discipline kept up in it, and that the persons who compose the army, for all offences in their military capacity, should be subject to a trial by their officers. That has induced the absolute necessity of a mutiny act accompanying the army. It has happened, indeed, at different periods of the Government, that there has been a strong opposition to the establishment of the army. But the army being established and voted, that led to the establishment of a mutiny act.

Hume, after speaking of the courts of the Star Chamber and High Commission, says: "[M]artial Law went beyond even these two in a prompt, and arbitrary, and violent method of decision. Whenever there was any insurrection or public disorder, the crown employed martial law, and it was during that time exercised not only over the soldiers, but over the whole people: any one might be published as a rebel, or an aider or abetter of rebellion, whom the provost marshal, or lieutenant of a county, or their deputies pleased to suspect."[20]

20. David Hume, *The History of England* (London: T. Cadell, 1822), 3: 246. [Eds. note: The Liebers seem to have cribbed from George Brodie's quotation of this passage, preserving his punctuation rather than Hume's. See George Brodie, *A History of the British Empire* (Edinburgh: Bell & Bradfute, 1822), 1: 204.]

These observations have reference to the time of Elizabeth, but it is doubtful whether, even at that day, this was regarded as a legal exercise of the prerogative. Hume refers to Lord Bacon's statement, that the trial at common law, granted to the Earl of Essex and his fellow conspirators, was a favor; for that the case would have borne and required the severity of martial law. But Mr. Brodie[21] calls attention to Bacon's own confusion with reference to the paper in which this statement was made—that it was written at the express desire of the Queen, was repeatedly perused and altered, both by her and her council, and that he only gave words and form of style in pursuing their directions.[22]

---

21. Brodie, *British Empire*, 1: 204–8. [Eds. note: **Robert Devereux** (1565–1601), the second Earl of Essex, was executed for plotting against Elizabeth. Before his death he was a friend and patron of Francis Bacon (1561–1626), a prominent jurist, philosopher, and author. Among Bacon's writings were letters of advice to George Villiers, first Duke of Buckingham (1592–1628); see below. See "Devereux, Robert, Second Earl of Essex (1565–1601)," *Oxford Dictionary of National Biography*, Oxford University Press, 2004; available at http://www.oxforddnb.com/view/article/7565; "Bacon, Francis, Viscount St Alban (1561–1626)," *Oxford Dictionary of National Biography*, Oxford University Press, 2004; available at http://www.oxforddnb.com/view/article/990; "Villiers, George, first duke of Buckingham (1592–1628)," *Oxford Dictionary of National Biography*, Oxford University Press, 2004; available at http://www.oxforddnb.com/view/article/28293.

22. It would seem, indeed, that Bacon was not insensible, for, in a letter "conceived to be written to the late Duke of Buckingham, where he first became a favorite of King James," we find him giving this advice: "I must not omit to put you in mind of the Lord Lieutenants, and Deputy Lieutenants of the Counties: their proper use is for ordering the military affairs, in order to an invasion from abroad, or a rebellion or sedition at home; good choice should be made of them, and prudent instructions given to them, and as little of the arbitrary power as may be left unto them; and that the muster masters, and other officers under them, in croach not upon the subject; that will detract much from the King's service." See *Cabala, Sive Scrinia Sacra: Mysteries of State and Government, in Letters* (London: Tho. Sawbridge, 1691), 37, 40.

It is well known that Elizabeth herself desired on more than one occasion to enforce martial law. Her proclamation against the introduction of papal bulls has already been noticed. She also wrote to the Earl of Sussex,* after the suppression of the Northern Rebellion, sharply reproving him because she had not heard of his having executed any criminals by martial law. Mr. Brodie thinks the very fact of criminals not having been executed by martial law in this case a striking proof of the general feeling and understanding of the age. An instance is also mentioned when Elizabeth ordered one Peter Burchet to be proceeded against by martial law for an ordinary common law offense, but was induced to revoke the order when told that martial law was usually confined to turbulent times.[23]

Perhaps the most correct presentation of the law, as then understood, is given by Sir Thomas Smith, Secretary of State under Edward VI, and afterwards under Queen Elizabeth. He says: "Militiae quoque & in castris princeps absolutam potestatem nullis legum repagulis coercitam habet. eius placita legis vim sustinent. ine aliqua processus iudicarii formula hos morte mulctare potest, illos poena, ubi quid deliquerint, corporis quantumlibet castigare. Usurpari quoque interdum ista suprema authoritas solita est, antequam belli facies se aperuerit, in subitis nimirum rebellium motibus, sed bonis et cor-

---

* **Thomas Radcliffe** (circa 1526–1583), the third Earl of Sussex, was president of the Council of the North during an uprising of other earls in 1569. He was criticized for a slow and insufficiently harsh response. See "Radcliffe, Thomas, Third Earl of Sussex (1526/7–1583)," *Oxford Dictionary of National Biography*, Oxford University Press, 2004; available at http://www .oxforddnb.com/view/article/22993.

23. Brodie, *British Empire*, 1: 210, 214–15, 222–23. [Eds. note: **Burchet** was a puritan who murdered a naval captain named Hawkins, whom he mistook for Queen Elizabeth's favorite Christopher Hatton.]

datis viris parum approbata, qui malum talis exempli exitum animo praevidentes, lege potius quam armis litem decerni voluerunt."[24]

Writing of this same period Stephens, in his introduction, to De Lolme's English Constitution, says: "Martial law . . . had only been legally exercised during the continuance of a rebellion, and when in force, any person was liable to be punished as a rebel, whom the provost martial, lieutenant of a county, or their deputies, suspected of guilt: but Elizabeth availed herself of this law, when no immediate danger to the state was apprehended."[25]

I have here referred to the leading authorities, and I believe I have, so far as they are concerned, presented both sides of the question to the reader. He will then be at least assisted in carrying the investigation further, and determining for himself the soundness of my conclusions. If these conclusions are correct it would seem that the precedents and authorities taken from the earlier periods of English history cannot be relied upon as proving the unqualified recognition of the legality of the prerogative which we have been discussing. A different view has been taken

24. Thomas Smith, *De Republica et Administratione Anglorum Libri Tres*, trans. Johannes Buddenus (London: Officina Nortoniana Londini, 1610), 65. [A contemporary English translation reads as follows: "In warre time, and in the field the Prince hath also absolute power, so that his worde is a law, he may put to death, or to other bodilie punishment, whom he shall thinke so to deserve, without processe of lawe or forme of judgement. This hath beene sometime used within the Realme before any open warre in sodden insurrections and rebellions, but that not allowed of wise and grave men, who in that their judgement had consideration of the consequence and example, asmuch as of the present necessitie, especiallie, when by anie meanes the punishment might have beene doone by order of lawe." Smith, *De Republica Anglorum* (London: Henrie Middleton, 1583), II.3.]

25. J. L. de Lolme, ed. A. J. Stephens, *The Rise and Progress of the English Constitution* (London: John W. Parker, 1838), 1: 265.

by several recent writers, but the weight of evidence seems to be against them. Looking upon it in this light, we are forced to the conclusion that a wrong use has, to a great extent, been made of such precedents and authorities. The prerogative was frequently exercised, but that its exercise was admitted to be legal is an inference which we cannot fairly deduce from the facts which have been given. A careful study of the growth of the English constitution seems to lead to a different result.

Martial Law—speaking of it as a legal principle—being founded in necessity must have always existed, when called forth by such necessity, but its definite recognition as a legal principle dates from a much more recent period than that concerning which we have been writing. This we can not trace back further than the close of the last century. From that time, however, it has become more and more firmly established, and better defined. The principles upon which it is founded have become better settled. Its legal operation has been separated from its illegal enforcement and abuse. Thus understood, its necessity has been recognized by, and it has received the confirmation of, a long list of able men—lawyers, statesmen and soldiers. Nor would it be fair to urge its previous non-recognition as an argument against its legal existence. Many of the principles upon which the English constitution rest have been of gradual development, and that this principle was not definitively recognized at an earlier period may be easily traced to the fact that it involved a temporary suspension of those guarantees of liberty, which had been illegally violated, and towards the establishment of which upon an inviolable basis the supports of the people were directed.[26] It was no time then

26. And to the further fact that it was generally understood to mean something more than a law of necessity.

to consider exceptional cases, but, these rights once secured, it became necessary to consider whether any circumstances would justify their temporary suspension, and the judgment of later days has unquestionably been in favor of the necessity of such suspension under certain circumstances.

This judgment would no doubt have been longer delayed but for the troubles in Ireland.* It was a judgment first given in the heat of passion, but it has been fully confirmed by the cooler deliberations of after years. It could not have been otherwise. Founded in necessity—whenever it can be shown that such necessity exists, it must find in it its legal justifications.

* See Chapter V.

Acts of Parliament, Recognizing the Legality of Martial Law

That Parliament has the power to authorize the enforcement of Martial Law can not be questioned. The existence of such a power is evident when we consider the nature of the English Constitution. That which is so called is no enacted or written constitution like our own. It is a collection of principles, developed at different times, and established by acts of Parliament, the decisions of courts of law, and immemorial usages. It is therefore cumulative,[1] and possesses the element of adaptability. It has

1. Dr. Francis Lieber, in his "Civil Liberty and Self-Government," makes the following observations: "They [enacted constitutions] are generally called written constitutions; but it is evident that the essential distinction of constitutions, derived from their origins, is not whether they are written or unwritten, which is incidental, but whether they are enacted or cumulative. The English constitution, that is the aggregate of those laws and rules which are considered of fundamental importance, and essential in giving to the state and its government those features which characterize them, or those laws and institutions which give to England her peculiar political organic being, consist in cumulated usages and branches of the common law, in decisions of fundamental importance, in self-grown and in enacted

"grown out of occasion and emergency; from the fluctuating policy of different ages; from the contentions, successes, interests, and opportunities of different orders and parties of men in the community."[2]

The English Constitution being of this character, it follows that no generation can impose upon succeeding ones an immutable supreme law. No parliament can bind future ones, and any act affecting to do so is void.[3] What one legislature has enacted, the next may repeal. "Subsequent Parliaments cannot be restrained by the acts of former ones. It is only necessary to repeal the ordinance to destroy the prohibition; and without a formal repeal, it seems that the act is *ipso facto* void. Some parts of Magna Charta, although it be expressly declared by the 42 Ed. 3, c. 2, that all statutes contrary thereto shall be

---

institutions, in compacts, and in statutes embodying principles of political magnitude. From these the Americans have enacted what has appeared important or applicable to our circumstances; we have added, expanded and systematized, and then enacted this aggregate as a whole, calling it a constitution—enacted, not by the legislature, which is a creature of this constitution, but by the people. Whether the constitution is written, printed, carved in stone, or remembered only, as laws were of old, is not the distinctive feature. It is the positive enactment of the whole at one time, and by distinct authority, which marks the difference between the origin of our constitutions and those of England or ancient Rome. Although the term written constitution does not express the distinctive principle, it was nevertheless natural that it should have been adopted, for it is analogous to the term lex scripta, by which the enacted or statute law is distinguished from the unenacted, grown and cumulative common law." Francis Lieber, *On Civil Liberty and Self Government* (Philadelphia: Lippincott, Grambo, and Co., 1853), 178–79.

2. A. J. Stephens, "Introduction," in J. L. De Lolme, *The Rise and Progress of the English Constitution* (London: John W. Parker, 1838), 1: 4; William Paley, *The Principles of Moral and Political Philosophy* (New York: B. and S. Collins, 1835), 2: 87.

3. Fortunatus Dwarris, *A General Treatise on Statutes*, ed. Platt Potter (Albany: William Gould & Sons, 1871), 75.

void, have been repealed, and other parts have been altered by subsequent statutes; yet such latter statutes, instead of being thus made void are said in Jenkin's Centuries, to have been constantly held to be in force."[4] The words "constitutional" and "unconstitutional" cannot, therefore, be applied to an act of Parliament in the same sense as it may be to an act of Congress, for an act of Parliament changing the constitution may be constitutional, whereas an act of Congress affecting to do so would be unconstitutional and void. The constitutionality of an act of Congress may become a question for the judiciary to decide. "The general and received doctrine certainly is, that an act of Parliament, of which the terms are explicit and the meaning plain, cannot be questioned, or its authority controlled, in any court of justice."[5]

Thus we find that, although the chief argument against Martial Law as an exercise of the prerogative power has been that it is in violation of the English Constitution, the power of Parliament to put it in place has not been questioned.

Upon this principle rests also the power of Parliament to pass indemnity acts, removing from those who have illegally exercised the power the legal consequences of their acts. Thus in 1796, (by the statute of 36 George III, c. 6.), and on one or two occasions subsequently and before the year 1798, the Irish Parliament passed acts indemnifying those who had exceeded their legal powers in suppressing insurrection in that island.*

* In the 1790s, partly due to inspiration from the French Revolution, a radical movement known as the United Irishmen grew among Irish Protestants. Amidst government repression and economic distress, this

4. Ibid.; see also Edward S. Creasy, *The Rise and Progress of the English Constitution* (London: Richard Bentley, 1853), 2.
5. Dwarris, *Treatise on Statutes*, 78.

Down to this time there had been no formal proclamation of Martial Law, but in 1798 the insurrection became so formidable that the Lord Lieutenant issued his proclamation to that effect, and Martial Law was put in force, and many persons executed. In November of that year one Wolfe Tone* was tried before a court-martial for complicity in the rebellion, and sentenced to be hanged. A writ of *habeas corpus*, intended to test the legality of these proceedings, was granted in his behalf, but, before the question thus arising could be determined, he put an end to his own life.[6] The Irish Parliament then passed an Act,[7] which being the first in which the power of executing Martial Law upon rebels is spoken of as an "undoubted prerogative," and being also that from which similar recitals were copied into the English statute book, it is important to examine somewhat fully.

Protestant-led movement allied with the Catholic "Defender" secret societies. This eventually culminated in the "Wexford War" of 1798, a rural uprising that produced several massacres before royal troops suppressed it, killing about ten thousand rebels and non-combatants in the process. The Irish Parliament responded with the Insurrection Acts, beginning in 1796. See Thomas Bartlett, *Ireland: A History* (New York: Cambridge University Press, 2010), 221–27; "Insurrection Act," in *The Oxford Companion to Irish History*, ed. S. J. Connolly, online ed. (Oxford: Oxford University Press, 2007); R. F. Foster, *The Oxford History of Ireland* (New York: Oxford University Press, 2001), 150–53.

* **Theobald Wolfe Tone** was a member of the United Irishmen who, after going into exile in France, encouraged the revolutionary government of that country to support Irish resistance. Two French expeditions failed in 1796 and 1798, and Tone was himself captured in an attempt to land at Lough Swilly. See Bartlett, *Ireland*, 224; Foster, *Oxford History of Ireland*, 151–53.

6. Thomas Howell, *A Complete Collection of State Trials* (London: Hansard, 1820), 27: 625.

7. 39 Geo. III, c. 11.

This act recites that: "Whereas a traitorous conspiracy for the subversion of the authority of his Majesty and the parliament, and for the destruction of the established constitution and government, hath unfortunately excited within the Kingdom for a considerable time, &c &c; and whereas for the more effectual suppression of the said daring and unprovoked rebellion, his excellency the said earl Camden did, on the 24th May, 1798, by and with the advice of the privy council, issue his orders to all general officers commanding his majesty's forces, to punish all persons acting, aiding, or in any manner assisting in the said rebellion, according to martial law, either by death or otherwise, as to them should some expedient, for the punishment and suppression of all rebels in their several districts, &c, &c: And whereas by the wise and salutary exercise of *his Majesty's undoubted prerogative in executing martial law, for defeating and dispersing such armed and rebellious force, and in bringing divers rebels and traitors to punishment in the most speedy and summary manner,* the peace of this Kingdom has been so far restored as to permit the course of the common law partially to take place; but the said rebellion still continues to rage in very considerable parts of this Kingdom, and to desolate and lay waste the country, by the most savage and wanton violence, excess and outrage, and has utterly set at defiance the civil power, and stopped the ordinary course of justice and of the common law therein; And whereas many persons who have been guilty of the most daring and horrid acts of cruelty and outrage in furtherance and prosecution of the said rebellion, and who have been taken by his Majesty's forces employed for the suppression of the same, have availed themselves of such partial restoration of the ordinary course of the common law to evade the punishment of their crimes, whereby it has become necessary for parliament to interpose; be it therefore enacted," that the Lord Lieutenant is authorized, "whether the ordinary courts of justice shall or shall not at such time be open to issue his or their orders to all officers commanding his Majesty's forces, . . . to take the most vigorous and effectual measures for suppressing the said rebellion, . . . and to punish all persons acting, aiding, or in any manner assisting in the said rebellion, or maliciously attacking or injuring the persons or properties of his Majesty's loyal subjects, in furtherance of the same, according to martial law either by death or otherwise, as to them shall seem expedient, for the punishment and suppression of all rebels in their several districts, &c &c."[8]

The act then provides, for the constitution of courts-martial for the trial of such persons; that acts done in pursuance of such orders shall not be questioned; that officers and soldiers shall be responsible to courts-martial only for acts done under such orders; and that when a writ of *habeas corpus* shall sue forth, it shall be a sufficient return that the party is detained by warrant of a person authorized under this act, &c, and then continues thus: "Provided always, and be it declared and enacted, that nothing in this act shall be construed to take away, abridge or diminish, *the acknowledged prerogative of his Majesty, for the public safety, to resort to the exercise of martial law against open enemies or traitors*, or any powers by law vested in the Lord Lieutenant, &c."

This act was accompanied by another,[9] granting indemnity to those who had been the instruments of enforcing Martial Law. Now, it might be asked, why, if it was an undoubted prerogative, was an act of indemnity required? Possibly the case of Wolfe Tone furnishes the answer. In that case the

8. Quoted in Thomas Simmons, *Remarks on the Constitution and Practice of Courts Martial*, 2nd. ed. (London: Pinkney, 1835), 574–78.
9. 39 Geo. III. c. 3.

military authorities seemed determined to carry into execution the sentence of the court-martial in defiance of the writ
of *habeas corpus*, yet the courts were open and it was then and
there a time of peace. His offense was one cognizable by the
civil courts, and, as Lord Coke says, when the common law
can determine a thing, the martial law should not. It may have
been with a view to cover such cases that the act of indemnity
was passed. That is to say, its intention may have been, and, by
its language seems to have been, to grant indemnity from acts
which, though done under color of martial law, were not justifiable under it. At any rate it can hardly be regarded as detract-
ing from the force of the recital as to the prerogative power, so
strongly expressed in the act above quoted.

The act of 39 Geo. III. c. 11, which was passed in 1799 by
the Irish Parliament, was followed in 1803—the Union having in the mean time been effected*—by that of the United
Parliament of 43 Geo. III. c. 117. This act provided:† "Whereas
a treasonable and rebellious spirit of insurrection now unfortunately exists in Ireland, &c &c, That from and after the passing of this Act, it shall and may be lawful to and for the Lord
Lieutenant, or other Chief Governor or Governors of Ireland,
from time to time during the continuance of the said rebellion, whether the ordinary courts of justice shall or shall not
at such time be open, to issue his or their orders to all officers
commanding his Majesty's forces in Ireland, and to all others
whom he or they shall think fit to authorize in that behalf, to

---

* Partly in reaction to the 1798 revolt, the Irish Parliament was abolished
and the kingdom unified with the United Kingdom on January 1, 1801. See
Bartlett, *Ireland*, 227–36; Foster, *Oxford History of Ireland*, 153–54.

† See Thomas Edlyne Tomlins, ed., *The Statutes of the United Kingdom of
Great Britain and Ireland* (London: George Eyre and Andrew Strahan, 1804),
1: 999–1000.

take the most vigorous and effectual measures for suppressing the said insurrection and rebellion in any part of Ireland,
which shall appear to be necessary for the publick safety, and
for the safety and protection of the persons and properties of
his Majesty's peaceable and loyal subjects, and to punish all
persons acting, aiding, or in any manner assisting in the said
rebellion, or maliciously attacking or injuring the persons or
properties of his Majesty's loyal subjects, in furtherance of the
same, according to Martial Law, either by death or otherwise,
as to them shall seem expedient for the punishment and suppression of all rebels in their several districts, and to arrest
and detain in custody all persons engaged in such rebellion,
or suspected thereof; and to cause all persons so arrested and
detained in custody to be brought to trial in a summary way
by courts-martial, &c." Then follow certain provisions similar to those of the Act of 39 George III. c. 11, relieving officers
from all responsibility, except to courts-martial, for acts thus
done, etc., and thus this proviso: "Provided always, and be it
declared and enacted, That nothing in this act contained shall
be construed to take away, abridge, or diminish *the acknowledged prerogative of his Majesty, for the publick safety, to resort
to the exercise of Martial Law against open enemies* or traitors,
or any powers by law vested in the said Lord Lieutenant, &c, to
suppress Treasons and Rebellion, &c, &c."

And again, in the Act of 3 & 4 William IV, c. 4., passed in
1833,* and entitled "An Act for the more effectual suppression

---

* The so-called "tithe war" began in 1830 in county Kilkenny before
spreading across southern Ireland. It was a combination of violent and non-
violent resistance to the British policy requiring cultivators—even Catho-
lics—to pay taxes in support of the Irish Protestant Church. After "rival massacres of tithe protesters . . . and of police," the tithe was commuted into a
charge added on to cultivators' rent, with an exemption for the least well-off

of local disturbances and dangerous associations in Ireland,"
we find a similar proviso:[10]

"Provided always, and be it declared and enacted, That
nothing in this act contained shall be construed to take away,
abridge or diminish the acknowledged prerogative of his Majesty, in respect of appointing and convening courts-martial
according to the provisions of the act for punishing mutiny
and desertion, or the *undoubted* prerogative of his Majesty, for
the public safety, to resort to the exercise of martial law against
open enemies or traitors, &c."

Here, therefore, we have the highest legislative sanction
for regarding the existence of this prerogative as an *"acknowledged"* and *"undoubted"* fact. These positive recitals certainly
cannot be reconciled with the opinions of authorities already
quoted.* How then are we to account for them? In seeking for
the answer to this question, we must take into consideration
the circumstances under which these acts were passed. We
must not forget what the relations between the English and
the Irish were. With hatred on the one hand, and if not equal
hatred—at least great bitterness on the other, may we not look
to see these passions reflected in the legislation of the times?

---

tenants. Thus "[t]ithe had not been abolished, but it was now made invis-
ible." The legislative response replaced the earlier Insurrection Acts with the
new Coercion Acts. See Bartlett, *Ireland*, 270–71; "Coercion Acts," in *The
Oxford Companion to Irish History*; Hansard HL Deb., vol. 15, col. 932–947
(Feb. 19, 1833); Hansard HL Deb., vol. 16, col. 1294–1332 (April 1, 1833).

 * The Liebers are referring to their Chapter IV discussion of authorities
such as Hale and Blackstone, along with figures like Lord Loughborough
and David Hume, who relied on them. See Chapter IV above.

 10. See *A Collection of the Public General Statutes Passed in the Third and
Fourth Year of the Reign of His Majesty King William the Fourth* (London:
Eyre and Spottiswoode, 1833), 25.

Nevertheless, this legislative recognition of the prerogative is of great weight, and from that day the prerogative which we are considering seems to have become more and more firmly established as an element of the English Constitution.

Mr. Hargrave makes, in his "Jurisconsult Exercitations," * some observations, which are pertinent, and valuable. His learning and manifest sincerity entitle them to especial consideration. Having been consulted with reference to the high treason attainder of Cornelius Grogan, after his death, by the Irish Act of 6th October 1798, he says:[11]

> I am impressed also, that his having been tried and put to death under a proceeding called *martial law*, so far from being a ground for inducing an act *for attaining him after his death*, should have operated in preventing such an *extraordinary* rigour. I so express myself; because that extremity was resorted to against him, previously to the Irish Statute made in the 39th of his present Majesty for suppression of the rebellion in Ireland; and so as I conceive

* **Francis Hargrave** (1740/41–1821), lawyer and legal historian, is best known for arguing and winning *Somerset's Case* (1772), which established that slavery was not recognized in England under common law. Thereafter he made a career drafting legal arguments for leading figures like Attorney General Edward Thurlow. Hargrave was also a prolific antiquary who published modern editions of legal manuscripts and collections of state trials. His three-volume *Jurisconsult Exercitations* (published between 1811 and 1813) brought together much of his previous written and oral work. See William Fletcher, ed., *English Book Collectors* (London: Kegan Paul, 1902), 3: 267–69; Daniel Hulsebosch, "Nothing but Liberty: Somerset's Case and the British Empire," *Law and History Review* 24, no. 3 (Fall 2006): 647–57.

11. Francis Hargrave, *Jurisconsult Exercitations* (London: W. Clarke and Sons, 1811), 1: 401–3.

was applied, when the doctrine, attributing to the
crown in the time of rebellion a prerogative right of
authorizing the trial arrested rebels before a court
martial and by a martial law, and the punishment
of them by death or otherwise as to the members
of such court martial should seem meet, had not,
as I apprehend, received legislative sanction even
in Ireland. Had I been consulted before the passing of that act, I should have deemed it fully open
to me, to express at least a doubt,—whether the
prerogative of proclaiming and authorizing martial
law in time of actual invasion by a foreign enemy,
or in time of actual rebellion, was not merely refer-
able to the law for governing the royal army and all
connected with it, that is, for governing those employed in defending the country against invasion
and in suppressing rebellion. I should have deemed
it fully open to me to express at least a doubt,—
whether, under martial law, to try persons seized in
rebellion, or seized upon suspicion of being rebels,
before a court martial constituted by the king's authority, and to punish them by death or otherwise
at the discretion of the members of such a court,
was not an extension of martial law beyond its real
object; and being so was not an infringement of the
law of England in a point of the most serious kind.
But the Irish act of the 39th of the present King, for
suppression of the Irish rebellion, makes a vast difference; for in effect it contains recitals, which not
only recognized a royal prerogative of authorizing
the trial and punishment of rebels by martial law,

in the very harsh latitude I have already mentioned, but expressly authorized such application of martial law by new provisions for that purpose: and this act, which was temporary, was afterwards continued for a further time by a subsequent Irish act, and since the union of Great Britain and Ireland has been further continued with some amendments by acts of the parliament of the United Kingdom, the first of which is the 41st of the present King, chapter 15. With these statutes before me, I am forced to resist any contrary impression I may have as to the real boundary of martial law. However too, from previous settled notions, I may see these statutes as amounting to a melancholy change, first most unhappily generated in the code of Irish legislation by the heated atmosphere of civil convulsions in Ireland, and then insensibly as it seems insinuated into the code of English law, through statutes of the united kingdom of Great Britain and Ireland, not so much as stating the terrible prerogative I point at, but engrafting it by continuing Irish statutes, which, being mentioned by the title only, are probably at this moment little known even to practising lawyers in England: yet to such high authority—I must succumb.

Having reached this point in English history, it remains for us to examine some of the more recent instances of the application of martial law. These will be found full of instruction, and, as the sources from which the information with reference to them has been derived, may not be accessible to all the readers of these pages, one of the principal objects of this work will be best attained by pursuing the plan already adopted of making as full extracts as its limits will allow. This chapter may be fittingly closed with the observations of Henry Hallam.* The English Constitution has no historian entitled to greater weight.

> There may indeed be times of pressing danger, when the conservation of all demands the sacrifice of the legal rights of a few; there may be circumstances that not only justify, but compel, the temporary abandonment of constitutional forms. It has been usual for all governments, during an actual rebellion, to proclaim martial law, or the suspension of civil jurisdiction. And this anomaly, I must admit is very far from being less indispensable at such unhappy seasons, in countries where the ordinary mode of trial is by jury, than where the right of decision resides in the judge. But it is of high importance to watch with extreme jealousy the disposition, towards which most governments are prone, to introduce too soon, to extend too far, to retain too long, so perilous a remedy. . . .
>
> It is an unhappy consequence of all deviations from the even course of law, that the forced

---

*Henry Hallam (1777–1859) was a prominent Whig historian, best known for his *Constitutional History of England* (1827). See Timothy Lang, "Hallam, Henry (1777–1859)," *Oxford Dictionary of National Biography*, Oxford University Press, 2004, available at http://www.oxforddnb.com/view/article/12002.

acts of over-ruling necessity come to be distorted into precedents to serve the purposes of arbitrary power.[12]

We thus seem to have reached the period when, this prerogative power being recognized, the question no longer is,—can it ever be exercised? It has now been reduced to this,—when and to what extent may it be enforced?

12. Henry Hallam, *Constitutional History of England*, (London: John Murray, 1876), 1: 240–42.

CHAPTER VI

Wall's Case, and the Demerara, Ceylon, and Jamaica Cases

W all's case has sometimes been referred to as strongly illustrating the harshness of martial law.[1] It is therefore important to examine it.[2]

Joseph Wall was, in 1782, Commandant of the garrison of Goree [Gorée, an island off Senegal]. On the 10th of July of that year there occurred what he claimed to have amounted to a mutiny. The facts appear to have been these: Governor Wall had announced his intended departure for England on the 11th, and was to be accompanied by the paymaster. The garrison having been for some time on a short allowance of provisions, and it being customary to compensate the men, by

1. *Annual Register* (London: Wilks, 1803), 560–68. J. W. Gordon's argument before the Military Commission in the so-called "Indiana Treason Trials." [Eds. note: These military commission trials eventually reached the Supreme Court in *Ex parte Milligan*, 71 U.S. 2 (1866). See Jonathan W. Gordon, *An Argument against the Jurisdiction of Military Commissions to Try Citizens of the United States* (Indianapolis: Hall & Hutchinson, 1865), 13–14.]

2. Martial Law was also resorted to in New Zealand in 1845, and 1860; at Ballaarat in Victoria, in 1854; at Lambing Flat, New South Wales, in 1861.

an equivalent in money, for such cutting down of their allowance, when the time drew near for the paymaster's departure,
some of the soldiers started for his quarters with the view of obtaining a settlement. They were stopped and ordered to return
by the Governor, and this order they obeyed. Soon afterwards
several—amongst them one Armstrong—again started for the
paymaster's quarters, but were again stopped by the Governor
who addressed certain remarks to Armstrong. The latter made
a statement of the grievances complained of, and then retired,
without apparently evincing any mutinous disposition. After
that there was no disorder of any kind, but later in the day the
"long roll" was beaten, and the men, having fallen into rank,
were ordered to form in a circle. It was claimed for the defence
at Wall's trial that he then ordered a drum-head court-martial
for the trial of Armstrong, and that the punishment which was
inflicted upon him was by virtue of the sentence of this court.
Be this as it may—Armstrong was stripped and eight hundred
lashes inflicted upon him under circumstances of unusual barbarity, approved by the Governor. From the effects of this treatment Armstrong died. It was a significant fact that although this
alleged mutiny, the suppression of which, it was claimed, required such extreme measures, occurred on the 10th, yet it was
not sufficient to interfere with Governor Wall's departure on the
11th. He sailed on that day, and, arriving in England, made his
official reports, which contained no reference to the mutiny.*

* This account seems to be based on the attorney general's statement for
the prosecution in Wall's 1802 murder trial, and to a lesser extent on Wall's
defense. By "unusual barbarity," Lieber refers to the attorney general's emphasis on Wall's employment of "black men" in place of ordinary soldiers
to inflict the punishment on Armstrong. See T. B. Howell & Thomas Jones
Howell, ed., *A Complete Collection of State Trials* (London: T. C. Hansard,
1820), 28: 51–178.

Fearing arrest Wall subsequently absented himself from England, and did not return until after the lapse of eleven years,* when he was immediately apprehended, and brought to trial for murder.

Lord Chief Baron Macdonald, in summing up, said:

> On the one hand . . . when a well-intentioned officer is at a great distance from his native country, having charge of a member of that country, and it shall so happen that circumstances arise which may alarm and disturb the strongest mind, it were not proper that strictness and rigour in forms and in matters of that sort should be required, where you find a real, true, and genuine intention of acting for the best for the sake of the public. . . .
>
> But, on the other hand, it is of consequence, that where a commander is so circumstanced,— that is, at a distance from his native country,—at a distance from inspection,—at a distance from immediate control,—and not many British subjects being there,—if he shall, by reason of that distance, wanton with [his] authority and his command, it will certainly be the duty of the law to control that, and to keep it within proper bounds. The protection therefore of subjects who are serving their country at that distance, on one hand, is one of the objects you are to have in view to-day; the protection of a well-intentioned officer,—if such he be,— who does not by his conduct disclose a malevolent

---

* This number seems to be incorrect, as it was 1801 when Wall returned to England and turned himself in. See ibid., 62.

mind, but may disclose human infirmity to a certain extent, who being in trepidation and alarm of mind, overlooks some things he ought otherwise to have regarded,—such a man's case is, on the other hand, deserving of great attention.

The crime imputed to the prisoner is, the murder of Benjamin Armstrong: The indictment charges . . . that malice is to be discovered in the heart of that person who is accused.[3]

Then, after defining malice, he continues:

I would also mention to you, that in all cases of corporal punishment, as I conceive, where there is lodged a discretion, regard is to be had to the extent of that punishment and to the means of inflicting it; because legitimate punishment may be inflicted in such a manner as to shew, that the infliction of the punishment was made the ground of wilfully carrying it to an extent and excess that would be attended with the destruction of him who is the object of it. . . . It is perfectly clear, that many persons have authority to correct in a certain degree. A master has to correct his servant. A parent has not only the power, but it is his duty to correct the child; but let me suppose that instead of inflicting five or six strokes with a few birch twigs upon that child, you inflict five or six hundred; although the

3. Ibid., 143–59. [Eds. note: The Liebers have omitted parts of the quotation, slightly altered a few words and punctuation, and Americanized MacDonald's spelling.]

instrument be a legal instrument, and cannot be quarreled with, yet the extreme excess of the quantity may denote an intent to do mischief, not bridled by that which ought to bridle human actions.

Or, he says, the instrument may be improper, and then, applying the rule to courts martial he continues: "I take it, they are bound to inflict that measure of punishment which has been known ordinarily to be inflicted and borne; and it may be a question, whether, if the quantity be inordinate in proportion to the instrument, that may not be evidence of such malice as may constitute that which would otherwise be justifiable, a murder according to the definition of the law of England."

And, after receiving the evidence, and referring to the conflict of testimony as to the alleged mutiny, he says:

If there were no [such] mutiny, and if there were no court-martial of any kind even the best that could be had (as is sworn by the witnesses for the prosecution), and this man was, by the command of the gentleman at the bar, tied up and received so large a punishment as eight-hundred lashes, with an instrument so unusual in its nature, the effect of which is in evidence, and which must necessarily be very different from that of nine loose strings, instead of one solid elastic mass; there is certainly ground to infer malice, according to the description I gave at the outset.

If it shall appear to you that there was a mutiny—if it shall appear to you that there was such a court-martial as could be had—and that there was reasonable notice to the deceased, that he was so and so charged, and was called upon to say how he came to be one of those mutineers (as to which evidence does not seem to have been examined, the prisoner perhaps trusting to the notoriety of it, in the shape the witnesses for him say it existed, namely in a notorious shape)—I have the attorney general's liberal authority for saying, in this case before us, that if you are satisfied of that, and do not derive from the degree of punishment and the mode in which it was inflicted by the instrument used, a malicious intent to destroy this man, or a wilful disregard of human life;—in case you see all the circumstances in that light, you will give the benefit of such a view of them to the prisoner, and acquit him. I see no medium between that and a conviction of murder. . . .

If you are of opinion that there was no mutiny, there was then no ground for anything that followed; if you are of opinion there was a mutiny, you are then to consider the degree of it, and whether there was as much attention paid to the interest of the person accused as the circumstances of the case would admit, by properly apprising him, and giving him an opportunity for justifying himself if he could, as the prisoner's witnesses have stated. Next you will consider the extent of the punishment. &c.[4]

4. The case of Commander Mackenzie, of the U.S. Navy, will suggest itself to many readers. Mackenzie being, in 1842, in command of the Somers, had, whilst at sea caused Midshipman Philip Spencer, and two of the crew to be hung at the yard arm for mutiny. For this he was brought before a

Wall was convicted of murder, and executed, but his conviction only proves that his acts were illegal—that it was an
illegal enforcement of military power. Beyond this it proves
nothing. It does not prove that there might not have been
circumstances which would have justified a use of military
authority which, under ordinary circumstances, would have
been illegal. It was a solemn decision that there was no such
necessity in this case as called for a departure from the laws by
which personal liberty is protected. No one who reads the remarks made by Lord Chief Baron Macdonald in summing up
can fail to be impressed by the conviction that—from amounting to a condemnation under all circumstances of such extraordinary application of military authority—they distinctly
recognize circumstances which may justify it. The abuse of
a power is no proof that the power does not exist. "Military
oppression," say the American "Instructions," "is not Martial
Law; it is the abuse of the power which that Law confers."[5]

In August 1823 a servile insurrection broke out in Demerara, owing in a great measure, it would seem, to the action
of the authorities. The precise causes of these disturbances it is
unnecessary to consider, but it is not to be overlooked that the
disturbances were not of a rebellious character. They were not
aimed at the overthrow of the government; they were not treasonable; but were, in fact, a resistance of slaves to the authority

---

court-martial, charged with murder. He admitted the killing, but claimed
that it was demanded by duty, and justified by necessity. The court found
the charge "not proven," and the finding was "confirmed" by the President.
[Eds. note: See, e.g., *Proceedings of the Court of Inquiry* (New York: Gree-
ley & McElrath, 1843); "The Somers Affair," *United States Naval Academy
Nimitz Library*, available at http://cdm16099.contentdm.oclc.org/cdm/
landingpage/collection/p15241coll1.]

5. G.O. 100, art. 4.

of the slaveholders. On the 19th of August Martial Law was proclaimed, and it continued in force until January 15th, 1824, although the revolt was suppressed before the end of August. Whilst it lasted many slaves were executed, and many others subjected to corporal punishment.

The humbleness of their position was the safe-guard of their oppressors. There was one case, however, which could not be so easily suppressed.

During the time when Martial Law was in force Rev. John Smith, a missionary, was arrested, and, after being kept in confinement for some time, was, on the 14th of October, brought before a court-martial. The charges upon which he was arraigned were—creating dissatisfaction among the slaves; concealing the intended revolt; and corresponding with the leaders of the revolt whilst it was in progress. Upon these charges he was condemned, and sentenced to be executed, but the sentence was not carried out—Mr. Smith dying in prison. The question of his rights was one, however, which his death did not set at rest. On the 1st of June, 1824, Lord Brougham addressed the Commons with reference to what he conceived to be the flagrant violation of law in Mr. Smith's case. In the course of his remarks he said:[6]

> Suppose I were ready to admit that, on the pressure of a great emergency, such as invasion or rebellion, when there is no time for the slow and cumbrous proceedings of the civil law, a proclamation may justifiably be issued for excluding the ordinary tribunals, and directing that offences should be tried by a military court: such a proceeding might

6. Hansard HC Deb., Second Series, vol. 11, col. 976 (June 1, 1824).

be justified by necessity; but it could rest on that
alone. Created by necessity, necessity must limit its
continuance. It would be the worst of all conceiv-
able grievances—it would be a calamity unspeak-
able—if the whole law and Constitution of England
were suspended one hour longer than the most im-
perious necessity demanded. And yet martial law
was continued in Demerara for five months. In the
midst of tranquillity, that offence against the Constitution was perpetrated for months, which nothing but the most urgent necessity could warrant for
an hour. An individual in civil life, a subject of his
majesty, a clergyman, was tried at a moment of perfect peace, as if rebellion raged in the country. He
was tried as if he had been a soldier. I know that
the proclamation of martial law renders every man
liable to be treated as a soldier. But the instant the
necessity ceases, that instant the state of soldiership
ought to cease, and the rights, with the relations, of
civil life to be restored.

Sir James Mackintosh said:[7]

The only principle on which the law of England tolerates what is called martial [Law], is necessity: its
introduction can be justified only by necessity; its
continuance requires precisely the same justification of necessity; and if it survives the necessity on

7. Ibid., col. 1046–1049; see also *The Miscellaneous Works of the Right
Honourable Sir James Mackintosh* (New York: D. Appleton & Co., 1871),
540–41.

which alone it rests for a single minute, it becomes
instantly a mere exercise of lawless violence. When
foreign invasion or civil war renders it impossible
for courts of law to sit, or to enforce the execution
of their judgments, it becomes necessary to find
some rude substitute for them, and to employ, for
that purpose, the military, which is the only remaining force in the community. While the laws are si-
lenced by the noise of arms, the rulers of the armed
force must punish, as equitably as they can, those
crimes which weaken their own safety and that
of society: but no longer; every moment beyond,
is usurpation: as soon as the laws can act, every
other mode of punishing supposed crimes is itself
an enormous crime. If argument be not enough on
this subject; if, indeed, the mere statement be not
the evidence of its own truth; I appeal to the highest and most venerable authority known to our law.
"Martial law" says sir Matthew Hale, "is not a law,
but something indulged, rather than allowed, as a
law. The necessity of government, order, and discipline in an army, is that only which can give it
countenance. Necessitas, enim, quod cogit defendit. Secondly: this indulged law is only to extend
to members of the army, or to those of the opposite
army, and never may be so much indulged as to be
exercised or executed upon others. Thirdly: the exercise of martial law may not be permitted in time
of peace, when the King's courts are" (or may be)
"open." The illustrious judge on this occasion appeals to the Petition of Right, which, fifty years before, had declared all proceedings by martial law, in

time of peace, to be illegal. He carries the principle back to the cradle of English liberty, and quotes the famous reversal of the attainder of the Earl of Kent, in the first year of Edward the third, as decisive of the principle, that nothing but the necessity arising from the absolute interruption of civil judicatures by arms, can warrant the exercise of what is called martial law. Wherever, and whenever, they are so interrupted, and as long as the interruption continues, necessity justifies it. No other doctrine has ever been maintained in this country, since the solemn parliamentary condemnation of the usurpations of Charles 1st, which he was himself compelled to sanction in the Petition of Right. In none of the revolutions or rebellions which have since occurred, has martial law been exercised, however much, in some of them, the necessity might seem to exist. Even in those most deplorable of all commotions which tore Ireland in pieces in the last years of the eighteenth century; in the midst of ferocious revolt and cruel punishment; at the very moment of legalising these martial jurisdictions, in 1799, the very Irish statute which was passed for that purpose did homage to the ancient and fundamental principles of the law, in the very act of departing from them. The Irish statute 39 Geo. 3rd, c. 2, after reciting that martial law has been successfully exercised to the restoration of peace so far as to permit the course of the common law partially to take place, but that the rebellion continued to rage in considerable parts of the kingdom, whereby it has become necessary for parliament to interpose, goes on to enable the lord

lieutenant "to punish rebels by courts-martial."*
This statute is the most positive declaration, that,
when the common law can be exercised in some
parts of the country, martial law cannot be established in others, though rebellion actually prevails
in these others, without an extraordinary interposi-
tion of the supreme legislative authority itself.

I have already quoted from sir Matthew Hale
his position respecting the two-fold operation
of martial law, as it affects the army of the power
which exercises it, and as it acts against the army
of the enemy. That great judge happily unused to
standing armies, and reasonably prejudiced against
military jurisdiction, does not pursue his distinction through all its consequences, and assigns a
ground for the whole which will support only one
of its parts. "The necessity of order and discipline
in an army" is, according to him, the reason why
the law tolerates this departure from its most valuable rules; but this necessity only justifies the exercise of martial law over the army of our own state.
One part of it has since been annually taken out of
the common law; and provided for by the Mutiny
act, which subjects the military offences of soldiers
only to punishment by military courts, even in
time of peace. Hence we may now be said annually to legalize military law; which, however, differs
essentially from martial law, in being confined to

* This apparently refers to the Irish Parliament's acts for indemnity and
suppressing rebellion, 39 Geo. III c. 11 and 40 Geo. III c. 2. See *Index to Acts
in Force, Extending and Relating to Ireland* (London: C. Baldwin, 1829), 334.

offences against military discipline, and in not extending to any persons but those who are members
of the army.

Martial law exercised against enemies, or rebels, cannot depend on the same principle; for it is
certainly not intended to enforce or preserve discipline among them. It seems to me to be only a
more regular and convenient mode of exercising
the right to kill in war; a right originating in self-
defence, and limited to those cases where such killing is necessary, as the means of insuring that end.
Martial law put in force against rebels, can only be
excused as a mode of more deliberately and equitably selecting the persons from whom quarter ought
to be withheld, in a case where all have forfeited
their claim to it. It is nothing more than a sort of
better-regulated decimation, founded upon choice,
instead of chance, in order to provide for the safety
of the conquerors without the horror of undistin-
guished slaughter; it is justifiable only where it is
an act of mercy. Thus the matter stands by the law
of nations. But by the law of England it cannot be
exercised except where the jurisdiction of courts of
justice is interrupted by violence.

Mr. Tindal, afterwards Chief Justice, is reported to have said:[8]

Before the House could pronounce an opinion that
there had been a gross violation of law in the pro-

8. W. F. Finlason, *The History of the Jamaica Case* (London: Chapman
and Hall, 1869), lv–lvi; W. F. Finlason, *A Review of the Authorities as to the
Repression of Riot or Rebellion* (London: Stevens & Sons, 1868), 156–57. [Eds.

ceedings of the court-martial, it must found such an opinion upon one of these grounds—either that the court was without jurisdiction, or that the measure of punishment inflicted was too heavy, or that the conduct of the court was partial and unjust. He conceived that the court was competent to the performance of the duties imposed upon it, and to award the punishment of death in the case. He agreed that, as a court-martial under the Mutiny Act, it was only the proclamation of martial law which would justify it. But the proclamation of martial law at once superceded all civil process, and made it necessary that some other courts should be established in its stead.[9] It was asked whether it was to have an *ex post facto* operation, and whether under it all bygone offences were to be tried? Certainly not; it would not be lawful to try an offence committed at any previous time, when it had a character distinct and separate from the circumstances which occasioned the proclamation of martial law. But here the case was different, as the charge was a guilty knowledge of the meditated rebellion, and was it not too nice and subtle a distinction to say

---

note: Both of Finlason's works record this quotation, and the Liebers have drawn on the punctuation, paraphrasing, and (incorrect) citations Finlason gives for both. While they cite "Annual Register, 1832. p. 137," the correct citation is *Annual Register* (London: Baldwin and Cradock, 1825), 93. The order of the cases they discuss here also seems to be drawn from Finlason.]

9. And Sir G. Cockburn, then attorney general, maintained the same view in the Ceylon case, when he said that "where martial law is in force the ordinary criminal courts cease to have jurisdiction." Hansard HC Deb., Third Series, vol. 117, col. 246 (May 29, 1851). [Eds. note: This is paraphrased, not directly quoted.]

that it was a bygone offence, and not cognizable by
the court-martial, there being then, under martial
law, no other court, by which it could be tried?

The Attorney General (Copley)* remarked that: "with
respect to the proclamation of martial law, no person could
justify that measure, but upon the ground of absolute necessity, he admitted, that the doctrine laid down by lord Hale,
which had been already stated, was the correct law on the subject. Unless gentlemen, therefore, were satisfied, that a case of
necessity existed, no justification could be made out of [for]
that measure."[10]

Lord Brougham having moved an address to the King
condemning the proceedings in Demerara as illegal, and pray-
ing for the adoption of such measures as would protect the
persons concerned from oppression, the motion was, on the
11th of June, defeated by a vote of 146 ayes to 193 noes.

The next instance of martial Law which attracts our attention is what is known as the "Ceylon case." In 1848 a rebellion broke out in that island, the precise causes of which
it is also not necessary to enquire into.† Suffice it to say that

* **John Singleton Copley**, who served 1824–1826. Gareth H. Jones, "Copley, John Singleton, Baron Lyndhurst (1772–1863)," *Oxford Dictionary of
National Biography*, Oxford University Press, 2004; http://www.oxforddnb
.com/view/article/6272.

† This revolt originated largely among peasants in the central region
of Kandy, as a response to increasing British taxation and perceived disrespect for Buddhist temples and traditions, alongside anxieties over the
expansion of coffee plantations and the arrival of Indian indentured laborers to work them. The governor, George Byng (the seventh Viscount
Torrington) declared martial law, killing two hundred rebels while losing

10. Hansard HC Deb., Second Series, vol. 11, col. 1261 (June 11, 1824).

the Governor—Lord Torrington—was apprehensive that it
would become formidable unless summarily checked, and accordingly issued his proclamation of Martial Law. This act was
formally approved on the 24th of October of that year by the
Colonial Secretary, Earl Grey, and this approval was made the
occasion of an attack upon the ministry. The whole matter was
by the Commons referred to a select committee on Ceylon,
but, the committee having had it under consideration for two
years without any satisfactory result, Mr. H. Baillie,* on the
27th of May, 1851, again brought the subject to the attention of
the Commons in a speech which, although it seems generally
to have been overlooked, stands pre-eminent for its advanced
views. The duke of Wellington's remarks made in the course of
the debate on the Ceylon case have often been quoted, but he
spoke—and professedly so—only with regard to the *occupatio
bellica*.[†] Earl Grey[‡] however did not recognize the distinction.
"I was glad," he said, "to hear what the noble Duke said with
reference to what is the true nature of martial law. It is exactly
in accordance with what I myself wrote to my noble Friend

---

only one British soldier. In addition to the debate over martial law that the
Liebers trace here, Parliament also launched an inquiry into the rebellion's
causes—eventually repealing most of the contested taxes. See Sujit Sivasundaram, *Islanded: Britain, Sri Lanka, and the Bounds of an Indian Ocean
Colony* (Chicago: University of Chicago Press, 2013), 309–10; Nira Wick-
ramasinghe, *Sri Lanka in the Modern Age: A History of Contested Identities*
(Honolulu: University of Hawai'i Press, 2006), 35.

　　* **Henry Baillie** (a member of the House of Commons from Inverness).
See "Mr Henry Baillie," *Hansard 1803–2005, People*, http://hansard.millbank
systems.com/people/mr-henry-baillie/.

　　† Military occupation.

　　‡ **Henry George Grey** (the Colonial Secretary from 1846 to 1852). See
Peter Burroughs, "Grey, Henry George, third Earl Grey (1802–1894)," *Oxford
Dictionary of National Biography*, Oxford University Press, 2004, available at
http://www.oxforddnb.com/view/article/11540.

[Torrington] at the period of those transactions in Ceylon. I
am sure that was not wrong in law, for I had the advice of Lord
Cottenham, and Lord Campbell, and the Attorney General,*
and I explained to my noble Friend that what is called proclaiming martial law is no law at all, but merely, for the sake
of public safety in circumstances of great emergency, setting
aside all law, and acting under the military power; a proceeding which requires to be followed by an act of indemnity when
the disturbances are at an end."[11]

If the last sentence were true, it would at once dispose of
the whole question, and there would be no use in prosecuting
this investigation further. It may sometimes be convenient to
pass acts of indemnity when that which they are intended to
cover is not in itself illegal, but nevertheless exposes the persons doing it to prosecutions against which it is desirable to
guard them, but it cannot in that case be said that an act of indemnity is *required*. Such an act can only be *required* when the
proceeding was illegal. But if martial law is always illegal that
ends the question. No matter how imminent the danger it can
never become a duty to do an illegal act and run the chances

* **John Jervis**, who served from 1846 to 1850. Joshua S. Getler, "Jervis, Sir
John (1802–1856)," *Oxford Dictionary of National Biography*, Oxford University Press, 2004, available at http://www.oxforddnb.com/view/article/14795.

11. Hansard HC Deb., Third Series, vol. 115, col. 23–25 (March 17, 1851);
Hansard HL Deb., Third Series, vol. 115, col. 843–882 (April 1, 1851); Hansard
HC Deb., Third Series, vol. 117, col. 6–33 (May 27, 1851). [Eds. note: These
remarks came from the same debate on martial law referred to in Chapter I.
The Liebers' wording might leave the impression that Wellington and Grey
spoke in the same session as Baillie, but this is not the case. In fact, Bail-
lie's motion was discussed in the House of *Commons* on March 17, while
Wellington and Grey responded in the House of *Lords* on April 1. Baillie
then went on to give another speech on the topic of Ceylon in May—but the
Liebers mention only this speech, not the dates of the others.]

of an indemnifying act. Again, if illegal, it is not an undoubted prerogative, as Parliament had declared it to be. Singularly in advance of this erroneous conception of Martial Law were the views of the Baillie. It being one of the principal objects of this work to collect and present in a compact form the most important opinions which have been pronounced upon the subject of martial law, no excuse is made for the following liberal quotation from Mr. Baillie's remarks as reported in Hansard's Parliamentary Debates.[12]

> When the Ceylon Committee first commenced their inquiry, they thought it advisable to request the attendance of Her Majesty's Judge Advocate General,* in order that they might have the benefit of his great legal knowledge and experience; and in the course of the evidence which that right hon. Gentleman gave to the Committee, he stated it to be his opinion that martial law ought never to be imposed except in cases of the most extreme necessity; and that, he (Mr. Baillie) supposed, was an opinion from which no right-minded man would be inclined to differ. But the right hon. Gentleman the Judge Advocate General, went on to say that martial law was no law at all, that it was the absence of all law; but with every possible deference to the great legal knowledge of the right hon.

* **William Goodenough Hayter**, who served 1847–1849. G. C. Boase, "Hayter, Sir William Goodenough, first baronet (1792–1878)," rev. H. C. G. Matthew, *Oxford Dictionary of National Biography*, Oxford University Press, 2004, available at http://www.oxforddnb.com/view/article/12790.

12. Hansard HC Deb., Third Series, vol. 117, col. 16–17 (May 27, 1851).

Gentleman, he (Mr. Baillie) could not concur in
that interpretation, or rather in that definition, of
martial law, at least without great qualification. It
might be perfectly true that martial law, as they
usually understood it, might not be a written law.
No more was the common law of England a written
law. The common law of England was governed by
precedents, and so to a certain extent must martial law be governed by precedents. An officer employed in carrying out martial law would have no
more right to assume that the lives and fortunes of
Her Majesty's subjects might be dealt with according to his supreme will and pleasure than a Judge
in Westminster Hall had to assume that, because
he was the interpreter of the common law of England, he was at liberty to bend that common law
at his own will and pleasure, to the prejudice of the
people. There were two modes in which trials by
court-martial were to be conducted. The first was
when hostile armies were in the field, when war
was actually raging; then, indeed, trials took place
under martial which were very summary in their
nature.

Persons were sometimes tried by what was
termed a drumhead court-martial, sentenced and
executed upon the spot, without any appeal or reference to superior authority. This was a species of
Lynch-law, justified only by the necessities of the
case, and by the usages of war. That was one mode
sanctioned by precedent. Another case was when a
district of [a] country was placed under martial law
in consequence of a supposed disaffection or rebel-

lious spirit among the people. This might only be a measure of prevention, and the ordinary tribunals might or might not be suspended according to the necessity of the case, and according to all former precedent, whether upon the Continent or in England. Prisoners, under these circumstances, had always been allowed a fair trial by court-martial under the provisions of the Mutiny Act. They had been allowed judge-advocates to assist in their defense, the courts had been properly constituted, and the sentences, referred for approval to the Commander-in-Chief.

There was another mode of conducting trials when a city or district was placed under martial law, as was frequently done on the Continent as a supplementary measure of security. In this case the ordinary tribunals of the Country might be suspended or not, according to the necessity of the case. In 1814 the Duke of Wellington established martial law in the south of France; but then the ordinary tribunals of the country were not suspended, and the law was administered by the civil functionaries as usual. In the other case, namely, when the ordinary tribunals of the Country were suspended, the precautions to which he had adverted—the appointment of a judge-advocate and the transmission of the proceeding of courts-martial to the Commander-in-Chief for perusal, was always adopted. Such was the mode in which martial law was administered in Ceylon in the years 1817 and 1818, during the rebellion, when Sir Robert Brownrigg was

Governor.* On that occasion he issued a warrant
to certain officers of rank, commanding them to
hold courts-martial in their district. These warrants were accompanied by a letter of instructions, detailing the mode in which these trials
were to take place, in order to ensure a fair trial
to the accused. He (Mr. Baillie) did not mean to
say that, upon that occasion, some irregularities
were not committed; but if they were it was not
the fault of Sir Robert Brownrigg, but it was in
consequence of the misconduct of individual officers, who acted in direct violation of the orders
of the Commander-in-Chief. But in the present
case, what they complained of was, that all the irregularities which occurred were occasioned by
the orders of the Ceylon Government, and were
committed under the immediate sanction of the
Governor. For example, after the disturbances had
been suppressed, and when the country was quite
quiet, the Supreme Court was appointed to hold a
special session in the town of Kandy, for the trial
of persons engaged in these disturbances.

Simultaneously with the appointment of the
Supreme Court to hold these sessions, courts-

* **Robert Brownrigg**, who served as British governor on the multi-
religious island between 1811 and 1820, conquered the Sri Lanka's interior
in 1815 and deposed the monarchy of Kandy. Two years later, his appointment of the first Muslim as chief of the inland regions of Uva and Vellassa/
Wellassa spurred a rebellion in support of a claimant to the defunct throne.
Brownrigg's troops suppressed the revolt in a bloody year-long campaign.
See Sivasundaram, *Islanded*, 126–27, 212; Geoffrey S. Powell, "Brownrigg,
Sir Robert, first baronet (1759–1833), *Oxford Dictionary of National Biography*, Oxford University Press, 2004, available at http://www.oxforddnb.com/
view/article/3718.

martial were also appointed to assemble in the towns of Kandy, Kornegalle, and Matelle, for the trial of persons, many of whom were accused of high treason. &c &c.

A motion was made:[13]

That this House is of opinion, that the execution of eighteen persons, and the imprisonment, transportation and corporal punishment of one hundred and forty other persons on this occasion, is at variance with the merciful administration of the British Penal Laws, and is not calculated to secure the future affections and fidelity of Her Majesty's Colonial subjects:—That this House is of opinion, that these severities are the more sincerely to be deprecated as they were exercised after the suppression of the disturbances, during which none of Her Majesty's troops or public servants were killed, and only one soldier slightly wounded:—That this House is of opinion, that the conduct of the late Governor of Ceylon, in keeping in force Martial Law for two months, after his chief legal adviser had recommended its discontinuance, and during which period the Civil Courts were sitting without danger or interruption, and also his refusal to allow a short delay in the execution of a priest, at the request of the Queen's Advocate, who wished further investigation into the case, was in the highest degree arbitrary and oppressive:—That this House is

13. Hansard HC Deb., Third Series, vol. 117, col. 253–254 (May 29, 1851).

> therefore of opinion, that the conduct of Earl Grey, in signifying Her Majesty's approbation of the conduct of Lord Torrington during and subsequent to the disturbances, was precipitate and injudicious, tending to establish precedents of rigour and severity in the government of Her Majesty's Foreign Possessions, and injurious to the character of their Country for justice and humanity.

This motion passed in the negative.

So ended the Ceylon Case, and the subject of Martial Law can hardly be said to have been again prominently before the English people until 1865, when it was enforced in the Island of Jamaica. It then became for several years a fruitful topic of discussion. As a result of the questions raised we have two charges to grand juries—that of Mr. Justice Blackburn, in the Queen's Bench, on the prosecution of Governor Eyre, and that of the Chief Justice of England, at the Central Criminal Court, in the case of the Queen against Nelson and Brand, to which it will be necessary to invite attention. The Chief Justice (Lord Cockburn) gives in the latter charge the following sketch of the insurrection:[14]

> In the year 1865, a spirit of discontent and disaffection, and of hostility to the authorities, had manifested itself among the negro population in parts of the island of Jamaica. On the 7th of October, in the year 1865, some disturbance took place, on the occasion of a magisterial meeting, at

14. Frederick Cockburn, *Charge of the Lord Chief Justice* (London: William Ridgway, 1867), 4–8.

the Court House in Morant Bay. . . . [I]t seems to
have brought this insurrectionary spirit to a crisis.
Immediately after it the negroes in the neighbourhood were evidently in an excited state, and were
making preparations for an outbreak; so much so,
that on the 10th of October it was thought necessary by the local authorities to communicate with
the Governor [Eyre], and to apply to him for military assistance. On the 10th, warrants having been
issued against one or two of the persons who had
taken part in the disturbance on the 7th, upon
those warrants being attempted to be put into execution, forcible resistance was offered, and on the
11th, the insurgents, to the number of several hundreds, made their appearance, more or less in arms.
They attacked the Court House at Morant Bay, in
which a vestry meeting was being held. The volunteers came to the assistance of the magistrates,
but they were overpowered; the Court House
was stormed, no less than eighteen persons were
killed, and upwards of thirty wounded; and from
that moment the negro population in the neighbourhood was in a state of rebellious insurrection.
This spread itself rapidly. The insurgents attacked
the neighbouring estates, destroying property, in
two instances taking life, in others inflicting severe
wounds, in others seeking victims, who, however,
managed to escape, and declaring their intention
to destroy the male part of the white population,*

---

* Here the Liebers omit a footnote from the source: "They were reported
to have declared their intention to reserve the white women for a worse fate;
but as to this see note, p. 157, *post*." In the referenced note, Cockburn noted

and to take possession of all the property in the island. This state of things, as one would naturally
have expected, excited in the minds of the white
population the greatest consternation and alarm.
The military force in the island was but small; the
number of the white population small, very small,
in proportion to that of the black; and the result
was, of course, that terror and alarm pervaded the
whole island. Under these circumstances, the Governor, with the concurrence of a council of war,
which he was bound to call, and which he did call,
declared the county of Surrey—Morant Bay, where
this insurrection broke out, being in the county of
Surrey—under martial law, with the exception . . .
of the town of Kingston, which is the principal
town in that county.

A small military force of 100 men, which had
been dispatched in consequence of the application
made to the Governor on the 10th, was very soon
upon the scene of action, and was followed by other
troops; and the force so sent, although in point of
number comparatively small, was able at once to
suppress and crush this outbreak. The moment the
soldiers appeared in the field, the whole insurrection collapsed. The negroes everywhere fled, and
the only business of the military appears to have
been to pursue and take them, and when martial
law had been proclaimed, to bring them before the

---

that "the proof on which this charge against the insurgents rests is but slight."
Ibid., 5, 157–58.

military tribunals. Martial law was proclaimed by
the Governor upon the 13th of October.[15]

Mr. G. W. Gordon, a British subject . . .* was
generally believed by the authorities and by the
white population to have been the instigator of this
rebellion, and to be an accomplice of those who
were actually engaged in it. He resided generally
at a short distance from the town of Kingston, but
had a place of business at Kingston, and was there
for three or four days before his arrest.

Martial law had been proclaimed in the county
of Surrey, but Kingston had been specially excepted.
Warrants having been issued against Mr. Gordon,
and that fact having come to his knowledge, it appears that, on the 17th of October, he proceeded to
the house of the General in command of the Forces
in Jamaica, General O'Connor, at Kingston, for the
purpose of giving himself up. The Governor, and
the Custos of Kingston—the Custos being the title
of the principal magistrate in each of the parishes
of Jamaica—. . . came to the General's house, and
apprehended Mr. Gordon. They took him on board

* The Liebers omit a short discussion of Gordon's culpability, and this
paragraph is rearranged and paraphrased from Cockburn's discussion.

15. The proclamation contained the following language: "We do hereby,
by the authority to us committed by the laws of this our island, declare and
announce to all whom it may concern that martial law shall prevail throughout the said county of Surry, except in the city and parish of Kingston; and
that our military forces shall have all power of exercising the rights of belligerents against such of the inhabitants of the said county, except as aforesaid,
as our military forces may consider opposed to our government, and the
well-being of our loving subjects."

a war steamer; they conveyed him to Morant Bay, where he arrived on the evening of the 20th; and, on the day after his arrival, he was put upon his trial before a court-martial, ordered by . . . Colonel Nelson, who was at the time, with the title of Brigadier-General, in command of the troops which had been sent to Morant Bay for the purpose of suppressing this insurrection. The court-martial was composed of Lieutenant Brand . . . , a Lieutenant in her Majesty's Navy; of a Lieutenant Errington, also a Lieutenant in her Majesty's Navy; and of . . . Ensign Kelly, an officer in her Majesty's 6th West India Regiment. Before these officers Mr. Gordon was arraigned upon a charge of high treason, and of complicity with those who had broken out in rebellious insurrection against the Government at Morant Bay. Upon this charge he was found guilty and sentenced to be hanged. The sentence was sent for approval and ratification to Colonel Nelson. It was by him approved and ratified, but sent to his superior officer, the General commanding the Forces, General O'Connor, to be by him submitted to the Governor, to see whether the Governor would approve of the sentence, and of its being carried into effect. The Governor did approve of the sentence, and expressed his opinion that it ought to be carried into effect, and, accordingly, on the morning of Monday, the 23d, Mr. Gordon was hanged.

Lord Cockburn's statement of the facts in Gordon's case has been given in detail because of the prominence of that case, but it was by no means an isolated instance of trial by martial law at the time of this insurrection. On the contrary many other persons were thus tried, and many sentences executed, a very considerable number being capital,[16] and others severe punishments, and martial law was in fact kept in force for thirty days, which was the utmost limit to which it could be extended under a local Act then in force.[17]

On the 30th of December, 1865, the Queen appointed a Commission, consisting of Major General Sir Henry Knight Storks, Russell Gurney Esq., Recorder of London, and John Blossett Maule Esq., Recorder of Leeds, to inquire respecting the disturbances in Jamaica, and the measures taken in the course of their suppression. The result of this inquiry is to be found in two folio volumes printed by order of Parliament, to whom the report was submitted.

With regard to the proclamation of Martial Law the commissioners "were of opinion that" (in advising it) "the Council of War had good reason for the advice which they gave, and that the Governor was well justified in acting upon that advice."[18] In commenting upon the manner in which the trials by court-martial were conducted, (military commissions being unknown in English practice,) they say:

The number of executions by order of Courts-martial appeared to us so large that it became very

16. Three hundred fifty-four persons were put to death by sentence of courts martial.

17. Charge of Mr. Justice Blackburn in *Queen v. Eyre*. See W. F. Finlason, ed., *Report of the Case of the Queen v. Edward John Eyre* (London: Chapman and Hall, 1868).

18. "Report of the Jamaica Royal Commission, 1866," in *Papers Laid before the Royal Commission of Inquiry by Governor Eyre* (London: George Edward Eyre and William Spottswoode, 1866), 19.

important to ascertain, as far as we were able, the
principles upon which the members constituting
the Courts acted, and the sort of evidence upon
which their decisions were pronounced.

It would be unreasonable to expect that in the
circumstances under which these Courts were assembled there should be the same perfect regular-
ity and adherence to technical rules which we are
accustomed to witness in our ordinary tribunals;
but there are certain great principles which ought
under no circumstances to be violated, and there
is an amount of evidence which every tribunal
should require before it pronounces a judgment
which shall affect the life, liberty or person of any
human being. . . .[19]

The Commission found in a great majority of cases the evidence unobjectionable, but also cases in which the finding or
sentence were "not justified by any evidence appearing on the
face of the proceedings."

With reference to Gordon's case they found that "although . . . it appears exceedingly probable that Mr. Gordon,
by his words and writings, produced a material effect," &c &c,
yet they "could not see, in the evidence which had been adduced, any sufficient proof either of his complicity in the outbreak at Morant Bay, or his having been a party to a general
conspiracy against the Government."[20]

They then discuss the duration of martial law as follows:

19. Ibid., 27; see also W. F. Finlason, *Commentaries upon Martial Law,
with Special Reference to Its Regulation and Restraint* (London: Stevens &
Sons, 1867); 19–20.
20. "Report of the Jamaica Royal Commission," 38.

The number of persons concerned in the original outbreak, and in the deeds of violence by which it was accompanied and followed, was undoubtedly large; the number also of those who availed themselves of a time of disorder to plunder their neighbours was far larger; but the punishments inflicted seem to us to have been far greater than the necessity required. Nor can we shut our eyes to the fact that among the sufferers during the existence of martial law there were many who were neither directly or indirectly parties to the disturbances which it was the object of those placed in authority to suppress.

We fear that this to a certain extent must ever be the case when the ordinary laws, framed for the suppression of wrong-doing and the protection of the well-doer, are for a time suspended.

The circumstances which are supposed to render necessary their suspension are almost sure to be such as to excite both fear and passion; and some injustice, and we fear some cruelties will be certain at such times to be perpetrated; but we think that much which is now lamented might have been avoided if clear and precise instructions had been given for the regulation of the conduct of those engaged in the suppression, and every officer had been made to understand that he would be held responsible for the slightest departure from those instructions.

It does not seem reasonable to send officers upon a very difficult, and perfectly novel, service without any instructions, and to leave everything to their judgment.

But as under any circumstances, however carefully instructions may be prepared, and however implicitly obeyed, the evils of martial law must be very great, we are driven to consider whether martial law might not have been terminated at an earlier period than the expiration of the 30 days allowed by the statutes.

We know how much easier it is to determine this question after than before the event, and we are aware, too, that sometimes the success of the measures adopted for the prevention of an evil deprive the authors of those measures of the evidence they would otherwise have had of their necessity.

We have endeavoured therefore to place ourselves as far as is possible in the position of the Governor and his advisers at the time their determination was arrived at. It was not till the 21st of October that the Maroons marched to Torrington, which evidently was the stronghold of the insurgents, and which place, from the marks of preparation found there, it had been intended to defend.

After, however, firing a few shots, they fled at the approach of the Maroons, and on the following Monday, the 23^d Paul Boyle was apprehended with his few remaining followers, and on the 24th, was conveyed a prisoner to Morant Bay.

From this time it must have been clear to all that the rising in St. Thomas-in-the-East was put down, and that the only thing to be feared was simultaneous risings in other parts of the Island. The question to be considered in deciding upon the conduct of the Government is not whether such risings were in fact likely to take place, but whether the Government, with the information then in their hands, had reasonable grounds for apprehending that they might take place.

It will be seen that they were receiving almost daily reports from different parts of the Island, which must have led them to the conclusion that considerable danger of such risings existed. They could not at the time investigate, as we have, the grounds on which those reports rested.

They were forwarded by the custodes of different parishes, in whom the Government was bound to place a certain amount of confidence, and they would have incurred a serious responsibility if, with this information before them, they had thrown away the advantage of the terror which the very name of martial law is calculated to create in a population such as that which exists in this Island.

But there was a course which might have been pursued by which that advantage would have been secured, and yet many of the evils ordinarily attendant upon martial law avoided.

On the 30th of October it was formally stated by the Governor that the wicked rebellion lately existing in certain parts of the County of Surry had been subdued, and that the chief instigators thereof and actors therein had been visited with the punishment due to their heinous offences, and that he was certified that the inhabitants of the districts lately in rebellion were desirous to return to their allegiance.

From this day at any rate there could have been no necessity for that promptitude in the

execution of the law which almost precluded a
calm inquiry into each man's guilt or innocence.

Directions might and ought to have been
given that courts-martial should discontinue their
sittings; and the prisoners in custody should then
have been handed over for trial by the ordinary
tribunals.[21]

And the Commissioners arrived at the following conclusions amongst others:

That the disturbances in St. Thomas-in-the-East
had their immediate origin in a planned resistance
to lawful authority.

That praise is due to Governor Eyre for the
skill, promptitude, and vigour which he manifested
during the early stages of the insurrection; to the
exercise of which qualities its speedy termination is
in a great degree to be attributed.

That by the continuance of martial law in its
full force to the extreme limit of its statutory operation the people were deprived for a longer than the
necessary period of the great constitutional privileges by which the security of life and property is
provided for.

That the punishments were excessive.

1) That the punishment of death was unneces-
sarily frequent.

2) That the floggings were reckless, and at
Bath positively barbarous.

21. Ibid., 39–40.

3) That the burning of 1000 houses was wanton and cruel.[22]

In one case, to which the Commissioners called attention, a prosecution for murder was attempted against a provost-marshal who, without orders from superior authority and apparently without justification, had caused a man to be hanged. This prosecution elicited from a colonial judge, Mr. Justice Ker, the following exposition of the principles of Martial Law. After saying that the act would have been murder under the ordinary law, he continues:—

Does the prevalence of martial law, then—of the temporary suspension and setting aside of ordinary law—make any difference? Undoubtedly it does. The object of martial law being the repression of insurrection, and the restoration of law and order, whatever is necessary towards that end is permitted, even to the destruction of human life. Martial law is the recurrence to physical force for the bringing about of a result beyond the scope and capabilities of the ordinary law, the ordinary law requiring, as one of its distinguishing peculiarities, a certain amount of delay and compliance with certain forms.

Unless they were for the time dispensed with revolt would gain head, and eventually, perhaps, triumph. It is requisite, therefore, that it should be temporarily suspended. Acts, accordingly, which in

22. Ibid., 41. [Eds. note: The Liebers omit many of the commission's conclusions.]

other circumstances would be unlawful, are now
held justified by the special exigency of the case.
Cases are judged rather by their own peculiar circumstances than by references to more than a few
great leading rules and principles. Nor will the law
scrutinize too closely particular acts, if only, without violating any of those rules and principles, they
forwarded or tended to forward the great end of
martial law—the suppression of armed outbreak.
It is manifest that every government must, in the
interest of those under its care, possess the power
of resorting to force in the last extremity. The want
of such a power would place the very existence of
the state at the mercy of organized conspiracy. The
public safety, therefore, which is the ultimate cause,
confides to the supreme authority in every country
the power to declare when the emergency has arisen.
But martial law, though it dispenses with the forms
and delays which appertain to ordinary criminal
jurisdiction, does not, therefore, authorize or sanction every deed assumed to be done in its name. It
stops far short of that. For if it did not, lawless men,
under colour and pretense of authority, might commit acts abhorrent to humanity, and might gratify
malice and revenge, hatred, and ill-will. No greater
error exists than to suppose that the subjecting of a
district to military power authorizes excess on the
part of those who administer that power. Deeply,
therefore, is it in the interest of the public welfare
that it should be understood what martial law sanc-
tions, and what it does not. It allows, in one word,
everything that is necessary towards putting down

resistance to lawful authority. It further requires that the acts of its members should be honest and *bona fide*. And it further fastens a condition upon its agents that their acts should be adjudged to be necessary in the judgment of a moderate and reasonable man. Reason and common sense must approve the particular act. It is not sufficient that the party should unaffectedly believe such and such an act to be called for, the belief must be reasonably entertained, and such as a person of ordinary understanding would not repudiate.

If these conditions are not fulfilled, the act becomes unlawful, with all the consequences attending to illegality. It then takes rank with those acts to which the privilege and protection of martial law are not allowed.

The vindictive passions are prohibited as absolutely during military rule as in the most orderly and tranquil condition of human affairs. Excess and wantonness, cruelty and unscrupulous contempt for human life, meet with no sanction from martial law any more than from ordinary law. No amount of personal provocation will justify or excuse vindictive retaliation. Were it otherwise, an institution which, though stern, is yet beneficial, would degenerate into an instrument of mere private malice and revenge.[23]

Governor Eyre was recalled, but when the report of the Commissioners was presented, public interest in the subject,

23. Finlason, *Review of the Authorities*, 168–69.

says Mr. Finlason, had been almost exhausted, especially as it appeared at the same time with a change of ministry.

Under an Act of Parliament "for the trying and punishing in Great Britain persons holding employment for offences committed abroad,"[24] prosecutions were however attempted against Governor Eyre, for illegally proclaiming and enforcing Martial Law, and against Colonel Nelson and Lieutenant Brand for their part in the trial and execution of Gordon. The indictments in both cases were ignored, but the views expressed by Chief Justice Cockburn and Mr. Justice Blackburn in their charges to the Grand Juries deserve careful consideration. Several points came up in connection with the Jamaica Insurrection which have no practical application in this country, and these remarks will therefore be restricted to so much of the charges of these distinguished lawyers as relates to the subject of Martial Law in general.

Lord Cockburn says:[25]

> The execution of persons taken in arms, or taken in pursuit, and put to death as rebels, is not in question here.[26] [. . .] What we are considering is whether, for the suppression of a rebellion, you may subject persons not actively engaged in it, and whom you therefore cannot kill on the spot, to an anomalous and exceptional law, and try them for their lives without the safeguards which the law ought to afford. We may therefore dismiss the cases in which

24. Criminal Jurisdiction Act 1802, 42 Geo. III c. 85.
25. Cockburn, *Charge of the Lord Chief Justice*, 84–86. [Eds. note: The Liebers omit a number of lines here.]
26. The fallacy of this view has already been remarked upon.

it is permitted to put men to death without process of law, as altogether foreign to the purpose, and come back to the question as to what martial law in the proper sense of the term really is.

Two views are put forward: the one that martial law applied to the civil subject is neither more nor less than the law applicable to the soldier applied to the civilian. . . . The other is, that while the law martial—as Coke, and Hale, and Blackstone call it—or, as it is the fashion now-a-days to term it, the military law—as applicable to the soldier, is a precise, accustomed, and well-defined law, martial law, when applied to the civilian, is no law at all, but a shadowy, uncertain, precarious something, depending entirely on the conscience, or rather on the despotic and arbitrary will, of those who administer it.

Then, after giving a short sketch of the development of military law, and of the courts administering it—remarking with reference to courts-martial, that "perhaps there are no tribunals in the world in which justice is administered with a higher sense of the obligation which the exercise of judicial functions imposes, with a higher sense of honour, or a greater desire to do justice"[27]—he continues:

Now, if such be the law as applied to the soldier, why should it not be the law applicable to the civilian? Why are we to be told that when you come to deal with a civilian by martial law, it is to be

27. Cockburn, *Charge of the Lord Chief Justice*, 99.

something different from the martial law which is applied to the soldier? I confess myself at a loss for any reason that can be given for that assertion, and certainly before I adopt the doctrine that a law, if it may be called a law, of the uncertain and arbitrary character which martial law is said to be, can be administered in this country, and that Englishmen can be tried for their lives under it, I shall require something more than assertion unsupported by authority. Of this I am perfectly sure—namely, that in those repertories of the law of England which have been compiled by the sages and fathers of the law, and which have been handed down to us with the sanction of their great names, to inform us, and those who are to come after us in future ages, what the law of England was and is, no authority for anything of the sort can be found.

No one, says Lord Cockburn, can deny the power of Parliament to enact that Martial Law shall be put in force.[28] So far as the power of the Crown to resort to it is concerned, he is unconvinced. The opinion of so eminent a lawyer is entitled to great weight; and this charge is interesting in its historical details, instructive in its interpretation of authorities, and suggestive of many important points, but as an exposition of the law it is not decisive. Lord Cockburn does not say—there is no such thing as Martial Law by virtue of the prerogative; he only says—the arguments hitherto advanced in support of it fail to convince him, and he awaits further proof. The extracts above given do not, indeed, show a true conception of what

28. Ibid., 53.

Martial Law really is. "Why," he says, "are we to be told that
when you come to deal with a civilian by martial law, it is to
be something different from the martial law which is applied
to the soldier?"[29] The answer is—such is not the case. The soldier is always subject to military law—the law put forth for the
government of the army, and having for its object the maintenance of military discipline. To this law the civilian is not subject. But when in time of war the necessity arises and martial
law is put in force, it covers with its jurisdiction the soldier as
well as the civilian. The soldier is still subject to military law,
but in addition thereto he may then also become amenable
to a different law—equally applicable to him and the civilian.
Martial Law does not in England spring from the Mutiny Act.
It may there come into existence by virtue of a legislative act—
but, in the absence of legislation, it must exist by virtue of the
prerogative, when called forth by necessity.

Mr. Justice Blackburn was also very cautious in charging
the Grand Jury on the subject of Martial Law in the case of the
Queen v. Eyre. He said:[30]

Now you, all of you, know, that by the laws of this
country, beginning at Magna Charta and getting
more and more established, down to the time of
the Revolution, when it was finally and completely
established, the general rule was that a subject was
not to be tried or punished, except by due course
of law; all crimes are to be determined by juries,

29. Ibid., 99.
30. Finlason, *Report of the Case,* 69–75. [Eds. note: Finlason quotes the
same statement, with somewhat different punctuation and wording, in *Review of the Authorities,* 213–15.]

subject to the guidance of the judge: that is the general rule, and is established law. But from the earliest times there was this, also which was the law, and is the law still, that when there was a foreign invasion or an insurrection, it was the duty of every good subject, in obedience to the officers and magistrates, to resist the rebels, and for the purpose of resisting them the executive officer could call them out, and, in point of fact, raise an army in order to fight them. In modern times that has become of little consequence, because we have, under the Mutiny Acts, and the Militia Statute and others, an armed force which can be raised and subject to the control of the law according to the statutes; and it is of very little practical consequence now, but in old times, in the age of Magna Charta, which was finally confirmed by Henry III.; during all the barons' wars, and afterwards, when there was no regular army, when there was an insurrection, to meet it, there were persons intrusted with Commissions of Array from the Crown to raise an army to fight the insurgents. As to that, everybody must feel at once that an armed force that was only to be punished by juries would be an intolerable nuisance, and could not be endured at all. Consequently, the prerogative was claimed by the Crown, that the Crown by its prerogative might direct that its armed force should be kept in order by summary process; not by a despotism which would authorise its officers to kill anyone they pleased, but summary process, not waiting for the ordinary process of the common law, to keep the soldiers in order;

and in that sense there was a martial law, terribly liable to be abused no doubt, but which Lord Hale has said, in a passage frequently quoted, was tolerated and excused because it was really the absence of all law; and that prerogative existed certainly, I think, in time of war, and the Crown had that prerogative over that armed force which it had gathered together for the purpose of fighting the enemy, whether a foreign enemy or an army in insurrection; and to that extent I think the Crown had the power to exercise martial law in time of war, and in time of war only. Further than that, there was what comes on very debateable ground indeed: in such a case as that of insurrection prevailing so far that the courts of law cannot sit, there must really be anarchy unless there is some power to keep the people in order. Supposing an invading army, for instance, took possession of Dover, and an English army lay opposite to them, you could have no Court of Quarter Sessions sitting in Kent and no Assizes there: and really unless you were to have some power to keep order there would be total anarchy. Upon that principle, the Crown claimed the prerogative in those early times (most fortunately now we have not the occasion to consider this question at all) to exercise summary proceedings by martial law, as they called it, in time of war, when this disturbance was going on, over others than the army. And further than that, the Crown made this further claim against the insurgents, that whilst it existed, pending the insurrection, and for a short time afterwards, the Crown had, and *de facto* exercised, the power to proclaim martial law, in the sense of using summary proceedings, to punish the insurgents; and to check and stop the spread of the rebellion by summary proceedings against the insurgents, so as, to adopt a modern phrase, "to stamp out the rebellion." Now no doubt the extent to which the Crown had power to do that has never been yet decided. Our law has been declared from time to time, and has always been a practical science; that is, the judges have decided so much as was necessary for the particular case, and that has become part of the law. But it never has come to be decided what this precise power is. The Crown did in fact exercise that power to some extent, at least in time of war, and in a way which was productive frequently of immense oppression. . . .*

I think, therefore, it would be an exceedingly wrong presumption to say that the Petition of Right, by not condemning martial law in time of war, sanctioned it, still it did not in terms condemn it.

There never has been since that time any case in which it has become necessary to consider judicially what were the limits of the powers of the prerogative in time of war. This much, I think, I may safely say, that in time of peace the Crown has no such power. Lord Hale, in a work, I believe, never published by him, but found amongst his papers after his death, "The Analysis of the Law," says the Crown, by its prerogative, has the power of punish-

* The Liebers omit a significant discussion of martial law under Queen Elizabeth I.

ing rebels "during the rebellion, but not after." I am quoting from memory, but I think that is it, and then, in a passage which you find often quoted in his "History of the Common Law," he in effect says "Martial law is that which is the absence of all law, tolerated for necessity, where necessity requires it, but confined strictly to the army on the part of the Crown and those who are against them." That is the substance, but it would seem he had changed his mind somewhat during that time, and he has put down very different views. Then, when he came to publish his great work, "The Pleas of the Crown," his deliberately and carefully prepared work, he was very cautious indeed. In a passage which has been cited, 1st vol. p. 347, he puts it, after citing the case of the Earl of Lancaster, "From this record it will appear that in time of peace the Crown cannot enforce martial law"; and further, that *"regularly,* when the King's Courts are open it is a time of peace in judgment of laws."[31] He is very cautious, you will observe, and puts it there in this way, and that is certainly the opinion I have come to myself, that it has not been quite settled what is the Crown's prerogative in such cases, and what not. But I think this much is settled, that it is by no means that unbounded, wild, and tyrannical prerogative which

31. Matthew Hale, *The History of the Pleas of the Crown* (London: Nutt and Gosling, 1736), 1: 347. [Eds. note: The first quotation differs from Hale's statement: "in time of peace no man ought to be adjudged to death for treason, or any other offense without being arraigned and put to answer." Later on he also writes that in the Earl of Lancaster's case, "the exercise of martial law in point of death in time of peace is declared murder." Ibid., 500.]

some persons have lately been saying that it is. It must, if it exist at all, be strictly limited to necessity, and I think you cannot doubt that Mr. Eyre, in keeping up martial law, for thirty days; after all armed resistance had been put down in a day or two,—so that there was really a period of three or four weeks after all armed resistance had ceased, when it would have been quite practicable to try any óne by the ordinary tribunals; there can be no reasonable doubt that he did exceed much that would be authorised on the most extended view of the prerogative. To that extent, [I think, I am bound to go; more than that,] I think is unnecessary in this case.

Beyond what I have said I will leave the case to be decided when it arises, without being biased by any weight of authority that might be attached to what I say, but to that extent, I think, I am bound to express an opinion. Therefore, if it stood solely and entirely on the question of what was the power which Mr. Eyre had in exercising the common law prerogative of the Crown, I think I should be obliged to say to you that, though there might be very good reasons for an Act of Indemnity or for a pardon, that you must find this bill.

CHAPTER VII

Martial Law in U.S. History*

artial Law was twice proclaimed by the English during the American Revolution—once by General Gage at Boston, June 12th, 1775, and once by Governor Dunmore in Virginia, on the 7th of November of the same year. It met in both cases with severe denunciation from the American people. Whether legally or illegally enforced, it is however true that it has always been denounced by those who were under its immediate operation.

The arraignment of the King of England in the Declaration of Independence has also been referred to, showing that the men, who were willing to go to war on the issues there

---

* The material denominated here as Chapter VII appears at this point in the manuscript in the National Archives, but is not denominated with a chapter number. It is chronologically and conceptually prior to the material in the next chapter, here denominated as Chapter VIII, and so we have characterized it as Chapter VII. Guido Norman Lieber later published some of this material (including minor quotation errors corrected here) under the title "Martial Law during the Revolution," *The Magazine of American History with Notes and Queries* (New York: A. S. Barnes & Company, 1877), 1: 538–41.

made, could never have admitted the truth of the principles involved in a proclamation of Martial Law. There is no stronger proof that it is a necessary accompaniment of war than the fact that our fore-fathers were themselves compelled to resort at the very beginning and throughout to it in the revolution. Thus we find the Congress of 1775 adopting (November 7th) the following resolution:

> All persons convicted of holding a treacherous correspondence with, or giving intelligence to the enemy, shall suffer death, or such other punishment as a general court-martial shall think proper.[1]

And December 27th, 1776, the following:

> *Resolved,* . . . The unjust, but determined, purpose of the British court to enslave these free states, obvious through every [delusive insinuation to the contrary],* having placed things in such a situation, that the very existence of civil liberty now depends on the right execution of military powers, and the vigorous, decisive conduct of these, being impossible to distant, numerous, and deliberative bodies: This Congress, having maturely considered the present crisis; and having perfect reliance on the wisdom, vigor, and uprightness of general Washington, do, hereby,

* These five words are illegible in the manuscript but interpolated from the source.

1. *Journal of the Proceedings of the Congress, Held at Philadelphia, May 10, 1775* (London: J. Almon, 1776), 113.

Resolve, that general Washington shall be, and he is hereby, vested with full, ample, and complete powers to raise and collect together, in the most speedy and effectual manner, . . . 16 battalions of infantry . . . [, &c]; to take, wherever he may be, whatever he may want for the use of the army, if the inhabitants will not sell it, allowing a reasonable price for the same; to arrest and confine persons who refuse to take the continental currency, or are otherwise disaffected to the American cause, and return to the states of which they are citizens, their names, and the nature of their offences, together with the witnesses to prove them.[2]

Here, therefore, we have a clear recognition of the necessity of Martial Law. The resolution empowers General Washington to do certain acts under it. At first sight it might perhaps seem that the authorized seizure of private property was an exercise of the right of *eminent domain*, but such is not the case. Washington was empowered to take whatever he might want, meaning, evidently, whatever might be necessary. It was

2. *Journals of the American Congress: From 1774 to 1788* (Washington, D.C.: Way and Gideon, 1823), 1: 584–85. [Eds. note: Many slightly varying editions of this letter were published before the Liebers wrote, but none match the precise wording or punctuation of the Liebers' quotation. It has been corrected here to match one edition which is close to their usage, and which might have been available to them. The deleted portions of the quotation, detailing other measures to support the Continental Army, were noted elsewhere on a scrap of paper kept with the manuscript. Much of this section also seems to draw on David Dudley Field's arguments for Lambdin Milligan at the Supreme Court in *Ex parte Milligan*, 71 U.S. (4 Wall.) 2 (1866); see D. F. Murphy, ed., "Appendix," in *Argument of David Dudley Field, Esq. for the Petitioners, March 12 and 13, 1866* (New York: William J. Reed, 1866).]

the law of necessity[3] applied in war to the country to which the army belonged—*i.e.* Martial Law Proper. When a house is blown up to prevent the spread of a conflagration, that is an application of the law of necessity. So when property is taken *flagrante bello* for the necessary uses of the army, it is an exercise of the war power under the law of necessity—not of the right of eminent domain.

On the 8th of October, 1777, Congress adopted the following resolution, which was only to remain in force until January 1st, 1778, but was extended by a resolution of December 29th:

> Whereas, it is of essential consequence to the general welfare that the most effectual measures should be forthwith pursued for cutting off all communication of supplies or intelligence to the enemy's army now in, and near the city of Philadelphia; and whereas, it has been found by the experience of all States that, in times of invasion, the power of the municipal law is too feeble and dilatory to bring to a condign and exemplary punishment persons guilty of such traitorous practices:
>
> *Resolved*, That any person, being an inhabitant of any of these States, who shall act as a guide or pilot by land or water for the enemy, or shall give or send intelligence to them, or in any manner furnish them with supplies of provisions, money,

3. The distinction between the law of "overruling necessity" and the right of eminent domain is discussed in William Lawrence, "The Laws of War. The Constitution and the War Power. The Liability of the Government to Pay War Claims," *American Law Register* 13, no. 22 (January–December 1874): 265–84, 337–45.

clothing, arms, forage, fuel, or any kind of stores, be
considered and treated as an enemy and traitor to
these United States; and that General Washington
be empowered to order such persons, taken within
thirty miles of any city, town, or place in the States
of Pennsylvania, Jersey, or Delaware, which is, or
may be in the possession of the enemy's forces, to
be tried by a court-martial, and such court-martial
are hereby authorized to sentence any such persons
convicted before them of any of the offences aforesaid to suffer death or such other punishment as to
them shall seem meet.[4]

Under this resolution one Joseph Murill, an inhabitant
of Pennsylvania, was tried for giving intelligence, and acting as a guide to the enemy, found guilty, and sentenced to
be executed. General Washington, in an order issued from his
Headquarters at Valley Forge, in 1778, approved the sentence,
and ordered it to be carried into effect. Murill's execution was,
however, subsequently indefinitely postponed.[5]

On the 3[d] of April, 1778, Washington also approved and
ordered the execution of the sentence of William Morganan, an inhabitant of Pennsylvania, who had been convicted,

4. Murphy, "Appendix," 64–65. [Eds. note: Similarities in punctuation
and wording suggest that the Liebers drew this quotation from Field's argument in *Milligan*. For the resolution itself, see *Journals of the American
Congress*, 2: 281.]

5. "Appendix," 64–65. [Eds. note: Here again the Liebers are quoting from
Field's *Milligan* argument rather than from the originals. For Washington's
orders, see Henry Whiting, ed., and John Whiting, *Revolutionary Orders of
General Washington, Issued during the Years 1778, '80, '81, & '82* (New York:
Wiley and Putnam, 1844), 25–27.]

under the same resolution, of coming out of Philadelphia and attempting to steal and carry back a horse. The sentence in this case was, "to be kept at hard labor during the contest with Great Britain, not less than thirty miles from the enemy's camp, and if he is caught making his escape, to suffer death."[6]

Orders dated March 25th, and April 13th, 1778, approve the sentences in several similar cases, none, however, being capital.[7] Again, on the 27th of February, 1778, Congress resolved:

> That whatever inhabitant of these states shall kill or seize, or take any loyal citizen or citizens thereof, and convey him, [her,] or them, to any place within the power of the enemy, or shall enter into any combination for such purpose, or attempt to carry the same into execution, or hath assisted or shall assist therein; or shall, by giving intelligence, acting as a guide, or in any other manner whatever, aid the enemy in the perpetration thereof, he shall suffer death by the judgment of a court-martial, as a traitor, assassin, and spy, if the offence be committed

6. "Appendix," 66; *Revolutionary Orders*, 49–50. [Eds. note: According to the order, Morganan had completed the theft of the horse, so "attempting" applied only to carrying it off.]

7. "Appendix," 65, 67; *Revolutionary Orders*, 39. [Eds. note: In the earlier order, Abel Jones of Pennsylvania was sentenced to hard labor for trading with and supplying the enemy, and passing counterfeit currency; five other Pennsylvanians—Matthew Tilson, Henry Norrice, Thomas Bailey, John Campbell, and Jesse Harburn—were sentenced to one month's service and restitution; and two soldiers, Thomas Coskel and Samuel Burris, were sentenced to be whipped for attempting to desert to the enemy. In the later order, Philip Calp was sentenced to fifty lashes and to "be employed on some public works," for trying to carry flour into the city of Philadelphia.]

within 70 miles of the headquarters of the grand or
other armies of these states, where a general officer
commands.[8]

The effect of this Resolution—and it did not escape observation at the time—was to suspend, for instance in Boston
and other parts of Massachusetts, which were not the seat of
war, but were within seventy miles of Providence, where a general officer commanded a small army, the judicial authority
of the state in particular cases, and to subject criminals to a
trial by court-martial instead of leaving them to the laws of
the state.

It was under this Resolution that Joshua H. Smith was
tried, before a court-martial which assembled September
30th, 1780 for complicity with Major André.* After André's

* **Major John André** (1750–1780) was a British army officer who, dur-
ing the War of American Independence, conspired with the American spy
General Benedict Arnold to betray the fortress at West Point, New York, to
the British. In September 1780, he left the British headquarters in New York
City and went up the Hudson River, aboard the ship *Vulture*, to meet with
Arnold. American forces captured him, while he was in disguise, and he was
quickly tried and hanged. See John Fabian Witt, *Lincoln's Code: The Laws of
War in American History* (New York: Free Press, 2012), 24–25; Richard Gar-
nett, "André, John (1750–1780)," rev. Troy O. Bickham, *Oxford Dictionary of
National Biography* (Oxford University Press, 2004), available at http://www
.oxforddnb.com/view/article/512.

8. *Journals of the American Congress*, 459–60. [Eds. note: Based on the
punctuation and wording of their draft, the Liebers seem to have drawn this
quotation from the arguments of John Bingham in the trial of those accused
of conspiring to assassinate Abraham Lincoln. See *Argument of John A.
Bingham* (Washington: Government Printing Office, 1865), 28. The female
pronoun placed in brackets in the quotation appears in the original *Journals*
in 1778. It also appears in Bingham's quotation from it in 1865. The Liebers
dropped it in their post–Civil War draft.]

first interview with Arnold, he did not return to the *Vulture*, sloop of war, which had taken him up the river, but went to Smith's house where he spent a night and a day. Smith went on board the *Vulture* on a mission from André, and when the latter started on his fatal trip he wore a suit of Smith's clothes. The court-martial being of opinion that it had jurisdiction under the Resolution of February 27th, 1778, the following charge was exhibited against Smith:

> [F]or aiding and assisting Benedict Arnold, late a major general in our service, in a combination with the enemy, for the purpose of taking, seizing and killing such of the loyal citizens and soldiers as were in garrison at West Point and its dependencies.[9]

The finding of the court was, that

> The evidence produced on the trial and the prisoner's defence being fully and maturely considered by the court, they are of opinion, that notwithstanding it appears to them, that the said Joshua H. Smith did aid and assist Benedict Arnold, late major general in our service, who had entered into a combination with the enemy for the purposes which the charge mentions, yet they are of opinion, that the evidence is not sufficient to convict the said Joshua H. Smith

9. Joshua Hett Smith and Anna Seward, *An Authentic Narrative of the Causes Which Led to the Death of Major André* (London: Mathews and Leigh, 1808), 201–2. [Eds. note: Based on the punctuation and word choice in the quotation, the Liebers seem to have drawn it from Smith's and Seward's works. However, in their original footnote they instead cited a newer work, which reproduced the quote differently: Peleg W. Chandler, *American Criminal Trials* (Boston: Charles C. Little and James Brown, 1844), 2: 189.]

of his being privy to, or having a knowledge of the said Benedict Arnold's criminal, traitorous and base designs. They are, therefore, of opinion, that the said Joshua H. Smith is not guilty of the charge exhibited against him, and do acquit him [of it].[10]

Washington subsequently delivered over the prisoner to the government of New York with a view to his trial by civil process if deemed advisable, but whilst thus held he effected his escape, and was not recaptured.

Shays' Rebellion in Massachusetts, and the Whiskey Insurrection in Pennsylvania, were not cases of martial law, but were put down by the military power acting in subordination to, and in aid of, the civil.*

* Shays' Rebellion took place in 1786 and early 1787 in western Massachusetts, where indebted farmers were frustrated by the state government's refusal to enact debt relief measures. Led by Daniel Shays, agrarian protesters shut down courts in the western half of the state to stop the collection of debts. The state militia responded with force and routed the rebellion. Nonetheless, men like Alexander Hamilton and James Madison went to Philadelphia for the Constitutional Convention a year later committed to addressing the "excess of popularity" and the "unruly temper of the people" that Shays' Rebellion had revealed. See Michael J. Klarman, *The Framers' Coup: The Making of the United States Constitution* (New York: Oxford University Press, 2016), 86–101. The Whiskey Rebellion broke out eight years later, in 1794, in western Pennsylvania, and spread to western Maryland and the back country of Virginia and Kentucky. As the name implied, the rebellion was directed at federal officials who collected excise taxes on liquor. The Whiskey Rebellion reflected anxieties over the new federal government's authority, and it echoed the tensions between the eastern (coastal) and western (inland) regions that had appeared in Shays' Rebellion. President George Washington suppressed the rebels by taking personal command of an army roughly the same size as he had commanded in the War of Independence. See Thomas P. Slaughter, *Whiskey Rebellion: Frontier Epilogue to the American Revolution* (New York: Oxford University Press, 1986).

10. Chandler, *American Criminal Trials*, 2: 264.

Thus we find Martial Law at that time distinctly recognized and enforced. It was, indeed, called into action by Congress but the reason of that was that there was no central executive holding the war power. Under the political system then in operation that power was in Congress. But, it was, nevertheless, an exercise (whether justifiable or not) of the same war power which, under the Constitution of the United States, has been confided by [Article 2, section 2] to the President as Commander-in-Chief.

The war of 1812 furnishes several instances of the application of Martial Law. The first to be mentioned is Stacy's case.[11] In July, 1813, a *habeas corpus* was, by a commissioner of the Supreme Court of the State of New York, directed to Isaac Chauncey, Commandant of the Navy of the United States on Lake Ontario, and Morgan Lewis, commanding the troops at Sacket's harbor, and all under them, requiring them to produce one Samuel Stacy. To this General Lewis returned that the prisoner was not in his custody. Royal Torrey, provost-marshal returned a copy of the order upon which he held the prisoner, signed by the Assistant Adjutant General of the command, the headquarters of which were at Sacket's Harbor, and directing him to receive such prisoner from Commodore Chauncey, he being charged with high treason committed in the territory of Great Britain.[12]

Chief Justice Kent delivered the opinion of the Supreme Court of New York* before which the matter came on a motion

---

* Note that as in Lieber's time and in ours, Chief Justice Kent's Supreme Court was a trial court of general jurisdiction, not the state's highest court.

11. *In re Stacy*, 10 Johns. 328 (N.Y. 1813).
12. See Joel Parker, *Habeas Corpus and Martial Law: A Review of the Opinion of Chief Justice Taney in the Case of John Merryman* (Cambridge:

for an attachment or a rule to show cause why an attachment should not issue, against General Lewis, Torrey, &c. He said that the return of Gen. Lewis was evasive; that he should have returned that the prisoner was not in his possession or power; that it was contradicted by the return of the provost-marshal; that the affidavit of the officer who served the writ showed that it was intentionally disregarded; and that the attachment—being process to bring the party to answer for alleged contempt—should be immediately awarded. And he added:

> The pretended charge of treason, (for upon the facts before us we must consider it as a pretext,) without being founded upon oath, and without any specification of the matters of which it might consist, and without any color of authority in any military tribunal to try a citizen for that crime, is only aggravation of the oppression of the confinement.[13]

Of this case Judge Parker remarks that the attention of the court does not seem to have been directed to the question whether the existence of war at that time could have had any effect upon the right of the military power to arrest and hold, and as Gen. Lewis did not claim the right to be exempt from the operation of the *habeas corpus*, he may be said to have waived it. "[I]t is not to be inferred," he says, "that no distinction exists in respect to the duty of obedience to the writ of *habeas corpus* in time of war and in time of peace, merely

---

Welch, Bigelow, and Company, 1861), 17. [Eds. note: The Liebers' account of Stacy's case is very closely paraphrased from Parker's.]

13. *In re Stacy*, 10 Johns. at 333.

because that distinguished tribunal failed to make one, when
its attention was not called to the subject."[14]

The next case deserving attention is that of *Smith v.
Shaw*, 12 Johns. 257 (N.Y. 1815) which grew out of the same
war. Shaw, a naturalized citizen of the United States brought
an action in New York against General Smith, an officer in
the military service of the United States, for assault and battery, and false imprisonment. At the trial in July, 1814, it was
proved that Shaw was arrested by two military officers, and,
after being kept in confinement for a certain time at Sacket's
Harbor, where General Smith was in command, was released
by him. This case was carried up to the Supreme Court of New
York on error, the defendant below having offered to prove
that plaintiff was committed to the provost-guard by the officers referred to, charged with having excited mutiny among
the citizens of the United States, violating his parole as a prisoner, engaging in an illicit trade, and furnishing the enemy
with necessaries, and being a spy, and the court having refused
to admit this evidence in *justification*, though deciding that it
might be received in mitigation of damages.

The jury found for the plaintiff below for $779.25. Thomp-
son, chief justice, delivering the opinion of the court, held, that
"[n]one of the offences charged against Shaw were cognizable
by a court-martial, except that which related to his being a spy;
and, if he was an American citizen, he could not be charged
with such an offence. He might be amenable to the civil authority for treason; but could not be punished, under martial
law, as a spy. There was, therefore, a want of jurisdiction, either
of the person or of the subject matter, as to all the offences alleged against the plaintiff."[15] And, it being held that there had

14. Parker, *Habeas Corpus*, 19.
15. *Shaw*, 12 Johns. at 265.

been a direct and positive exercise of authority in the case by Smith, judgment was affirmed. Spencer, J., differed as to Smith's responsibility, but admitted that the officers making the arrest were trespassers.[16]

When, in 1814, General Jackson was in command at New Orleans, that city being besieged by the English, he proclaimed Martial Law. Whilst it was in force one Louallier, a member of the Legislature and a Frenchman by birth, was arrested and placed in confinement for conspiring to aid the enemy, and to incite treason and mutiny. A writ of *habeas corpus* was, on the 5th of March, 1815, attained from Judge Hall, the United States District Judge, requiring General Jackson to appear in person and produce Louallier. He refused to obey the writ, but arrested the judge, and sent him beyond the lines. The emergency, which called for the proclamation of Martial Law having passed, and the supremacy of the civil law being restored, Judge Hall returned and immediately, and without meeting with resistance, caused General Jackson to be brought before him, and fined him $1000 for contempt of court. This is said to have produced such exasperation that General Jackson was obliged to interpose for the protection of the court.*

---

* During the War of 1812 Andrew Jackson declared martial law in New Orleans, in part because he feared capitulation or disloyalty from the city's civilian elite. Jackson ordered French citizens dismissed from the militia and banished from the city, though he later rescinded the decision. Louis Louallier, a Louisiana state senator, anonymously published a letter in the *Louisiana Courier* protesting the order. Jackson learned Louallier's identity and had him arrested. Louallier was not apparently charged with treason, but with "mutiny, exciting mutiny, general misconduct, being a spy, illegal and improper conduct and disobedience of orders, writing a willful and corrupt libel, and, finally, unsoldier-like conduct." A court-martial dismissed

16. Id. at 268–73 (Spencer, J., dissenting).

The question of the validity of this proclamation came before the Supreme Court of Louisiana in *Johnson v. Duncan et al.'s Syndics*, 3 Mart. (o.s.) 530 (La. 1815) and Martin, judge, said:

> The Constitution of the United States, in which everything necessary to the general and individual security has been foreseen, does not provide, that in times of public danger, the executive power shall reign, to the exclusion of all others. It does not trust into the hands of a dictator the reins of the government. The framers of that charter were too well aware of the hazards to which they would have exposed the fate of the republic by such a provision; and had they done it, the states would have rejected a constitution stained with a clause so threatening to their liberties. In the meantime, conscious of the necessity of removing all impediments to the exercise of the executive power, in cases of rebellion or invasion, they have permitted Congress to suspend the privilege of the writ of habeas corpus in those circumstances, if the public safety should require it. . . .

---

most of the charges and acquitted Louallier of the rest. Jackson nonetheless detained Louallier until the end of fighting in the city. Jackson did pay the fine Judge Hall had imposed, and he did move to quiet supporters who protested Judge Hall's contempt order—though he also later tried unsuccessfully to have Hall impeached. In the 1840s, Congress refunded Jackson his one thousand dollars. See Matthew Warshauer, *Andrew Jackson and the Politics of Martial Law* (Knoxville: University of Tennessee Press, 2006); Matthew Warshauer, "The Battle of New Orleans Reconsidered: Andrew Jackson and Martial Law," *Louisiana History* 39, no. 3 (1998): 261–91; George M. Dennison, "Martial Law: The Development of a Theory of Emergency Powers, 1776–1861," *The American Journal of Legal History* 18, no. 1 (1974): 52–79.

Under the Constitution and laws of the United States, the president has a right to call, or cause to be called into the service of the United States, even the whole militia of any part of the Union, in case of invasion. This power, exercised here by his delegate, has placed all the citizens subject to militia duty under military authority, and military law. That I conceive to be the extent of the martial law, beyond which, all is usurpation of power. . . .

But the counsel for the appellant, to support his assertion, that in the circumstances then existing, the court could not administer justice, went further, and said, that the city of New Orleans had become a camp, since it had pleased the general of the seventh military district to declare it so, and that within the precincts of a camp there can exist no other authority than that of the commanding officer. If the premises were true, the consequence would certainly follow; but the abuse of words cannot change the situation of things. A camp is a space of ground occupied by an army for their temporary habitation, while they keep the field. That space has limits: it does not extend beyond the ground actually occupied by the army. The camp of the American army during the invasion of our territory by the British, was placed at a distance of four miles below the city. During that time, the city might be considered a besieged place, having an entrenched camp in front. But the transformation of the city itself into a camp, by the mere declaration of the general, is no more to be conceived, than would the transformation of a camp into a city by the same means.

It is, therefore, our opinion that the authority
of courts of justice has not been suspended of right,
by the proclamation of the martial law, nor by the
declaration of the general of the seventh military
district that the city of New Orleans was a camp; and
we now repeat what we declared when the subject
was discussed, "that the powers vested in us by law
can be suspended by none but legislative authority."[17]

To the debates in Congress we may naturally look for
the expression of conflicting views. The question had already
(January 10th, 1814) come before the House of Representatives
in the following resolution introduced by Mr. Wright:

Resolved, That a Committee of the whole House
be instructed to inquire into the expediency of extending the 2^d section of the act for the establishment of rules and articles for the government of the
armies of the United States, relative to spies, to the
citizens of the United States.[18]

17. *Johnson v. Duncan et al.'s Syndics*, 3 Mart. (o.s.) 530, 549–53 (La. 1815).
See *Lamb's Case*, 4 N.C. (1 N.C. Law Repository) 314 (1816). [Eds. note: *Lamb's
Case* arose out of the trial by court-martial of a member of the South Carolina militia for insubordination. After a conviction, the accused Mr. Lamb
sought a writ of habeas corpus on the ground that the court-martial lacked
jurisdiction over him. The court in *Lamb's Case* agreed and ordered him
released, expressing a dim view of military suspension of the courts: "such
a monster could not exist in the land of liberty and freedom." *Lamb's Case*, 1
N.C. Law Repository at 330–31. The Liebers likely drew the citation to *Lamb's
Case* from Murphy, *Argument of David Dudley Field*, 65, where Field discusses this case alongside *Johnson*. The quoted material at the end of the long
block quote from *Johnson* in the text comes from an earlier passage in the
Johnson opinion; see *Johnson*, 3 Mart. (o.s.) at 548.]
    18. *The Debates and Proceedings of the Congress of the United States*
(Washington: Gales and Seaton, 1854), 881.

Messrs. Webster,[19] Stockton and Grosvenor opposed the resolution. Mr. Stockton hoped that the House would not sanction the resolution so far as to deliberate upon it. "The principle contained in it," he said,

> is so monstrous that I do hope no reference will be made of it. The amount of it is simply this, whether the citizens of the United States, who are entitled to all the benefits and privileges of the Constitution, are to be placed under the jurisdiction of a court martial, and subject to military law. This appears to me a monstrous principle without the least necessity for its exercise. Whence, sir, is the necessity of subjecting our citizens to martial law? If any citizen is found aiding and assisting the enemy, in the language of the Constitution adhering to the enemy, giving them aid and comfort, he is guilty of treason, and can be tried for the same in our courts of justice, where he will be entitled to the inestimable privilege of a trial by a jury of his country. . . . This resolution goes to subvert every principle of civil liberty, to place the citizens under the ban of martial law, to prostrate courts of justice and the trial by jury . . . and I hope the House will not so far sanction it as to refer it to any committee.[20]

But, it is to be observed that in this debate, as well as in *Smith v. Shaw*, Martial Law is spoken of as a general substitute

19. An extract from Mr. Webster's remarks will be found in a note to Chapter VII. [Eds. note: The extract is actually found in the body of the chapter, which we have here converted from Chapter VII to Chapter VIII.]

20. The question, being taken by yeas and nays, was determined in the affirmative by 86 to 77. See *Debates and Proceedings*, 881, 887.

for the ordinary trial for treason, without reference to the emergency of individual cases. As such it would seem to be indefensible.[21]

In 1844 a bill was introduced into Congress refunding to General Jackson the amount of the fine imposed by Judge Hall.[22] Stephen A. Douglas strongly advocated it, and in the course of his remarks, (delivered January 6th) said:

> I am not one to admit that General Jackson vio-
> lated the Constitution, or the law, at New Orleans.
> I deny that he violated either. I insist that the Gen-
> eral rightfully performed every act that his duty
> required, and that his right to declare martial law,
> and enforce it, resulted from the same source, and
> rested on the same principle, that the gentleman
> from New York (Mr. Barnard) asserted, from which
> Judge Hall derived the authority to punish for con-
> tempt, without trial, without witnesses, without
> jury, and without anything but his own arbitrary
> will. The gentleman asserted that the power to pun-
> ish for contempt was not conferred by the statute,
> or by the common law, but was inherent in every
> judicial tribunal and legislative body; and he cited
> the authority of the Supreme Court to support the

21. As a principle grounded in necessity it is, however, not assailed in the remarks above quoted. [Eds. note: In a crossed-out passage, the Liebers write that "Martial Law Proper rests upon necessity alone," and promise to return to the subject of its relationship to treason trials hereafter. The next chapter takes up the hypothesis that martial law is not a substitute for trea-son trials.]

22. *Cong. Globe*, 28th Cong., 1st sess. (Dec. 29, 1843), p. 87. [Eds. note: The Liebers attributed the Jackson indemnification bill to 1844, which is when most of the debate took place.]

assertion. He said that this power was necessary to the Courts, to enable them to perform the duties which the laws intrusted to them, and arose from the necessity of the case. Now, it was from the same source that the power to declare martial law was derived—its necessity in time of war for the defense of the country. The defense of the lives and liberties of the people, as well as their property, being all intrusted to the discretion of the commanding General, it became his duty to declare martial law, if the necessity of the case required it. If it became necessary to blow up a fort, he was authorized to do it; if it became necessary to sink a vessel, he was authorized to do it; and if it became necessary to burn a city, he was authorized to do it. The necessity of the case was the law to govern him; and he, on his responsibility must judge of the existence of that necessity. It was the first law of nature which authorized a man to defend his own person, and his wife, and his children, at all hazards. It was that law which authorized this body to repel aggression and insult, and protect itself in the exercise of its legislative functions; and it was that law which authorized courts of justice to defend themselves and punish for contempts. He acknowledged that this was a high-handed and despotic power—one that was only to be exercised when necessary, and which ceased when the necessity no longer existed. Such was the power under which General Jackson declared martial law at New Orleans. . . .

Talk about illegality! Talk about formalities! Why, there was but one formality to be observed;

and that was the formality of directing the cannon, and destroying the enemy, regardless of the
means whether it be by the seizure of cotton bags,
or the seizure of persons, if the necessity of the case
required it. The God of nature has conferred this
right on men and nations; and therefore let him not
be told that it was unconstitutional. To defend the
country, let him not be told that it was unconstitutional to use the proper means. The Constitution
was adopted for the protection of the country; and
under that constitution the nation had the right to
exercise all the powers that were necessary for the
protection of the country. If martial law was necessary to the salvation of the country, martial law
was legal for that purpose. If it was necessary for a
judge, for the preservation of order, to punish for
contempt, he thought it was necessary for a general
to exercise control over his cannon, to imprison
traitors, and to arrest spies, and to intercept communication with the enemy. If this was necessary,
all this was legal. . . .

General Jackson did not exercise any unnecessary arbitrary authority. He did not suspend the
civil law nor close the civil tribunals, any farther
than was necessary for the carrying out of the military defense of the country. To this extent he did do
it, and to this extent it was right that he should do
it. In other respects, the civil law, and the courts,
were in full force.[23]

23. *Cong. Globe*, 28th Cong., 1st sess. (Jan. 6, 1844), 113. [Eds. note: The
Douglas speech appears in the *Congressional Globe*, but the alteration of

Mr. A. V. Brown, speaking with reference to the same bill, said:

> The city to be defended was his whole camp. Within
> that camp what law must prevail, or ought of neces-
> sity to prevail? Why, martial law. But it prevailed
> no further than was necessary for the defence of
> the city. He might here give various illustrations
> to enforce his position. For instance: when it was
> necessary to defend a mountain pass, and main-
> tain it from the assaults of an enemy, you may send
> your army to take possession of it; and though a
> few shepherds' huts may be there, the general is
> not bound to permit the ingress and egress of the
> inhabitants to carry intelligence to the enemy, be-
> cause their constitutional rights may be in the way;
> and if the general, in such a case, should abridge
> the personal liberty of the citizens, and override
> their constitutional rights, it would be monstrous
> to suppose that a judge could come with his civil
> process, and break up the defence of a pass, upon
> the maintaining of which the safety of the country
> depended.[24]

Mr. Payne, of Alabama, held that martial Law was unknown to the Constitution and laws, but rested upon the principle of self-defense, which rises paramount to all written laws.

some words in the excerpt suggests that the Liebers took it from Benn Pitman's transcript of the trial of Lambdin Milligan. See Benn Pitman, ed.,
Trials for Treason at Indianapolis (Cincinnati: Moore, Wilstach & Baldwin,
1865), 259–60.]

24. *Cong. Globe*, 28th Cong., 1st sess. (Jan. 8, 1844), 118.

"The justification of the officer who assumes the responsibility of acting on that principle, must rest," said he, "upon the necessity of the case."[25]

The original "fine indemnity" bill was, in the Senate, reported back from the judiciary committee with a proviso to the effect that nothing in the act should be construed to express or imply any censure of the conduct of Judge Hall. Senator Robert J. Walker, however, made a minority report, in which he said: "The law which justified this act was the great law of necessity; it was the law of self-defense. This great law of necessity—of defense of self, of home, and of country—never was designed to be abrogated by any statute, or by any Constitution." The proviso was rejected by a vote of eighteen to twenty six.[26]

A similar proviso was proposed in the House, and Mr. Barnard, of New York, moved as an amendment, to strike out the proviso, and insert—"that it is hereby declared that this remission of the fine imposed shall not be deemed or taken as an expression of the legislative opinion, affirming in any way the right of a military commander to proclaim martial law in this country, or to interrupt or forcibly suspend, by military power, the exercise of the civil authority."[27] This amendment was, however, withdrawn. Mr. Stephen's amendment which contained the proviso was then rejected, there being 38 ayes to 122 noes. The original bill passed the House by a vote of 158 to 28, and the Senate by 30 to 16.[28]

25. Pitman, *Trials for Treason*, 15.
26. Ibid.
27. *Cong. Globe*, 28th Cong., 1st sess. (Jan. 6, 1844), 115.
28. Ibid., 120. In a debate in the House of Representatives in 1842, on an appropriation bill, John Quincy Adams, referring to General Jackson's fine indemnity bill, then before Congress, said: "And here I recur again to

Thomas Jefferson and John Quincy Adams have both left us their views upon the subject of Martial Law. In a letter addressed to T. B. Colvin, September 20th, 1810, the former says:

> The question you propose, whether circumstances do not sometimes occur which make it a duty in officers of high trust to assume authorities beyond the law, is easy of solution in principle, but sometimes embarrassing in practice. A strict observance of the written laws, is doubtless *one* of the high duties of a good citizen: but it is not *the highest*. The laws of necessity, of self-preservation, of saving our country when in danger, are of higher obligation. To lose our country by a scrupulous adherence to written law, would be to lose the law itself, with life, liberty, property, & all those who are enjoying them with us; thus absurdly sacrificing the end to

---

the example of General Jackson. What are you now about in Congress? You are about passing a grant to refund to General Jackson, the amount of a certain fine imposed upon him by a judge under the laws of Louisiana. You are going to refund him the money with interest, and this you are going to do, because the imposition of the fine was unjust. And why was it unjust? Because General Jackson was acting under the laws of war; and because the moment you place a military commander in a district which is the theatre of war, the laws of war apply to that place." [Eds. note: The Liebers seem to have borrowed the quotation from J. W. Gordon's argument on behalf of Lambdin Milligan's codefendant, William Bowles. See J. W. Gordon, *An Argument Against the Jurisdiction of Military Commissions to Try Citizens of the United States* (Indianapolis: Hall & Hutchinson, 1865), 16. Adams had been making this point since at least 1836 in his defense of a federal war power over slavery. See generally William Lee Miller, *Arguing about Slavery: John Quincy Adams and the Great Battle in the United States Congress* (New York: Knopf, 1996); Witt, *Lincoln's Code*, 204.]

the means. When, in the battle of Germantown, Genl Washington's army was annoyed from Chew's house, he did not hesitate to plant his cannon against it, altho' the property of a citizen. When he besieged Yorktown, he levelled the suburbs, feeling that the laws of property must be postponed to the safety of the nation. While that army was before York, the Govr of Virginia took horses, carriages, provisions & even men, by force, to enable that army to stay together till it could master the public enemy; & he was justified. A ship at sea in distress for provisions meets another having abundance, yet refusing a supply; the law of self-preservation authorises the distressed to take a supply by force. In all these cases the unwritten laws of necessity, of self-preservation, & of the public safety controul the written laws of meum and tuum. . . .

To proceed to the conspiracy of Burr, & particularly to Genl Wilkinson's situation in New Orleans. In judging this case we are to consider the state of the information, correct & incorrect, which he then possessed. He expected Burr and his band from above, a British fleet from below, and he knew that there was a formidable conspiracy within the city. Under these circumstances, was he justifiable 1. in seising notorious conspirators? On this there can be but two opinions; one, of the guilty & their accomplices the other, that of all honest men. 2. In sending them to the seat of Government when the written law gave them a right to trial in the territory? The danger of their rescue, of their continuing their machinations, the tardiness and weakness of the law, apathy of the judges, active patronage of the whole tribe of lawyers, unknown disposition of the juries, an hourly expectation of the enemy, salvation of the city, and of the Union itself, which would have been convulsed to its center, had that conspiracy succeeded, all these constituted a law of necessity & self-preservation, and rendered the salus populi supreme over the written law. The officer who is called to act on this superior ground, does indeed risk himself on the justice of the controuling powers of the Constitution, and his station makes it his duty to incur that risk. But those controuling powers, and his fellow citizens generally, are bound to judge according to the circumstances under which he acted. . . .

From these examples & principles you may see what I think on the question proposed. They do not go to the case of persons charged with petty duties, where consequences are trifling, and time allowed for a legal course, nor to authorise them to take such cases out of the written law. In these the example of over-leaping the law is of greater evil than a strict adherence to its imperfect provisions. It is incumbent on those only who accept of great charges, to risk themselves on great occasions, when the safety of the nation, or some of its very high interests are at stake. An officer is bound to obey orders: yet he would be a bad one who should do it in cases for which they were not intended, and which involved the most important consequences. The line of discrimination between cases may be difficult; but the good officer is bound to draw it at

his own peril, & throw himself on the justice of his
country and the rectitude of his motives.[29]

"The powers incidental to war are derived," said John Quincy
Adams,

> not from their internal municipal source, but from
> the laws and usages of nations. . . . There are . . . in
> the authority of congress and of the executive two
> classes of powers, altogether different in their na-
> ture, and often incompatible with each other—the
> war power and the peace power. The peace power
> is limited by regulations, and restricted by provi-
> sions, prescribed within the constitution itself. The
> war power is limited only by the laws and usages
> of nations. This power is tremendous; it is strictly
> constitutional, but it breaks down every barrier so
> anxiously enacted for the protection of liberty, of
> property, and of life. . . . [T]he powers of war are all
> regulated by the laws of nations, and are subject to
> no other limitation.[30]

29. [Eds. note: The Liebers drew Jefferson's Colvin letter from H. A.
Washington, ed., *The Writings of Thomas Jefferson*, 9 vols. (New York: Riker,
Thorne, & Co., 1853–1855), 5: 542–44. We have made modest edits to con-
form the text of the Colvin letter as it appears here to the modern scholarly
edition, Thomas Jefferson to John B. Colvin, September 20, 1810, in *The Papers of Thomas Jefferson Digital Edition*, ed. James P. McClure and J. Jefferson
Looney (Charlottesville: University of Virginia Press, Rotunda, 2008–2017).]

30. Speech of John Quincy Adams in the House of Representatives,
May 25, 1836, in *Niles' Weekly Register*, June 18, 1836, pp. 276–77 . [Eds. note:
Adams's May 1836 speech was widely reprinted during the Civil War era in
debates over the constitutionality of Emancipation. On the basis of internal textual evidence, the Liebers probably drew the citation from William

The observations elsewhere made with reference to the opinion of the Supreme Court in *Ex parte Milligan* are intended to show the impossibility of restraining Martial Law within such territorial limits.* It is there maintained that, Martial Law (Proper) being a law of necessity, its jurisdiction is governed only by the necessity of the case.

In applying this case we must not forget that Martial Law was, in 1842, declared in Rhode Island by the Legislature, and the opinion of the Supreme Court treated it in this light, Chief Justice Taney expressly saying that he forbore remarking upon the commissions anciently issued by the Kings of England, because they bore no analogy to the declaration of martial law by the legislative authority of the State.[31]

In March, 1865, Hon. Hy. Winter Davis moved an amendment to the Miscellaneous Appropriations Bill,[32] which finally passed the House of Representatives by a vote of 79 to 64, in the following form:

> And be it further enacted, that no person shall be tried by court-martial, or military commission, in any State or Territory where the courts of the United States are open, except persons actually mustered, or commissioned, or appointed in the military or

* See Chapter I above.

Whiting, who (like the Liebers) misdated the speech to May 26. William Whiting, *The War Powers of the President* (Boston: John L. Shorey, 1862), 76–77. See also *The Abolition of Slavery the Right of Government under the War Power* (Boston: R. F. Wallcut, 1862), 7.]

31. *Luther v. Borden*, 48 U.S. (7 Howard) 1, 46 (1849).

32. *Cong. Globe*, 38th Cong., 2d sess. (1865), 1323.

naval service of the United States, or rebel emissaries charged with being spies.[33]

The Senate refused, on two votes, to pass this as an amendment to an appropriations bill, but its conference committee are said to have reported the sense of the Senate to have been in favor of the prohibition.*

The Dorr Rebellion furnishes an instance of Martial Law declared by legislative authority. By an act of June 25th, 1842, entitled "An Act establishing Martial Law, &c.," the General Assembly of the State of Rhode Island enacted as follows:

> Section 1. The State of Rhode-Island and Providence Plantations is hereby placed under Martial Law; and the same is declared to be in full force, until otherwise ordered by the General Assembly, or suspended by Proclamation of his Excellency the Governor of the State.[34]

The question of the legality of this act came before the Supreme Court of the United States in *Luther v. Borden* (48 U.S. (7 Howard) 1 (1849), upon which occasion Chief Justice Taney, delivering the opinion of the Court, said:

---

* For the procedural history of the 1865 amendment to the appropriations bill that would have limited the executive's authority to employ military commissions, see Edward McPherson, *The Political History of the United States of America during the Great Rebellion* (Washington, D.C.: Philp & Solomons, 1865), app. pp. 561–62.

33. Ibid., 1333.
34. Rhode Island General Assembly: Public Laws, June 1842 Adjourned Session (1842), p. 7.

[U]nquestionably, a State may use its military
power to put down an armed insurrection, too
strong to be controlled by the civil authority. The
power is essential to the existence of every government, essential to the preservation of order and
free institutions, and is as necessary to the states
of this Union as any other government. The State
itself must determine what degree of force the crisis demands. And if the government of Rhode Island deemed the armed opposition as formidable,
and so ramified throughout the State, as to require
the use of its military force and the declaration of
martial law, we see no ground upon which this
court can question its authority. It was a state of
war; and the established government resorted to
the rights and usages of war to maintain itself, and
to overcome the unlawful opposition. And in that
state of things the officers engaged in its military
service might lawfully arrest any one, who, from
the information before them, they had reasonable
grounds to believe was engaged in the insurrection;
and might order a house to be forcibly entered and
searched, when there were reasonable grounds for
supposing he might be there concealed. Without
the power to do this, martial law and the military
array of the government would be mere parade,
and rather encourage attack than repel it. No more
force, however, can be used than is necessary to
accomplish the object. And if the power is exercised for the purposes of oppression, or any injury
willfully done to person or property, the party by

whom, or by whose order, it is committed would undoubtedly be answerable.[35]

Justice Woodbury gave, in the same case, a very full dissenting opinion, in which, however, he admits that there are some circumstances which justify a resort to martial law, for he says:

> [M]y impression is that a state of war, whether foreign or domestic, may exist, in the great perils of which it is competent, under its rights and on principles of national law, for a commanding officer of troops under the controlling government to extend certain rights of war, not only over his camp, but its environs and the near field of his military operations. (6 *Am. Archives*, 186.*) But no further, nor wider. (*Johnson vs. Duncan. et al's Syndics*, 3 Martin (o.s.) 530, 551–53 (La. 1815).)[†] . . .
>
> But in civil strife they are not to extend beyond the place where insurrection exists. (3 *Martin*, 551.) Nor to portions of the State remote from the

---

* Justice Woodbury's reference to volume 6 of Peter Force's *American Archives* is a reference to the debate in Parliament in November 1775 over the suspension of trade into Boston Harbor. Lord North is quoted there saying that there was no need to repeal the bill for the administration of justice in Boston because "being in actual war, martial law took place, and there were no courts of justice in which [the administration of justice] could operate." See "Lord North's Prohibitory Bill," in Peter Force & M. St. Claire, *American Archives: Containing a Documentary History of the English Colonies in North America*, 4th ser. (Washington, 1837), 6: 186.

† For *Johnson v. Duncan et al's Syndics*, see above in this chapter.

35. *Luther*, 48 U.S. at 45–46.

scene of military operations,[36] nor after the resistance is over, nor to persons not connected with
it. . . . Nor, even within the scene, can they extend
to the person or property of citizens against whom
no probable cause exists which may justify it. (*Sutton vs. Johnston, 1 D. & E., 493, 549 (1786).*)* Nor
to the property of any person without necessity or
civil precept.[37]

---

* In *Sutton v. Johnston*, Lord Mansfield opined that a naval officer convicted in a court-martial for his refusal to follow orders in a naval engagement with the French in 1781 could not bring a cause of action in the common law courts to seek a remedy on the grounds that he had been convicted
without probable cause.

36. I have already spoken of the impossibility of giving it this territorial
restriction. [Eds. note: See Chapter I above.]
37. *Luther*, 48 U.S. at 83–84 (Woodbury, J., dissenting).

CHAPTER VIII

Has Martial Law
Jurisdiction of Treason?

That the true theory of Martial Law was not recognized, at an earlier day in England, is, in a great measure, due to the fact that it was generally resorted to as a substitute for the ordinary trial for treason. From the trial of Lancaster down to that of Gordon such has been the case, and, indeed, statutes have recognized this as its legitimate object. But treason is a crime known to, and defined by, the ordinary law, and which, under that law, has its appropriate tribunal, proof, and punishment. What qualifications, then, can there be for an exercise of the war power with reference to an act thus provided for? Two theories have been advanced, viz: first, that when war exists, a war power, *ipso facto*, springs up, which supersedes the ordinary law as to all matters which involve a violation of the common law of war; and, secondly, that when the ordinary law is silent, it becomes necessary to substitute Martial Law in its stead. The first proposition is believed to be entirely untenable. Laws which can be enforced in war as well as in peace have no silent reservation restricting their operation to times of peace. Whatever cases they reach, to them they apply. It is only when they cannot be enforced, or when, for reasons unforeseen by the legislature[1] they are inadequate to the protection of the country, as where the lesser civil offense is merged into the greater war crime, that an exercise of the war power may become necessary, and justifiable.[2] The second theory would clearly not apply to districts not immediately affected by military operations, or where the courts are open, and the administration of justice unobstructed. Nor would it justify the trial of rebels by Martial Law after the suppression of the rebellion. Yet this has occurred on more than one occasion in English history, and has been defended on the ground of the necessity of preventing further outbreak. It has even been extended to the suppression of incipient rebellions.

An act ordinarily triable as treason may under certain circumstances become an offense against the common law of war, but this ceases to be the case with rebels treated as belligerents. They remain guilty of the political crime of treason, but are no longer guilty of the war crime involved in it. When rebellion becomes wide-spread and organized humanity requires that the rules of the just war should be applied to it. Otherwise—the rebellious subjects possessing the power of retaliation—it would degenerate into a warfare of savages.

Dr. Bluntschli in his valuable work on the Law of Nations, says that an armed party, which has not been empowered by any existing government to resort to arms, is, nevertheless, to be regarded as a belligerent when it is organized

1. See Chapter I.
2. There is no limit to the possible encroachments upon liberty which might result from a contrary doctrine.

.✗. note to preceding page)   S mall print   4

The following many excellent observations appeared
in the New York Times, at the beginning of our Civil War, over the signature "York"

"I read in the newspapers that there is a division of
opinion in the National Cabinet upon the question
whether or not the Southern insurgents should be
treated as "belligerents".

Belligerents are those who carry on war. Does
it admit of doubt that we are engaged in a war
with the (so styled) Confederates? If not, why should
we not acknowledge it? We can neither alter the fact,
nor deceive any one by denying it.

The boundaries that separate a mere insurrection
from a civil war may not always be very obvious,
but there can be no doubt that they have been
passed in the present case. Exclusive possession,
with trivial exceptions, of a country containing seven
hundred thousand square miles, and more than
nine millions of people; the existence of a regular
Government, imposing taxes and levying troops;
numerous battles, a great victory by the insurgents,
the capital of the nation in a state of siege - these
things surely constitute war. We can neither hide
them nor diminish their force by a denial.

Lord Palmerston (or perhaps it was Lord John
Russell) justly expressed the rule of international
law when he said that when an insurrection had
reached a certain height the insurgents were
entitled to be treated as belligerents. He may
have been premature in the application of the rule,
but its existence is undeniable. Nor was there

Figure 3. A sample page from Chapter VIII (Chapter VII
in the Liebers' original). Source: National Archives.

as an independent military power, and, in place of the State, honestly contends for a principle of public law. When, he says, the criminal law has lost its power, and it, in point of fact, becomes necessary to wage war for political objects, it is then more logical to suspend the application of the penal laws, and to regard and treat the adversary as an *enemy*, both in a political and military point of view. It is, therefore, he continues, to be regarded as an evidence of the progress of modern international law that it is disposed to treat rebels, as well as organized free-corps, as belligerents, notwithstanding that they have no national organization, provided: 1st, that they have a military organization; 2dly, that they themselves respect the laws of war; and, 3dly, that they are in good faith contending for a political principle.[3]

The following excellent observations appeared in *The New York Times*, at the beginning of our Civil War, over the signature "York":[4]

> I read in the newspapers that there is a division of opinion in the National Cabinet upon the question whether or not the Southern insurgents should be treated as "belligerents."
>
> Belligerents are those who carry on war. Does it admit of doubt that we are engaged in a war with the (so styled) Confederates? If not, why should we

3. See J. C. Bluntschli, *Das Moderne Völkerrecht der civilisirten Staten* (Nördlingen: C. H. Beck, 2d ed. 1872), 287.

4. York, "Question of Belligerent Rights; A Legal Investigation of the Entire Subject," *The New York Times*, August 27, 1861, available at http://www.nytimes.com/1861/08/27/news/question-of-belligerent-rights-a-legal-investigation-of-the-entire-subject.html?pagewanted=all. [Eds. note: This article was almost certainly written by Francis Lieber under a pseudonym.]

not acknowledge it? We can neither alter the fact, nor deceive any one by denying it.

The boundaries that separate a mere insurrection from a civil war may not always be very obvious, but there can be no doubt that they have been passed in the present case. Exclusive possession, with trivial exceptions, of a country containing seven hundred thousand square miles, and more than nine millions of people; the existence of a regular Government, imposing taxes and levying troops; numerous battles, a great victory by the insurgents, the capital of the nation in a state of siege—these things surely constitute war. We can neither hide them nor diminish their force by a denial.

Lord Palmerston (or perhaps it was Lord John Russell) justly expressed the rule of international law when he said that when an insurrection had reached a certain height the insurgents were entitled to be treated as belligerents. He may have been premature in the application of the rule, but its existence is undeniable. Nor was there any good reason to take offense at his reference to the recognition, by England, of the belligerent rights of the Greeks in their insurrection against the Turks.*

---

* A revolt against the Ottoman Empire broke out among the empire's Greek-speaking Christian subjects in 1821 in the Peloponnesus and modern-day Romania, resulting in full-scale war and widespread atrocities throughout the 1820s. Francis Lieber himself fought briefly in this conflict as one of many European "philhellene" volunteers. Between 1821 and 1823, the British government wrestled with the question of whether to treat the fledgling Greek fleet—which often attacked British merchant ships accused of

The reference was for illustration, not comparison; and where the rules of [inter]national law have force (that is, among civilized nations,) their application in a state of war does not depend upon the justice of the cause or the character of the belligerents.

But the difficulty alleged is that if we acknowledge the rebels as belligerents, we must treat them as belligerents. And what does that mean? Simply, that we must conduct this war according to the rules of international law. I should be sorry if I supposed that there was an intention to conduct it otherwise. Let us prosecute this war with vigor; but let us prosecute it in a manner worthy of a great, humane and Christian nation.

International law makes no difference with respect to the mode of its prosecution between civil and foreign war. Those maxims of humanity and justice which the consent of civilized nations

---

carrying Ottoman goods—as illegal pirates, or as privateers authorized by a legitimate sovereign. Unwilling to execute them as pirates, but also, until 1830, unwilling to upset the geopolitical status quo by recognizing Greece as an independent state, British Secretary of State for Foreign Affairs George Canning found a middle way by recognizing Greece as a *belligerent*, entitled to use force under the law of war, but not as an independent sovereign. See Harold William Vazeille Temperley, *The Foreign Policy of Canning, 1822–1827: England, the Neo-Holy Alliance, and the New World* (London: G. Bell and Sons, 1925), 326; John Bew, "'From an Umpire to a Competitor': Castlereagh, Canning, and the Issue of Intervention in the Wake of the Napoleonic Wars," in *Humanitarian Intervention: A History*, ed. Brendan Simms and D. J. B. Trim (Cambridge: Cambridge University Press, 2011), 131; Will Smiley, "War without War: The Battle of Navarino, the Ottoman Empire, and the Pacific Blockade," *Journal of the History of International Law* 18, no. 1 (2016): 54–55; John Fabian Witt, *Lincoln's Code: The Laws of War in American History* (New York: Free Press, 2012), 174–75.

has established in the one case, are equally applicable in the other. We cannot escape the obligation
to observe them by denying an indisputable and
notorious fact. The obligation arises from the fact
of civil war, and not from our acknowledgement of
the fact.

But it will be found utterly impossible to escape the necessity of recognizing the insurgents
as belligerents. Our interests, no less than theirs,
demand the recognition. We have, indeed, so recognized them in various ways already. We have
declared and established a *blockade*, and that is a
belligerent right. We have seized a neutral vessel,
and caused her to be condemned as a prize for a
violation of the blockade. In order to obtain that
condemnation, it was necessary to establish that
the blockade was *legal*; and to establish the legality of the blockade, it was necessary to show the
existence of a war as a foundation for the exercise
of that belligerent right. It will be found, in my
judgment, utterly impracticable, (though this is going further than my argument requires,) to carry
on the war without treating the *States* that in their
corporate capacity have made themselves parties
to it—leaving not a vestige of a loyal Government
within their limits—as *belligerent States*. Otherwise,
we should be obliged to distinguish at every step,
between loyal and disloyal individuals, and should
find ourselves involved in a labyrinth of technicali-
ties. No State at war with another makes any discrimination, unless as a matter of grace and favor,
and for its own interest, between the citizens of the

State with which it is at war. To be *compelled* to do
so, would paralyze its energies. We are at war with a
(not *de jure* but *de facto*) State, or rather organized
community struggling to become a State. That is a
broad, flagrant *fact*; and we must adapt the Constitution to that fact in the best way we can. The case
is not to be determined by the subtleties of Courts.
I concede the constitutional difficulty of admitting
the idea of the nation being at war with States of
the nation; but so it is, and unless we can constitutionally prosecute such a war, the Constitution is a
felo-de-se. The case is novel, extraordinary, unforeseen, and the Constitution contains no express provisions applicable to it. We must accommodate its
provisions to the extraordinary condition of affairs,
so as to do it as little violence as possible, regarding it with the eye of a statesman, rather than of a
lawyer, looking to its hope and object, and remem-
bering that that Constitution must be absurd which
dooms it to dissolution by its own hand. If there is
repugnancy in its provisions, the lesser must yield
to the more important. We must not construe in-
junctions intended to preserve it in such manner
as to involve the necessity of its destruction. The
law of an Italian city prohibited, under penalty of
death, the letting of blood in the public streets; but
this was held not to apply to a surgeon who opened
a vein to save the life of a citizen.

We never shall be able to carry on war upon
the theory that there is no war. The door of the
temple of Janus must be either opened or shut.
Acknowledge war, and we have power adequate to

every emergency. Deny it, and we are involved in the [meshes] of a law-suit. Shall we never get beyond the *posse comitatus* and the militia ordered out to enforce process? Our Cabinet are lawyers, and they look upon war with the eyes of lawyers and not of soldiers. They seem solicitous lest Jeff. Davis should get some technical advantage over them. They are apprehensive, perhaps, of a motion to set aside the proceedings for irregularity.

They will find no other solution of the difficulties that perplex them than in the recognition of the Confederated insurgents, not as a State or nation, but as a rebellious community, seeking to make itself a State by war, and with which we are at war in order to prevent it from doing so. It is only upon this theory that the recent proclamation of the President, declaring non-intercourse with the seceded States, can be defended. What is this if not the exercise of a war power? Upon the supposition of a mob, a riot, a mere insurrection *within* a State (the State itself in contemplation of law remaining loyal,) the President certainly could not claim authority to place *the State*, or which is the same thing, all the citizens of the State, beyond the pale of constitutional protections—suspending acts of Congress and constitutional privileges, even of citizens of loyal States. War, an insurrection that has reached the height of war, renders this necessary and proper; but nothing else could make it either the one or the other. It is clear then that our necessities have already compelled us to exercise belligerent process; and it is absurd to suppose that we can claim the rights without being subject to the duties that that character implies. If we take the benefits we must bear the burdens. *Qui sentit commodum sentive debet et onus.* We cannot blow hot and blow cold. We cannot, as the Scotch lawyers say, *approbate and reprobate.* And, indeed, have we not already conceded to the enemy the rights of a belligerent? Have we not recognized his flags of truce and respected the inviolability of his heralds and messengers? Have we not treated his soldiers taken in battle as prisoners of war? The present question that agitates, as is said, the Cabinet is, whether we shall exchange prisoners with the enemy. Why not, since we hold the men as prisoners of war? If they are not prisoners of war we ought to hang them; if they are, I can see no reason why we should not exchange them. To be illogical where a benefit can be gained thereby, is not uncommon; but to stop short in a concession just where we should gain an advantage by carrying it to its legitimate consequence, is singular folly. We have discharged prisoners gratuitously or upon the empty form of an oath; shall we hesitate to discharge them when by doing so we can obtain the release of loyal citizens?

An absurd idea seems to be entertained that if we acknowledge the Confederates as belligerents, we thereby acknowledge their independence. Mr. Jefferson Davis advanced this notion in one of his messages, and, regarded as a quibble, it was rather amusing; but it appears to have done some execution, and the lawyers of the Cabinet seem to be dreadfully afraid of being caught in this secession snare. If the fact that the rebels have made war upon the Government gives them a title to be recognized as an independent nation, I know not how we can help it: but, if not, then a recognition of the fact can have no such consequence. We have gone to war to subdue the rebels—*ergo*, says Mr. Davis, we admit their independence. If so, our case is desperate; for peace would certainly admit their right to independence, and, what is more, secure it. It is scarce worth while to pursue such small game. War admits nothing. By war we dispute the claims of rebels; we can do so in no other way. And the question is to be determined by force of arms, and not by legal punctilities.*

To conclude, these propositions seem to me evident—

That we are engaged in a civil war, that by the law of nations we are bound to concede to the enemy the right of a belligerent, and that we cannot deny him these rights without incurring the censure of the civilized world and the condemnation of our consciences.

That we cannot carry on the war efficiently without exercising belligerent rights; and that we cannot exercise those rights without conceding them to our adversaries.

And finally, that by conceding to our adversary the character of a belligerent, we admit nothing more than that the insurrection has reached a

---

* Original: peurilities.

certain height, and do not in any respect admit to its legitimacy.

And, when the rebel is treated as a belligerent you clearly can not try him by martial Law for treason. In other words you cannot try him, whom you recognize as a belligerent, for being a belligerent. But this does not absolve him from his civil responsibility. "Treating, in this field, the rebellious enemy according to the law and usages of war has never prevented the legitimate government from trying the leaders of the rebellion or chief rebels for high treason, and from treating them accordingly, unless they are included in a general amnesty."[5] *Shortbridge et al. v. Mason* fully sustains this doctrine.* In that case Chief Justice Chase, delivering the opinion of the court, said:

> Nor can we agree with some persons, distinguished by abilities and virtues, who insist, that, when rebellion attains the proportions and assumes the character of civil war, it is purged of its treasonable character, and can only be punished by the defeat of its armies, the disappointment of its hopes, and the calamities incident to unsuccessful war.

* Chief Justice Salmon P. Chase held that a debt owed by a North Carolina citizen to a Pennsylvania citizen had not been discharged when, during the Civil War, the Confederate government of North Carolina forced the debtor to pay the debt to a state receiver. He also found that interest continued to accrue during the war. See "*Shortridge v. Mason*, U.S. Circuit Court, District of North Carolina," *American Law Review* 2 (1868): 95–100. The Liebers' version of the opinion is drawn from a footnote in Francis Wharton, *A Treatise on the Criminal Law of the United States*, 6th ed. (Philadelphia: Kay and Brother, 1868), 3: 298–302.

5. G.O. 100, Art. 154.

Courts have no policy, and can exercise no political powers. They can only declare the law. On what sound principle, then, can we say judicially that the levying of war ceases to be treason when the war becomes formidable? that war levied by ten men, or ten hundred, is certainly treason, but is no longer such when levied by ten thousand or ten hundred thousand? that the armed attempts of a few, attended by no serious danger to the Union, and suppressed by slight exertions of the public force, come, unquestionably, within the constitutional definition; but attempts by a vast combination, controlling several states, putting great armies in the field, menacing with imminent peril the very life of the Republic, and demanding immense efforts and immense expenditures of treasure and blood for their defeat and suppression, well [beyond] the boundaries of the definition, and become innocent in the proportion of their enormity?

But it is said that this is the doctrine of the Supreme Court. We think otherwise.

In modern times, it is the usual practice of civilized governments attacked by organized and formidable rebellion, to exercise and concede belligerent rights. Instead, under such circumstances, of punishing rebels when made prisoners in war as criminals, they agree on cartels for exchange, and make other mutually beneficial arrangements; and, instead of insisting upon offensive terms and designations in intercourse with the civil or military chiefs, treat them, as far as possible, without surrender of essential principles, like foreign foes engaged in regular warfare.

But these are concessions made by the legislative and executive departments of the government in the exercise of political discretion, and in the interest of humanity, to mitigate the vindictive passions inflamed by civil conflicts, and prevent the frightful evils of mutual reprisals and retaliations. They establish no rights, except during the war.

And it is true that when war ceases, and the authority of the regular government is fully reëstablished, the penalties of violated law are seldom inflicted upon many.

Wise governments never forget that the criminality of individuals is not always or often equal to that of the acts committed by the organization with which they are connected. Many are carried into rebellion by sincere though mistaken convictions, or hurried along by excitements due to social and state sympathies, and even by the compulsion of a public opinion not their own.

When the strife of arms is over, such governments, therefore, exercising still their political discretion, address themselves mainly to the work of conciliation and restoration, and exert the prerogative of mercy, rather than that of justice. Complete remission is usually extended to large classes by amnesty or other exercise of legislative or executive authority, and individuals not included in these classes, with some exceptions of the greatest offenders, are absolved by pardon, either absolutely or upon conditions prescribed by the government.

These principles, common for all civilized nations, are those which regulated the action of the Government of the United States during the war of the rebellion, and have regulated its action since rebellion laid down its arms.

In some respects the forbearance and liberality of the nation exceeded all example. While hostilities were yet flagrant, one act of Congress practically abolished the death penalty for treason subsequently committed, and another provided a mode in which citizens of rebel states maintaining a loyal adhesion to the Union, could recover, after war, the value of their captured or abandoned property.

The National Government has steadily sought to facilitate restoration with adequate guarantees of union, order, and equal rights.

On no occasion, however, and by no act have the United States ever renounced their constitutional jurisdiction over the whole territory, or over all the citizens of the Republic, or conceded to citizens in arms against their country the character of alien enemies, or admitted the existence of any government, *de facto*, within the boundaries of the Union, hostile to itself.

In the prize cases, the Supreme Court simply asserted the right of the United States to treat the insurgents as belligerents, and to claim from foreign nations the performance of neutral duties under the penalties known to international law. The decision recognized, also, the fact of the exercise and concession of belligerent rights, and affirmed,

as a necessary consequence, the proposition, that
during the war all the inhabitants of the country
controlled by the rebellion, and all the inhabitants
of the country loyal to the Union, were enemies re-
ciprocally each of the other. But there is nothing in
that opinion which gives countenance to the doctrine which counsel endeavor to deduce from it,
that the insurgent states, by the act of rebellion and
by levying war against the nation, became foreign
states, and their inhabitants alien enemies. . . .

Those who engage in rebellion must consider the consequences. If they succeed, rebellion
becomes revolution; and the new government will
justify its founders. If they fail, all their acts hostile to the rightful government are violations of law,
and originate no rights which can be recognized by
the courts of the nation whose authority and existence have been alike assailed.

If, then, the rebellion is successful, and ends in the establishment of a new national organization, the crime is wiped
out; but, if it be suppressed, those engaged in it may, or may
not—according to circumstances—be amenable for their political crime.* They certainly cannot be tried for the political

* After the Civil War Jefferson Davis was very nearly tried for treason,
in a case that would have defined the legal significance of secession; if Mis-
sissippi had legally seceded, Davis would have argued, then he owed no allegiance to the United States. The government abandoned the prosecution in
1869, and the Supreme Court instead ruled secession to have been unlawful
in *Texas v. White*, 74 U.S. 700 (1869). See Cynthia Nicoletti, *Secession on
Trial: The Treason Prosecution of Jefferson Davis* (Cambridge: Cambridge
University Press, 2017).

crime of treason by martial Law. I have already expressed the opinion that a citizen, not treated as a belligerent, cannot—in the absence of any reasons based upon the necessities of the case—be tried by a military court for Treason, or for a violation of the common law of war, when the treasonable act is the subject of the charge. When the courts are closed, and criminal justice cannot be administered according to law, there is a necessity of substituting Martial Law in its stead; but it may also be necessary to enforce Martial Law (Proper) when the courts are open, and the administration of justice undisturbed, if the law fails to furnish an adequate remedy. "Those courts," said Chief Justice Chase in *Ex parte Milligan*, "might be open and undisturbed in the execution of their functions, and yet wholly incompetent to avert threatened danger or to punish, with adequate promptitude and certainty, the guilty conspirators."[6]

Congress has, indeed, recognized that such may be the case. By the act of April 10, 1806, prescribing Rules and Articles of war for the government of the Army, Congress provided for the military trial and punishment of "all persons not citizens of, or owing allegiance to the United States of America, who shall be found lurking as spies."[7] This provision of the act referred to was, therefore, restricted to persons not citizens, and the reason for the restriction was that such an act committed by a citizen would be treason, over which the civil courts had jurisdiction.

---

6. *Ex parte Milligan*, 71 U.S. (4 Wall.) 2 (1866), 140–41.

7. An Act for Establishing Rules and Articles for the Government of the Armies of the United States, 2 Stat. 359, 371, § 2 (1806). [Eds. note: This language paralleled that passed by the Continental Congress in 1776. See William Winthrop, *Military Law and Precedents* (Washington: Government Printing Office, 2nd ed. 1920), 765–66, 985.]

But by an act approved March 3[d], 1865, Congress provided, "that *all persons* who, in time of war or rebellion against the supreme authority of the United States, shall be found lurking or acting as spies in or about any of the fortifications, posts, quarters, or encampments of any of the armies of the United States, *or elsewhere*, shall be triable by a general court-martial or military commission, and shall, upon conviction, suffer death."[8] Thus Congress distinctly recognized the necessity of extending military authority over a whole class of cases, ordinarily triable as treason under the law of the land.

The same is true with reference to the 56th Article of war (act of April 10, 1806), which provides that "whosoever shall relieve the enemy with [money,] victuals, or ammunition, or shall knowingly harbor or protect an enemy, shall suffer death, or such other punishment as shall be ordered by the sentence of a court-martial."[9]

So by the 57th Article of War Congress enacted that, "whosoever shall be convicted of holding correspondence with, or giving intelligence to, the enemy either directly or indirectly, shall suffer death, or such other punishment as shall be ordered by the sentence of a court martial."[10] "This article," says Judge Advocate General Holt, ". . . was adopted by the Congress of the Confederation, and its terms and effect

8. An Act for Enrolling and Calling Out the National Forces, and for Other Purposes, § 38 (1863). [Eds. note: This statute established the Union's conscription system. The Liebers' date is incorrect, as it was passed on March 3, 1863, not 1865. The language paralleled that of 1776 and 1806, as well as a February 1862 law. It was, with minor changes, included in the updated 1874 Articles of War. See Winthrop, *Military Law*, 766, 996.]

9. An Act for Establishing Rules and Articles for the Government of the Armies of the United States, § 1 (1806).

10. Ibid.

remained unchanged at the time of the formation of the Constitution. In 1806 a slight modification was introduced in its language—the substitution of the word 'whosoever' for the words 'all persons';—and then a Congress, composed probably of many of the founders of the republic, substantially reaffirmed the jurisdiction previously conferred."[11] Here again Congress recognized the necessity of this war power.

Nor must we lose sight of the fact that war creates new obligations, unknown in time of peace, and the violation of which constitutes—to a great extent—purely war crimes, and involves no civil liability. The safety of the country requires that all unlawful interference with its military operations should be suppressed, and, when this cannot be done in due course of law, a resort to martial law becomes a necessity.

But, where the courts are open for the administration of justice, Martial Law Proper cannot, under any circumstances take cognizance of an offense which is not a violation of the common law of war. Such an offense would not have that connection which is necessary in order to give it the character of a war crime. A discussion took place during the trial of the assassins of President Lincoln, which will serve to illustrate this point. The conspirators were tried by a Military Commission, and they were charged, amongst other things, with "traitor-

---

11. William Winthrop, ed., *Digest of Opinions of the Judge Advocate General of the Army* (Washington: Government Printing Office, 3d ed. 1868), 229–30. [Eds. note: Holt's reference to "the Congress of the Confederation" is confusing, because the original 1776 Articles of War were passed by the Continental Congress (Sec. XIII, Art. 19 was equivalent to Art. 57 on correspondence with the enemy). Holt may have meant that the Confederation Congress's 1786 repeal and replacement of Sec. XIV of the Articles of War implicitly recognized the other sections of the 1776 Articles. See Winthrop, *Military Law*, 22–23, 972.]

ously" doing certain acts. Mr. Ewing, counsel for one of the conspirators, asked: "By what code or system of Laws is the crime of 'traitorously' murdering, or 'traitorously' assaulting with intent to kill, or 'traitorously' lying in wait, defined?"

The Judge Advocate (Gen. Holt, Judge Advocate General of the Army) said in reply: "I think the common law of war will reach that case. This is a crime which has been committed in the midst of a great civil war, in the capital of the country, in the camp of the Commander-in-chief of our armies, and if the common law of war can not be enforced against criminals of that character, then I think such a code is in vain in the world."

Mr. Ewing: "Do you base it, then, only on the law of nations?"

The Judge Advocate: "The common law of war."*

Martial Law Proper, being an application of the law of war, knows no offenses other than violations of the common law of war, except in so far as a greater latitude of jurisdiction may become necessary in order to extend the protection of military authority to the inhabitants of districts within the theatre of active military operations in which the civil administration has been displaced.

The necessity in the latter case would be similar to that upon which the martial law of hostile occupation rests.

Whenever a civilian† or alien is engaged in practices which directly interfere with waging war, which

---

* See Edward Steers Jr., ed., *The Trial: The Assassination of President Lincoln and the Trial of the Conspirators, A Special Edition of the Trial Transcript as Compiled and Arranged in 1865 by Benn Pitman* (Lexington: University Press of Kentucky, 2003), 247. Holt relied upon Lieber's own G.O. 100, which he introduced into evidence. See Witt, *Lincoln's Code*, 294.

† In original: citizen.

directly affect military movements and operations,
and thus directly tend to hinder or destroy their
successful result, and when, therefore, these practices are something more than mere seditious or
traitorous designs or attempts against the existing
civil government, the President as Commander-in-
Chief may treat this person as an enemy, and cause
him to be arrested, tried and punished in a military
manner, although the civil courts are open, and although his offense may be sedition or treason, or
perhaps may not be recognized as a crime by the
civil courts.[12]

Military crimes, or crimes of war, include all acts
of hostility to the country, to the government, or to
any department or officer thereof; to the army or
navy, or to any person employed therein: *provided*
that such acts of hostility have the effect of opposing, embarrassing, defeating, or even of interfering
with, our military or naval operations in carrying
on the war, or of aiding, encouraging, or supporting the enemy.[13]

"This seems to me absolutely certain," said Dr. Lieber,[14]
"and it is probably admitted by almost all writers on the subject:

12. See John Norton Pomeroy, *An Introduction to the Constitutional Law
of the United States* (New York: Hurd and Houghton, 1868), 479–80.
13. See William Whiting, *War Powers under the Constitution of the United
States* (Boston: Lee and Shepherd, 43d ed. 1871), 188.
14. In the course of his lectures on the Laws and Usages of War, delivered
before the Law School of Columbia College. [Eds. note: The following is a

1. That Martial Law within the United States means, of course, the legality of everything absolutely demanded by military necessity, according to the General Law of War, e.g. hanging a spy, &c.
2. That it means the suspension of the privilege of the writ of *Habeas Corpus*, but only for the time of the war, or of the military necessity.
3. That it extends to police regulations.
4. That it does not extend to trials, except, I take it, such trials, as military necessity demand instanter—not, for instance, general trial for treason."

The question whether treason can be tried by Martial Law came up in the House of Representatives, during the War of 1812, on a resolution looking to the exclusion to citizens of the United States of the second section of the act for the establishment of rules and articles for the government of the armies of the United States, relative to spies. Upon that occasion Daniel Webster said:[15]

[T]his resolution proposes, in effect, to consider whether it is not expedient to try accusations for treason before military instead of civil tribunals. However glaring may be the idea, yet such is in

---

partial paraphrase of the original lectures, for which see "Dr. Lieber on the Laws and Usages of War," *New York Times*, March 17, 1862, available at http:// www.nytimes.com/1862/03/17/news/dr-lieber-laws-usages-war-martial -law-united-states-who-shall-suspend-writ.html.]

15. D. F. Murphy, ed., *Argument of David Dudley Field* (New York: William J. Read, 1866), 74.

truth the real nature of the proposition. It is to change the forum for the trial of treason. The mover of the resolution* and the gentleman from the State of Georgia, (Mr. Troup),† have not left any doubt on this subject. They have alluded to cases which they suppose the resolutions to embrace, and for which they deem it necessary to provide military punishment. But what is the nature of these cases? Are they not cases of treason? It is said information has been communicated to the enemy, very material to him, respecting the operations of our own forces, by citizens of the United States. . . . Do gentlemen suppose that the act of communicating to the enemy important intelligence, whether by signals or otherwise, whereby he is better able to defend himself, or attack his adversary, is not treason? Is not this giving to the enemy aid and comfort? May it not be in many cases the most important service which can be rendered him? Certainly, sir, all such offenses as gentlemen have mentioned are provided for by law, and adequate penalties annexed to the commission. The simple question before us

* **Robert Wright** of Maryland (1752–1826), a Democratic Republican who served in Congress, 1810–1817, and before that in the Senate, 1801–1806. "Wright, Robert (1752–1826)," *Biographical Directory of the United States Congress*, available at http://bioguide.congress.gov/scripts/biodisplay.pl?index=W000768; *Debates and Proceedings of the Congress of the United States* (Washington, D.C.: Gales and Seaton, 1854), 885.

† **George M. Troup** (1780–1856), a Democratic Republican who served in Congress, 1807–1815. He later served as a senator from Georgia from 1816 to 1818. "Troup, George Michael (1780–1856)," *Biographical Directory of the United States Congress*, available at http://bioguide.congress.gov/scripts/biodisplay.pl?index=T000382.

is, whether we will consider the propriety of taking the power of trying for these offenses from the
courts of law, where the Constitution has placed it,
and confer it on the military. Sir, the proposition
strikes me as monstrous, &c &c?

See *Smith v. Shaw*, 12 Johnson 257. Stacy's case, 10 Johnson 328.*
The question might arise whether a person who had been
tried by a civil court for treason, could, if arraigned before a
military tribunal for a war crime growing out of the same facts,
plead such trial in bar of further proceedings. In England a
trial by a civil court operates in bar of trial by a military court,
but in this country a different principle has been established.
Here—looking to this point alone—there appears to be no reason why such a person might not be held to a double liability.
Moore v. The State of Illinois (14 Howard's Rep.) confirms the
American principle of double liability.[16] The Supreme Court,
in that case, say:

An offense, in its legal signification, means the transgression of a law. A man may be compelled to make
reparation in damages to the injured party, and be
liable also to punishment for a breach of the public
peace in consequence of the same act; and may be

* See the previous chapter for the Liebers' discussion of *Smith v. Shaw*,
12 Johns. 257 (N.Y. 1815), and *In re Stacy*, 10 Johns. 328 (1813). The Liebers'
placement of this citation makes it appear to be part of Webster's speech,
but it is not.

16. *Moore v. Illinois*, 55 U.S. 13, 19–20 (1852). [Eds. note: The U.S. Supreme
Court ruled that it did not violate the constitutional prohibition on double
jeopardy to try a defendant under Illinois law for aiding a fugitive slave, even
though the same act was banned by federal law.]

said in common parlance to be twice punished for the same offense. Every citizen of the United States is also a citizen of a State or Territory. He may be said to owe allegiance to two sovereigns, and may be liable to punishment for an infraction of the laws of either. The same act may be an offense or transgression of the laws of both. Thus an assault upon the marshal of the United States and hindering him in the execution of legal process is a high offense against the United States, for which the perpetrator is liable to punishment; and the same act may be also a gross breach of the peace of the State, a riot, assault, or a murder, and subject the same person to punishment under the State laws for a misdemeanor or felony. That either or both may (if they see fit) punish such an offender, cannot be doubted. Yet it cannot be truly averred that the offender has been twice punished for the same offense, but only that by one act he has committed two offenses, for each of which he is justly punishable. He could not plead the punishment by one in bar to a conviction by the other; consequently this Court has decided, in the case of *Fox v. the State of Ohio*, (5th Howards, 432,) that a State may punish the offense of uttering or passing a false coin, as a cheat or fraud practiced upon its citizens; and in the case of the *United States v. Marigold*, (9th Howard, 560,) that Congress, in the proper exercise of its authority, may punish the same act as an offense against the United States.

This principle extends to offenses committed by persons subject to the Rules and Articles of War, which are at the same time transgressions of the civil law, and military offenses. Trial for the one is no bar to trial for the other, for the same act constitutes two distinct offenses, for each of which the law provides appropriate proceedings. (See *Bird's case*, in U.S. District Court for the District of Oregon, May 24, 1871.)* The same rule may be applied to crimes and offenses which are, at the same time, violations of the civil law, and of the common law of war; so that the fact that an act constitutes an offense cognizable by the civil courts, would not, in itself, be a legal impediment to the trial of the offender for the war crime involved in the act. But, although there is no legal difficulty in the rule, whether or not the occasion is one to justify its application would always remain a question of necessity.

When, however, the courts are in the uninterrupted discharge of their functions, and furnish adequate protection against the wrongs alone referred to, and there is no necessity

---

* This was not the main holding of *In re Bird*, 2 Sawy. 33 (D. Oregon May 24, 1871). There a federal judge upheld the military detention of a former soldier, William B. Bird, pending trial on manslaughter charges. Even though Bird had been dishonorably discharged before the offense by a different court-martial in 1869, the court found that discharge to have been nullified when the earlier conviction was overturned. Bird therefore remained a soldier, amenable to military authority, under law when he allegedly committed the manslaughter in 1870, and could be detained even after his original term of enlistment expired. The court implicitly accepted the same reasoning as *Moore*, noting that there "might be a good cause . . . why proceedings for the military offense of manslaughter . . . committed by the act of unlawful killing, should be postponed or suspended until the petitioner had been proceeded against in the civil courts for the greater and graver offense of murder, committed by the same act," *Bird*, 2 Sawy. at 40. The court noted that it was within the military authorities' sphere of discretion under the Articles of War to decide whether to suspend military proceedings in this manner—but the question of "double liability" was assumed; it was not a holding of the case.

for a more speedy and certain remedy, trial by martial law is unauthorized. Upon this point the two opinions in *Ex parte Milligan* perfectly agree.[17] Here we have an instance of a law, (the act of Congress of March 3, 1863, relating to *habeas corpus*, and regulating judicial proceedings in certain cases) made during the war with reference to a specific class of cases, and vesting in the Circuit and District Courts of the United States complete jurisdiction as to them.[18] Milligan's case was "within the precise letter and intent of the act of Congress."[19] The administration of the laws in Indiana, of which state he was a citizen, and in which he was arrested, remained unimpaired. Nevertheless he was brought before a military commission, tried and sentenced to death. His sentence was commuted, and he then applied to the Circuit Court for a writ of *habeas corpus*,* but the opinions of the judges being opposed, three questions were certified to the Supreme Court, which the latter court decided as follows: 1st, that a writ of *habeas corpus* ought to be issued; 2^d, that Milligan ought to be discharged from custody; 3^d, that the military commission had no jurisdiction legally to try and sentence him in the manner and form stated.

---

* The Liebers have inverted the order of events here: Milligan's military commission convened on October 21, 1864, and originally scheduled his hanging for May 19, 1865. On May 16, President Andrew Johnson delayed Milligan's sentence to June 1865, and then on May 30, he commuted the sentence to life in prison. Meanwhile, Milligan's *habeas corpus* petition was filed on May 10—before, not after, the commutation. See *Milligan*, 71 U.S. at 6–7; William Rehnquist, *All the Laws but One* (New York: Knopf, 1998), 104.

17. *Ex parte Milligan*, 71 U.S. (4 Wall.) 2 (1866), and *Ex parte Milligan*, 71 U.S. at 132 (Chase, C.J., concurring).

18. An Act Relating to Habeas Corpus, and Regulating Judicial Proceedings in Certain Cases, 12 Stat. 755 (1863).

19. *Milligan*, 71 U.S. at 134 (Chase, C.J., concurring).

This case, therefore, distinctly establishes the point we are considering—and in so far all of the questions concurred—that when the law of the land adequately provides for certain cases, and there is no obstruction to the enforcement of the law through its legal machinery, it cannot be set aside by the war power. The object being attainable without a resort to it, the reason of necessity in which it is grounded fails. To go further than this, is, as has already been intimated, to open wide the doors to limitless abuses.

Appendix
Francis Lieber's Annotated Lieber Code*

General Orders, No. 100} WAR DEPARTMENT, ADJUTANT
GENERAL'S OFFICE, *Washington, April 24, 1863.*

The following "Instructions for the Government of
Armies of the United States in the Field," prepared by FRANCIS
LIEBER, LL.D., and revised by a Board of Officers, of which
Major General E. A. HITCHCOCK is president, having been ap-
proved by the President of the United States, he commands
that they be published for the information of all concerned.

BY ORDER OF THE SECRETARY OF WAR:

E. D. TOWNSEND,
Assistant Adjutant General

———

INSTRUCTIONS FOR THE GOVERNMENT OF ARMIES
OF THE UNITED STATES IN THE FIELD.
SECTION I.
Martial Law—Military Jurisdiction—
Military necessity—Retaliation.

———

* This appendix, in the original manuscript, is a printed copy of G.O. 100,
annotated with handwritten notes.

GENERAL ORDERS, }   WAR DEPARTMENT,
No. 100. }   ADJUTANT GENERAL's OFFICE,
    Washington, *April 24*, 1863.

The following "Instructions for the Government of Armies of the United States in the Field," prepared by FRANCIS LIEBER, LL.D., and revised by a Board of Officers, of which Major General E. A. HITCHCOCK is president, having been approved by the President of the United States, he commands that they be published for the information of all concerned.

BY ORDER OF THE SECRETARY OF WAR:

E. D. TOWNSEND,
Assistant Adjutant General.

INSTRUCTIONS FOR THE GOVERNMENT OF ARMIES OF THE
UNITED STATES IN THE FIELD.

SECTION I.

Martial law—Military jurisdiction—Military necessity—Retaliation.

1. A place, district, or country occupied by an enemy stands, in consequence of the occupation, under the Martial Law of the invading or occupying army, whether any proclamation declaring Martial Law, or any public warning to the inhabitants, has been issued or not. Martial Law is the immediate and direct effect and consequence of occupation or conquest.

The presence of a hostile army proclaims its Martial Law.

2. Martial Law does not cease during the hostile occupation, except by special proclamation, ordered by the commander-in-chief; or by special mention in the treaty of peace concluding the war, when the occupation of a place or territory continues beyond the conclusion of peace as one of the conditions of the same. (*)

note (*) This was for instance, the case with several Prussian fortresses, which continued to be occupied by the French after the conclusion of the Peace of Tilsit, in between Alexander I, of Russia, Napoleon I of the French, and Frederic William III of Prussia, in the months of July, 1807. Nothing was stipulated in the treaty of peace concerning the martial law of in those fortresses, and the French commanders acted accordingly. War having ceased there was no longer any need for that severity which actual war often requires; the French authorities acted in conjunction with the Russian government, but arbitrary and oppressive measures would be resorted to, whenever the victorious government considered it its interest to do so.

Figure 4. Francis Lieber's annotations on a printed copy of G.O. 100 (FL manuscript). Source: National Archives.

1. A place, district, or country occupied by an enemy stands, in consequence of the occupation, under the Martial Law of the invading or occupying army, whether any proclamation declaring Martial Law, or any public warning to the inhabitants, has been issued or not. Martial Law is the immediate and direct effect and consequence of occupation or conquest.

The presence of a hostile army proclaims its Martial Law.

2. Martial Law does not cease during the hostile occupation, except by special proclamation, ordered by the commander-in-chief; or by special mention in the treaty of peace concluding the war, when the occupation of a place or territory continues beyond the conclusion of peace as one of the conditions of the same.

[the next page, presumably including articles 3-4, is missing]

5. Martial Law should be less stringent in places and countries fully occupied and fairly conquered. Much greater severity may be exercised in places or regions where actual hostilities exist, or are expected and must be prepared for. Its most complete sway is allowed—even in the commander's own country—when face to face with the enemy, because of the absolute necessities of the case, and of the paramount duty to defend the country against invasion.

To save the country is paramount to all other considerations.

6. All civil and penal law shall continue to take its usual course in the enemy's places and territories under Martial Law, unless interrupted or stopped by order of the occupying military power; but all the functions of the hostile government— legislative, executive, or administrative—whether of a general, provincial, or local character, cease under Martial Law, or

continue only with the sanction, or if deemed necessary, the participation of the occupier or invader.

Note to Article 2: Several Prussian fortresses continued to be occupied by the French after the conclusion of the Peace of Tilsit, between Alexander I, of Russia, Napoleon I of the French, and Frederic William III of Prussia, in the month of July, 1807.* Nothing was stipulated in the treaty of peace concerning the martial law in those fortresses, and the French commanders acted accordingly. War having ceased, there was no longer any need for that severity which actual war often requires; the French authorities acted in cooperation with the Prussian government, but arbitrary and oppressive measures would be resorted to, whenever the victorious government considered it in its interest to do so.

Note to Article 6: Martial Law is, here, treated of almost exclusively with reference to invaded or conquered territories, but it may be declared by a government within its own country, for a place, a district or province, or for the whole country. Martial Law within the government's own country forms the more difficult subject of the two, with free nations. In the nations under despotic sway, whether this consist in monarchical or democratic absolutism, there exists no theoretic difficulty. They may be said to live under perpetual martial law,

* The Treaty of Tilsit, signed on a raft in the middle of the River Neman, ended the 1806–1807 War of the Fourth Coalition, in which a British-led alliance (including Prussia and Russia) had opposed Napoleonic France. The agreement forged a Franco-Russian alliance, preserved the weakened but independent kingdom of Prussia (after Napoleon had conquered it), and revived an independent Poland as the "Duchy of Warsaw." See Dominic Lieven, *Russia Against Napoleon: The Battle for Europe, 1807–1814* (New York: Allen Lane, 2009), 47–51; James Dodsley, ed., *The Annual Register, or a View of the History, Politics, and Literature, for the Year 1807* (London: W. Otridge and Son et al., 1809), 720–24.

since the arbitrary will of the ruler or rulers passes for law. Writers have not always distinguished between martial law at home, and martial law in the enemy's country. There is but one term for the two conditions, and since the word Law is used, it has been often supposed that it ought to consist, or lays claim to consisting of a system of well established rules and digested precedents, as real branches of the law of any people do, while, in fact Martial Law consists chiefly in a negation of rights and legal protection, not in a collection of positive Laws; because it designates the state of things ensuing from a return to force.

It would have been better had the term Martial Law been restricted to the martial law at home, and which in French is called a "state of siege," and had the Martial Law in a hostile country, simply been called Martial Rule.

No other language has a corresponding general term for Martial Law. Such terms as State of War; *Raison de Guerre*, state of siege, Rule of War are used for the different subjects comprehended within the English term. So undefined are the ideas generally connected with the grave term Martial Law, that the duke of Wellington is reported to have said that martial law is the will of the commander-in-chief, while Blackstone says that it "is built upon no settled principles, but is entirely arbitrary in its decisions."[1]

Judge Joel Parker, now of the Law School of Cambridge [Harvard] University, Massachusetts has this passage in a valuable pamphlet, titled Habeas Corpus and Martial Law, a Review of the Opinion of Chief Justice Taney in the Case of John Merryman, Cambridge 1861, namely:[2]

1. Blackstone, *Commentaries*, 1: 413.
2. See Joel Parker, *Habeas Corpus and Martial Law* (Cambridge, MA: Welch, Bigelow, and Co., 1861), 38–39.

Martial Law, then, is that military rule and authority which exists in time of war, and is conferred by
the laws of war, in relation to persons and things
under and within the scope of active military operations in carrying on the war, and which extinguishes or suspends civil rights, and the remedies
founded upon them, for the time being, so far as it
may appear to be necessary in order to the full accomplishment of the purposes of the war; the party
who exercises it being liable in an action for any
abuse of the authority thus conferred. It is the application of military government—the government
of force—to persons and property within the scope
of it, according to the laws and usages of war, to the
exclusion of the municipal government, in all respects where the latter would impair the efficiency
of military rule and military action.

Founded upon the necessities of war, and
limited by those necessities, its existence does not
necessarily suspend all civil proceedings. Contracts
may still be made, and be valid, so long as they do
not interfere with or affect the military operations.
A mere trespass by A. upon the land of B., uncon-
nected with military service, is none the less a trespass, and does not require a military trial or determination. The courts are not necessarily closed, for
all actions relating merely to the private affairs of
individuals may still be entertained without detri-
ment to the public service; but it closes the consideration there of any action, suit, or proceeding in
which the civil process would impair the efficiency
of the military force.

This passage seems to mingle the Martial Law in hostile countries and domestic Martial Law. Treating of Martial Law it is necessary to distinguish between the two, and, in each of the two divisions between the operation of Martial Law in close vicinity of actual hostilities, and the operation of martial law at a distance from the combatting forces, or in disturbed districts where it has been declared, in order to aid the quelling of a revolt or insurrection. As to Martial Law in hostile countries it has been treated in the text. As to the Martial Law at home, which may become necessary in cases of foreign invasion as well as in cases of domestic troubles, it has full sway in the immediate neighbourhood of actual hostility. The military power may demolish or seize property, and may arrest persons, if indispensable for the support of the army or the obtaining of the military objects in view. This arises out of the immediate and direct physical necessity, as much so as the law of trespass is inoperative against those who forcibly enter a house in a case of conflagration. This operation of Martial Law is not exclusive or exceptional. Any immediate physical danger and paramount necessity arising from it dispenses with the forms of law, most salutary in a state of peace. The mentioned pamphlet of Judge J. Parker contains citations of cases and passages on this subject, to which the general reader will turn with advantage.

The subject of the greatest difficulty connected with Martial Law is its existence in a country distant from the scene of military action or in districts which are in a state of insurrection. How far may it extend in point of geographical limits? How far may it extend in intrinsic action? Can it be dispensed with under all circumstances? How can a people devoted to liberty limit its action so that it may not become a means of military despotism?

It cannot be dispensed with under all circumstances and if there were a law prohibiting it, it would break through the law in cases of direct and absolute necessity. The salvation of a country is like the saving of an individual life. It is paramount to all else. The danger that it may be used, and often has been used for the destruction not only of liberty but even of the common civil law, does not prove that it can be dispensed with. The more elementary the necessity of a thing is or the nobler a truth or principle is, the greater is their danger, in all places whatever. Free nations must guard against these dangers but they cannot dispense with martial law. The annihilation of liberty by declaring whole districts, and many of them in "a state of siege" has been discussed in Lieber's *Civil Liberty and Self-Government*.[3] A fact which it is hoped will be recorded in places more prominent than in an annotation to a code is this that on several occasions in the Civil War in the United States, the patriotic people of the North, assembled in large meetings, called, by solemn resolutions, on the government to proclaim martial law in their district.

It has been denied that the government has any right to proclaim martial law, or to act according to its principles, in districts distant from the field of action; or to declare it in larger districts than either cities or counties. This is fallacious. The only justification of martial law is the danger to which the country is exposed, and as far as the positive danger extends, so far extends its justification. The main action will always be, with free nations, the suspension of those guarantees against arbitrary arrest, which are called with us the privilege of the writ of habeas corpus; but it may extend

3. See Francis Lieber, *On Civil Liberty and Self-Government* (Philadelphia: Lippincott, Grambo and Co., 1853).

much further, because as the danger increases in intensity and extent, Martial Law comes to consist more and more of the application of the Law of War to a government's own and loyal people. When the Russian government in [1812]* found that it would be impossible to repel the French invasion, unless the fighting of the Russian troops were aided by starving the French army, the commanding Russian general gave order[s] that every village behind the retreating Russians should be burnt and a band of land many miles wide [missing word]. And ultimately the city of Moscow was given up to the flames. This severe act of Martial Law saved the country. The friends of the French complained of it, at the time, as an act of barbarity, as there have been persons who complained of our attempt to block up the harbor of Charleston, but it is now universally acknowledged as an act of high patriotic self-sacrifice without which the country would not have been saved.

The Civil War in the United States has occasioned a number of writings on the suspension of the writ of Habeas Corpus, granted as it is by the Constitution of the United States.

---

* The Liebers erroneously give the date as 1813. Napoleon invaded Russia in June 1812, and by December of that year, his rearguard had retreated back out of Russian territory. During the intervening six-month campaign in Russia, Napoleon advanced deep into Russia. After the French passed the city of Smolensk in August, Tsar Alexander I's forces began a "scorched-earth" policy to destroy shelter and supplies that could aid the invaders. When Napoleon reached Moscow on September 15, a six-day fire destroyed three-quarters of the city. Though the Russian commander Mikhail Kutuzov did not order this result, the conflagration probably began with smaller fires set as part of the Russian scorched-earth policy. See Dominic Lieven, *Russia against Napoleon: The Battle for Europe, 1807–1814* (New York: Allen Lane, 2009), 212–13, 283.

The following order of General Schenck is given to show how far an American commanding general the Martial Law ought to extend in a district endangered by the propinquity of actual hostilities and the well-known existence of treasonable persons within the district:*

---

* Schenck's order is found in Chapter I of the finished manuscript, accompanied by a reiteration of this paragraph on its significance.

Index

Illustrations are indicated by italicized page numbers.

Treaty of Tilsit (1807), 310
trials: fair trial by courts-martial,
    221, 222; by martial law, 138,
    220–21. *See also* drum-head
    court martial; jury trial, right
    to; military commissions/
    tribunals
Troup, George M., 300
Trump, Donald, 5, 56
Tyler, Wat, followers of, 142–43
tyranny as result of use of emer-
    gency powers or martial law,
    26, 37, 149

*United States v. See name of oppos-
    ing party*
U.S. Army's General Orders. *See all
    General Orders*

vagueness of Liebers' writing, 57
vindictive retaliation, 237
virtue as basic founding principle,
    57

Walker, Robert J., 268
Wall, Joseph, and his trial for
    handling of Senegal mutiny,
    42–43, 202–8
war, common law of. *See* common
    law
war crimes, 296, 298, 303
War of 1812, 23, 256–59, 299
War of the Fourth Coalition
    (1806–1807), 310
War of the Roses (1487), 142–43
war power: Adams (John Quincy)
    on, 269n28, 272; Congress and,
    256; Lancaster's trial and execu-

tion not considered an exercise
    of, 141; Lincoln's exercise of,
    286; *Milligan* case and, 28;
    necessity of, 99, 296; ordinary
    law's relationship to, 278–79;
    property taken for necessary
    use by army under, 250
Washington, George, 249, 251, 255,
    270
Webster, Daniel, 263, 299–300
Wellington, Duke of (Arthur
    Wellesley), 24, 41, 87–88, 217,
    218n11, 221, 311
West Point: law department
    headed by Norman Lieber, 3, 11;
    lectures by Francis Lieber, 2
Western Rebellion (1549), 144, 163
Westmoreland, Sixth Earl of
    (Charles Neville), 148
Wexford War (1798), 191
Wharton, Francis: *A Treatise on
    the Criminal Law of the United
    States*, 289
Whiskey Rebellion (1794), 255
Whiting, William, 273n30
Wilford, Thomas, 149–50
Wilkinson, James, 270
William III (also William of
    Orange), 109, 110, 118, 161, 181
Winthrop, William, 79
Wolfe Tone, Theobald, 191, 193–94
Woodbury, Levi, 95–96n27, 276
Wright, Robert, 300

Yerger, Ex parte (1868), 64n85
Yoo, John, 54
"York" Letter, 62n53